Good News
in Growing Churches

Contributors

Samuel Acosta
Erasto L. Arenas
Jerald W. Baker
Ned Barnes
Felix Carrion
Thomas R. Henry
Barry L. Johnson
Ardie Kendig-Higgins
James L. Kidd
John T. McFadden
Donald W. Morgan
Culver H. Nelson
Robert I. Rhoads
Arthur A. Rouner Jr.
Martha Swan
Jeremiah A. Wright Jr.
Otis E. Young

Good News in Growing Churches

Edited by ROBERT L. BURT

Foreword by LYLE E. SCHALLER
Postscript by JOHN H. WESTERHOFF III

The Pilgrim Press
Cleveland, Ohio

Scripture quotations are from the New Revised Standard
Version Bible, copyright 1989, Division of Christian
Education of the National Council of the Churches of
Christ in the United States of America, and are used by
permission.

Library of Congress Cataloging-in-Publication Data

Good news in growing churches / edited by Robert L.
Burt; foreword by Lyle E. Schaller;
postscript by John H. Westerhoff III.
p.   cm.
ISBN 0-8298-0872-8
1. Church growth—United Church of Christ—Case
studies. 2. Church growth—United churches—Case
studies. 3. Church growth—United States—Case studies.
I. Burt, Robert L. II. Westerhoff, John H.
BR515.G59   1990
254'.5—dc20   90-42144
CIP

This book is printed on acid-free, recycled paper to save
trees and help preserve the earth.

Printed in the United States of America

10 9 8 7 6 5 4 3 2

The Pilgrim Press, Cleveland, Ohio

"Whatever you do, do everything for the glory of God."
—1 Corinthians 10:31

CONTENTS

FOREWORD

Perhaps the greatest heresy in American Protestantism to surface during the 1960s was that every congregation must choose between two alternatives. One is to be faithful and obedient to God's call, to proclaim a prophetic message centered on social justice, and to watch as the numbers shrink. Social justice, not the Holy Spirit or the Eucharist or praise, should be the focal point of worship. When challenged by that prophetic approach to ministry, however, most people will silently disappear mumbling, "No, not me, Lord, that is too much to ask of me." It was widely assumed that a prophetic ministry and numerical growth were mutually exclusive goals.

The second alternative, according to this heresy, acknowledges that numerical growth is possible, perhaps even guaranteed, for those self-centered parishes that are controlled by the wants of the people, that ignore the needs of the poor and the oppressed, that preach a popular, self-improvement version of the gospel, and that spark a feeling of joy, optimism, and awe.

Perhaps the second great heresy of the past half century calls for the pastor to be an enabler or facilitator, not a leader who challenges the people with the high expectations that appear repeatedly in the teachings of Jesus.

This book demolishes both of these heresies. This book documents the centrality of Word and sacrament in corporate worship. This book underscores the importance of intercessory prayer. This book repeatedly lifts up the need for the pastor to challenge people. This book affirms the importance of the study of the holy scriptures. In chapter after chapter, this book illustrates how excellence in worship, faithfulness in prayer, high-quality care of the people, an active role in community outreach, involvement in the

1

worldwide ministry of the church, and numerical growth are compatible priorities.

Perhaps the most widely used excuses for the numerical decline of a congregation can be summarized in the word demographics. "Well, I can understand why your church is growing and ours is shrinking. Look at the difference in the demographics!" This book repeatedly points out the fallacy of that excuse. Vision, leadership, meaningful worship, prayer, hospitality, memorable sermons, sensitive pastoral care, hard work, and the Holy Spirit are shown to be far more influential than demographics in determining which congregations grow in numbers and which ones shrink.

For many readers the most disturbing book published in the 1980s may have been *The First Urban Christians* by Wayne A. Meek (1983). In this book the author, as he analyzes the letters of Paul, notes that the upwardly mobile people of that era were especially attracted by the gospel of Jesus Christ. That theme recurs throughout the history of the Christian churches. It also appears in chapter after chapter in this volume, especially in those that describe the immigrant and African American congregations, but it also is reflected in the accounts of the predominantly Anglo congregations.

Another thread that runs through this volume can be summarized by one three-letter word. That word is joy. When people who were reared in church-going families and subsequently "dropped out of church" are asked why, they offer a huge variety of answers. One of the most common, which is offered by those born after World War II, is that they find church boring. That is an accurate description of corporate worship in thousands of churches today. That may be the number one reason they are shrinking in size.

A close second, however, is given by those dropouts who find today's churches to be irrelevant to their journey.

This book illustrates in scores of ways how churches that are both sensitive *and responsive* to the needs of people, that speak to people on their personal and religious pilgrimage, and that are faithful in proclaiming the Good News of Jesus Christ are neither boring nor irrelevant.

It would be easy to describe this as another book on church growth, as a collection of success stories about a few nonrepresentative congregations. That would be a great oversimplification!

This is really not a book about church growth. It is a book that affirms the centrality of corporate worship, that describes the

2

power of music, that offers practical examples of how churches and pastors can and do carry out their public witness for social justice. It is a book that lifts up the impact on people's lives of the Good News of God's grace, that shows how congregations can challenge people to be engaged in ministry in their own backyard as well as in other parts of the world, that explains how congregations can relate to existing agencies in making this a better world, and that shows that growth is not an end in itself, but rather a byproduct of faithful ministry.

This is a book about patience, persistence, prayer, pilgrimages, the power of the Holy Spirit, vision, planning, goals, leadership, Jesus, Bible study, commitment, hard work, joy, spontaneity, long tenure for pastors, hospitality, surprises, love, and television. It is about specialized ministries, God, preaching, healing, team work, high expectations, music, youth, obedience, Christmas Eve, fear of the unknown, program, evangelism, church administration, faithfulness, singles, children, dreams, creativity, optimism, journeys, caring, justice, belief, and disappointments. Those are the themes that produce numerical growth. Those also are the themes that make this book fun to read, an inspiration to reflect on, and a collection of stories to share with others.

LYLE E. SCHALLER
Yokefellow Institute
Richmond, Indiana

ACKNOWLEDGMENTS

I wish to acknowledge my unrepayable debt to the seventeen pastors who took precious time out of their very busy schedules to write the stories for this volume: Sam Acosta, Erasto Arenas, Jerry Baker, Ned Barnes, Felix Carrion, Tom Henry, Barry Johnson, Ardie Kendig-Higgins, Jim Kidd, John McFadden, Don Morgan, Culver "Bill" Nelson, Bob Rhoads, Art Rouner, Martie Swan, Jerry Wright, and Otis Young.

I desire to express gratitude to the delegates of the Seventeenth General Synod, 86 percent of whom voted "Evangelism and Membership Growth" the chief priority of the United Church of Christ for the years 1989–1993, and to Tom Dipko, conference minister and executive of the Ohio Conference, who invited me to be the keynote speaker at the 1990 Ohio Conference annual meeting on the theme, "Growing a Good News Church." The former action motivated us to accelerate the production schedule of this book, and the latter inspired the choice of the book's title.

I want to convey my deep appreciation to two long-time mentors, Lyle Schaller and John Westerhoff, for their generous contributions and to two special colleagues, Jim Bidle and Alan Johnson, who played a major role in envisioning this collection and steering its preparation through the early stages. Particular words of thanks are given to artist-friend Diane Klann, who designed the cover and line drawings of the churches; to Wendy Fassett, my long-suffering administrative assistant, who retyped manuscripts; to Susan Winslow, the gifted Pilgrim Press editor whose professional counsel, illuminating comments, and good humor were indispensable; and to Larry Kalp and Barbara Withers, who from our initial conversation offered constancy of support every step along the publication journey.

My deepest thanks go to Charles Shelby Rooks, executive vice president of the United Church Board for Homeland Ministries, who by example encourages staff to engage in not-for-pay writing projects such as this, and to my wife, Delores, our son, Geoffrey, and daughter, Stephanie, who know very little about this project and had absolutely nothing to do with it, except lovingly to keep the home fires burning during my travels.

Finally, my fondest hope is that many of the pastors and lay leaders of the 6,362 local churches of the United Church of Christ, and the local churches of other denominations, will find in these pages stimulation and encouragement for their congregations' faithful Good News witness and growth in the years ahead.

R. L. B.

INTRODUCTION

I feel like the runner in the Septuagint of the Old Testament coming with the long-awaited news of victory. There hasn't been much lately! "Those Mainline Blues" has been the dominant story in recent years.

Reflecting on the membership trends in mainline denominations for over two decades, the headline writers have not found much good news to write about.

- "Mainline Church Self-Image Suffers"

- "Emphasis on Survival Becomes the Operational Priority"

- "Influence in the Larger Society Is Diminished!"

- "A Decrease in Income Is Inevitable"

- "Those of us known as 'Mainline' denominations are now called 'Old Line' and we are in trouble!"

- The real story of mainline churches today is about "aging donors, declining revenues, declining market share and a changing market."

The statistical sources for those statements can be found by comparing membership in 1965 with the membership numbers cited in the *1988 Yearbook of American and Canadian Churches*:

- The United Methodist Church dropped from a high of 11 million members in 1965 to 9.2 million.

- The Presbyterian Church, USA, has lost nearly 1 million members. Membership now stands at 3 million.

7

- The Christian Church, Disciples of Christ, has lost 1 million with a current membership of 1.1 million.

- The Episcopal Church membership declined from 3.4 million to 2.5 million members. There are now more Muslims than Episcopalians in the United States.

- The three largest Lutheran denominations lost more than half a million members.

- The United Church of Christ has had a net loss of 340,000 during this period. The Assemblies of God now have more members than the 6,362 local churches of the UCC.

Perhaps George Gallup Jr. and George O'Connell stated the mainline church's challenge most pointedly in their 1986 book, *Who Do Americans Say That I Am?*

> We boast Christianity as our faith, but many of us have not bothered to learn the basic biblical facts of our faith. We say rejoice in the *good news* that Jesus brought, but we are often strongly reluctant to share the gospel with others. In a typical day the average person stays in front of the TV set nearly 25 times longer than in prayer. We say we are believers, but perhaps we are only *assenters*.

"Assenters"? What a stark contrast to the earliest church. "Christianity burst on the scene with all the suddenness of Good News: Good News proclaimed with great enthusiasm and courage." That is how the evangelist teacher Michael Green describes what happened.

This was no ordinary Good News that rocked Palestine around the year A.D. 30. This was no first-century soap opera about a carpenter-teacher who had been executed under a Roman procurator. Observes Green, "This was nothing less than the joyful announcement of the long-awaited Messianic salvation, when God had come to the rescue of a world in need." The content of this message became known as *to euaggelion*, "the Good News"!

The Good News (the synonym is "gospel") was so basic, so central to the Christian experience, so much the essence of the Christian faith, that it became the life-changing, world-transforming proclamation of the early church. The Good News was the words picked to describe the great event of Jesus coming into the world to announce in his life, death, and resurrection what God had done for humanity—the gospel of Jesus Christ. This was the

8

Good News that the early church proclaimed and demonstrated in its preaching, teaching, and serving.

This Good News is intensely personal: "God loves you! And Jesus Christ is God's decisive revelation of that love. God calls you to love. And Jesus Christ is the decisive pattern of the way in which you can love. Accept this love; be reconciled; live in reconciliation; live to reconcile others."

Yet the Good News is always aimed at persons in community. As Albert Outler has reminded us, "The first great event in Christian history was the gathering of men and women whose love for God had been called out by an overwhelming demonstration of God's love for them." The first fruit of God's reconciling love was a new community of persons reconciled to God and to one another, *the church*, Christ's body, a community of hope in God's love revealed in Jesus Christ reaching out to share in God's good causes of love, justice, and peace in the world.

For twenty centuries the ministries of Christian churches have been energized by this life-changing, world-transforming Good News witness of the early church. Since that time, whenever Christian churches have put this Good News in the center of who they are and what they do, growth is the result.

For twenty-two years I have been honored to be a homeland missionary of the United Church of Christ. During those years it has been my privilege to visit countless local churches in one of the mainline denominations. I have encountered so many local churches where many varieties of growth are occurring. I have been struck again and again by how these growing churches exude joy. The growth is clearly the result of the energizing power of the Good News. The worship services, evoking a deep sense of active involvement, are uplifting, full of the proclamation and celebration of the Good News. The Bible-based preaching is stirring. The music touches the heart and inspires people with God's presence. People of all ages are being nurtured by the teaching ministries. Choices are being provided by programs that meet a range of spiritual and other needs. The outreach ministries into local communities express genuine care for hurting people. The pastors, laboring long and hard, are driven by a vision of a new tomorrow. The people are outgoing and inviting. The places are alive with expectation. Building facilities are being expanded. Even the environments seem to have taken on a quality of hospitality.

An increasing number of local churches appear to be going through a transformation from growing older and smaller to growing younger and larger. Where there is Good News, there is growth. Where there is growth, there is new life and vitality. These are congregations whose experiences and witness stand in stark contrast to the well-publicized perceptions of "Those Mainline Blues"-type analyses appearing in the public media.

Thus was born the idea of writing this book, selecting Good News stories of growing churches across the United Church of Christ. Each story was written by the pastor of the church described, and together they feature a rich variety of method, approach, and perspective. They are exemplary stories capturing denominators common to other local churches not only in the United Church of Christ but in all mainline denominations.

The stories come from a variety of contexts: rural and urban, racial/ethnic minority (African American, Filipino, Hispanic) and predominately Anglo, stable and rapidly growing communities. In age, they cover a broad spectrum, from one of the two fastest-growing new churches in the past decade to one of the historic churches of New England, organized in 1635. The size range covers the extremes from the largest-membership church in the United Church of Christ to a small-membership church whose average worship attendance increased from a dozen to more than a hundred in a four-year period. The geographical span is from Boston to the San Francisco Bay area, from the east coast of Florida to Phoenix, Arizona, from Chicago to Southern California, from Reading, Pennsylvania, to Lincoln, Nebraska, from Hartford to Minneapolis.

In these stories you will observe in action an evangelism that is empowering. You will *not* encounter simplistic and dogmatic definitions but rather styles of evangelism that blend consistency and flexibility and, above all, that reflect the integrity and power of the Christian message. These are local churches that are touching with the gospel the lives of seeking and searching people of all ages—children, youth, younger adults, adults, and older adults. They are effectively motivating people through invitation and welcome to experience God's Good News through Jesus Christ in their personal lives, within the community of believers and as disciples in the world.

For most of twenty centuries, the Christian churches have regarded Matthew 28:16–20 as the "Great Commission." For the last decade of this century and into the third millennium, perhaps we should regard this as the "Final Commission" and let that be the faithful witness of local churches in and to the world.

10

The "Final Commission," observed Eduard Schweizer, "is the instructions and promise to us of the one who has ascended his throne. The instructions are to bring about the fulfillment of a promise." Our instructions, in the period between Jesus' earthly ministry and the end of the age, are to impart his spirit to all peoples, so that all peoples will acknowledge him as Lord. The promise is that Jesus does not desert his disciples until all is fulfilled! With the authority given to him by God, Jesus empowers believers, *then* and *now* until the end of the age, to declare and demonstrate God's Good News declared in his life, death, and resurrection. In the "Final Commission" the rule of Christ over the entire world is associated with universal discipleship—"make disciples" of all peoples—going, baptizing, teaching. It was the basis for doing evangelism then. It is the basis for growing Good News churches today!

ROBERT L. BURT, general secretary
Division of Evangelism & Local Church Development
United Church Board of Homeland Ministries

How We
Set Ourselves
on Fire

First United Church of Christ, Jupiter, Florida

NED BARNES

As church starts go, it was not exactly your ordinary cup of tea. There was no land, no building, no people, but from the beginning there was a great spirit and an enormous amount of faith.

The time was Christmas 1982. I, my wife, Lynn, and our two young children arrived in Jupiter, Florida, with nothing except our household belongings and 150 donated hymnals packed into a U-Haul trailer. Our mission was to start a new church in North Palm Beach County for the United Church of Christ, as part of the denomination's New Initiatives in Church Development project.

In Jupiter, I began a one-man crusade of knocking on doors, conducting person-to-person visits, and having myself interviewed by newspapers and radio stations. I also bought ads that said, "A great new thing is happening in Jupiter. Come to the grand opening celebration."

On March 6, 1983, First United Church of Christ held its first

---

Ned Barnes in seven years has gathered a brand new church, whose membership today approaches a thousand. First United Church of Jupiter, Florida, is one of the fastest-growing new churches in the United Church of Christ. Previously Barnes was for six years the senior minister of North Congregational Church in Woodbury, Connecticut, which doubled in size during his ministry.

Sunday service for 140 worshipers on the top floor of the Jupiter Beach Hilton Hotel.

Just seven years later, First United Church of Christ in Jupiter had grown from no members to more than eight hundred adults and two hundred youth members. It has been the fastest-growing new church in its denomination, the fastest-growing church in Florida, and a two-time winner of the United Church Board for Homeland Ministries' Biennial Growth Award. Today, the church's ministries are strong and vital. The annual operating budget exceeds $400,000. Construction on First Church's new home has been completed, and plans are being made for expansion.

An Ocean View

When I first thought about starting a new church in southern Florida, my Connecticut friends were convinced I needed my head examined. Why would anyone want to leave a well-established, fast-growing church in beautiful New England for a hot, humid Florida town with no United Church of Christ congregation? I wonder about it myself sometimes. Even now, I feel the anxiety of those early times, the uncertainty of moving from a serene, stable community to a town where my family and I knew no one.

The date for our first church service was fast approaching. I was desperate for ushers. I had seen a fellow out jogging with his dog in the early morning, so I jogged along with him and introduced myself. "We're starting a new church," I said. "Could you possibly be an usher a week from Sunday?"

"That's my first wedding anniversary," he said. "But my wife and I are looking for a church. We'll be there." Five years later, my jogging friend is still with us. We've baptized his children, and the church celebrates his anniversary on our anniversary each year.

I ran an advertisement about our Sunday service in the local newspaper, and a woman called. She had belonged to a UCC church on the West Coast of Florida. "I'll drop by and visit you this afternoon," I said boldly. The woman, apparently having second thoughts, hung up the telephone. "What if this man is one of those fly-by-night operators?" she thought, as she later admitted to me. She promptly called the UCC conference office in Winter Park, Florida. "Is this guy legitimate?" she asked. Officials assured her I was, but they called me immediately. "What are you doing down there?" they demanded. "Stop scaring women who live alone!" The woman is now a close friend and a charter member and was our treasurer for the first five years.

14

Where could we hold our actual church services? The search was long and difficult. After being turned down by every available school, Elks Club, and vacant storefront in town, I wandered into the Jupiter Beach Hilton, a beautiful resort hotel on the ocean, on the off chance they might give me a lead. The sales representative was intrigued. "We've never booked a church," she said. "I'll show you what we have."

We rode the elevator to the top floor, and suddenly I found myself standing in the most magnificent glass-enclosed, ocean-front room you could imagine. "I'll take it," I quickly said.

"Don't you want to know how much it costs?" she asked. "It doesn't matter," I said. "I'll take it." For two years, that ocean-view room on the top floor of the Jupiter Beach Hilton served as our church home.

What an amazing location to start a new church! Every Sunday, worshipers drove to the beach, past beautiful palm trees and flowers. They parked by the ocean in the hotel's lot, punched the top-floor button on the hotel's elevator, and headed for the penthouse. When the elevator door opened, church greeters welcomed them and directed them down the hall. An usher showed them to a seat, and the first thing they saw was a breathtaking view of the Atlantic Ocean. To the north was Jupiter Inlet, with fishing boats heading out for the day. To the south was a dramatic view of the Palm Beach skyline. The sea was always crystal clear and turquoise blue. During silent prayer you could hear the waves crashing and the bathers cavorting on the beach below. Hardly a Sunday passed when something unexpected did not happen. Pelicans flew by at eye level, ogling our little congregation assembled behind the expanse of penthouse glass. The Coast Guard came by in helicopters to hover over boats and check for drugs. Airplanes pulled advertising banners—one read "Drink Coors Bear"—up and down the coast as we sang our hymns.

I will never forget the first Sunday at the hotel. There had been a lot of knocking on doors and telephoning the weeks before, to be sure. But very nervously I wondered if anyone would show up. "Let's set up sixty chairs," we said bravely. "Sixty chairs! What if we could really get sixty people to come!"

Early that morning we lugged everything to the Hilton—hymnals, organ, cross, flowers, and church-school equipment. We set up the sixty chairs and waited for a service scheduled to begin at 10:30 A.M. At 10:03 the first person appeared. By 10:15 the sixty seats were filled. At 10:20 our ushers quickly put into place another

15

sixty chairs. By 10:25 people were spilling out into the hallway, and by 10:30 more than 140 people had arrived.

One year later, 280 people came to the church's first anniversary service. During the festivities, I noticed another of those airplanes with a banner flying up the coast. "Oh, no," I thought. "In the middle of this great moment, here comes a beer commercial!" Slowly the plane came into view. The congregation began to laugh, point, shout, and jump out of their chairs. The plane's banner read, "HAPPY 1ST, UNITED CHURCH OF CHRIST."

The Greatest Thing in the World

Later, I was invited to Manhasset, Long Island, to speak before a group of people who were giving money to start new churches. I boasted about how great our people were, what a beautiful spot the Hilton was, and how fast we were growing. They seemed very impressed.

When I finished speaking, there was a question: "Mr. Barnes, it all sounds exciting. Why do you think you've been so successful in Jupiter?" Almost without thinking, I blurted out, "We're successful because we think what we're doing is the greatest thing in the history of the world. In Jupiter, we act as if our church is the biggest thing that's ever happened. We believe we're part of something that could one day change the world."

Change the world? Everyone at the party smiled politely. "Nice fellow," they probably thought, "a little crazy, but nice." The room was quiet. Finally someone said, "You really believe that, don't you?" "Yes," I replied, "I really do."

From our church's modest beginning we have maintained an incredible momentum by believing in what we are doing. From the start, we have dared to believe that God is calling us, that our church is unique and vital, that our ministry will touch, help, and change countless people.

I often think of the German poet who stood with a friend looking up at a magnificent old cathedral in Europe. "Why can't people build like that anymore?" asked the friend. "In those days, people had convictions," replied the poet. "Today we have opinions, and it takes more than opinions. It takes convictions to build a cathedral."

In the past few years, as the United Church of Christ started more new churches, I've become convinced that it won't work out at all if you don't believe in it with a passion. You have to move into town, rent the best place there is, and not worry about how much it costs. You have to scrape together every cent you have and advertise, call yourself a Great Church, invite everyone to a Grand Opening, and make it clear you're building something the likes of which the world has never known.

To me, the greatest words ever spoken on the subject of church growth were those of John Wesley, the founder of the Methodist Church. Wesley drew large crowds wherever he preached. When someone asked him why people seemed to be drawn to him almost like iron to a magnet, Wesley replied, "When you set yourself on fire, people love to come and watch you burn."

The United Church Board for Homeland Ministries' Division of Evangelism and Local Church Development once asked me to speak at a training institute for new-church ministries. "We want you to lay out the step-by-step program you've developed that makes your church grow so rapidly," they said.

"That's a problem," I replied. "We don't have a step-by-step program here. Even though we're the fastest-growing new church in the denomination, we don't have any plan at all. What we have is a guiding principle? 'When you set yourself on fire, people love to come and watch you burn.' " In every way we can, as often as possible in our church, we set ourselves alight with faith and hope, conviction and vision, love and joy, and that is what attracts people.

From the start, we raised eyebrows with our enthusiasm. The Florida conference board of directors met in Jupiter shortly after we began. On such occasions, as a courtesy they invite the local pastor and one or two key lay people to join them for dinner. I received such an invitation, but our church council's reaction was, "Two key lay people? We're all key lay people." So we invited everyone, and thirty-five of our new church members turned out to meet the board.

Two years later, we were received as a church with full standing in the United Church of Christ. "Bring a few important church people for dinner and the evening service," the organizer told me. "But we're all important!" said our church members. So we rented a bus and more than fifty of us traveled to join in the occasion.

The Secret of Our Success

The secret of church growth is twofold: Get people to come and get people to stay. A church needs something special to catch people's interest and draw them in. Why would a family want to attend our church rather than stay at home on Sunday morning?

For two years, we pushed our location. "Come to the church with the ocean view," we advertised. "Visit the church with two hundred oceanfront seats."

In Florida, churches often cater to the retired and the elderly. By contrast, we discovered that many young families were looking for a church for their youngsters. So we publish brochures with pictures of children having fun, and we emphasize our church school. We hold family events and we created a vacation Bible school at a local state park. And we advertise our youth programs in every way we can.

More than any other time, Christmas and Easter are when people look for a church to attend. We mail holiday announcements to ten thousand area residents, inviting them to our services. We publicize every special church event—our anniversary, a ground-breaking ceremony, a sermon on a family topic, ranging from solving marital problems to child development. We produce brochures with pictures and stories of our church and distribute them in the community several times each year.

We have found that all forms of communication—publicity, advertising, and tasteful and effective promotion—are crucial to church growth. Jesus Christ can change people's lives, but what difference does it make if no one knows? To draw people to church, we must send the work out, do it consistently, and persuade people we have something to offer.

When we invited members to the ground-breaking ceremony for our new building, we used a small, one-fold, invitation-size mailer. When you opened the flap, inside was a tiny toy metal shovel that we bought at a discount from a supplier. I worried about the cost of the promotion. "How can we afford it?" "How can you not afford it?" a friend asked. He was right.

I believe that everyone who tries our service for the first time must find something that makes that coming worthwhile. Hence, a powerful Sunday service is the most crucial ingredient in a growing congregation. As a new-church pastor, I spend a major part of my week preparing for Sunday morning. I can knock on doors all week and see very little return for my effort. But if I take time to prepare and preach a Sunday sermon that sticks with a visitor throughout the following week, often that person will return the following Sunday and bring his or her friends.

A story is told about an Indian chief on a reservation who was persuaded to attend church one Sunday. After the service, someone asked what he thought. The chief was disgusted: "Big wind, lotta dust, no rain."

Growing churches need rain on Sunday morning. Inspirational worship experiences are the key to keeping people coming. Here are four vital quotes that I find helpful in preparing for Sunday morning:

- "In a growing church, every Sunday should be Easter."

- "People do not drive to Riverside Church [Harry Emerson Fosdick's church] from all over New York to hear about the Jebusites or the Hittites. They come to hear about themselves and discover the Bible's answers for their own needs."

- "I will go to church this Sunday if you will take me to hear a preacher who will tempt me to do the impossible."

- "As I prepare for Sunday, I keep asking myself, 'So what?' If what I plan to say has no value to people, I drop it."

Land Ho!

By far the most difficult part of starting our new church was finding a building site in a central location we could afford. We rapidly outgrew the hotel penthouse and moved to the Jupiter middle school, but we wanted a place of our own. Our searches, trials, and disappointments over a four-year period were enough to write a book entitled "Real Estate in South Florida."

Time after time we would come close to a deal only to see it fall through at the eleventh hour. There was, for example, a small but suitable three-and-one-half-acre site on a heavily traveled road that was ready to blossom into development. However, our church had only a back-up agreement whereby we were standing second in line behind a developer who had the first option. Would he exercise it? He eventually did.

Our building and finance committees began dreaming the wildest dreams imaginable—not just 3 acres but 183 were available. Suppose we crafted a plan to build a sanctuary, an outdoor center, a community nursing home, a day-care center, a church camp, a massive recreation area, basketball courts for youngsters—and even idyllic nature trails on the property? There was no limit to the possibilities in our dreams.

But there was a limitation on financing such an overly ambitious project. How could we ever pay for it? In evening meetings, we brainstormed every possibility from selling off parcels of land to developers to selling building lots to our members. Or perhaps we could rent out camp sites to tourists paddling up and down the waterways within the nature-conservation area?

Much of our thinking and dreaming was blue sky, we realize today. Yet we felt challenged to examine the future potential for the United Church of Christ in addition to our local church as a whole.

Suddenly those blue-sky aspirations were brought to earth as yet another real estate developer bought up the 183 acres. Good-bye, outdoor center, nursing home, nature trails, and other hopes we had shared for using all that land.

That particular time, more than any other in the history of First Church, marked our lowest point, both spiritually and psychologically. Our four-year search had amounted to nothing but a steady series of major disappointments and frustrations. All our leads for land had been exhausted. What should we do now? Where could we turn? I had all but given up hope. In my prayers I would say, "God, I know you want this church to succeed, but can't you be more helpful here?" It was certainly the lowest point for me as well as the congregation.

Then one day, as I usually did on my way home, I drove by a parcel of empty land on Indian Creek Parkway that we had looked at years before. Back then, the developer simply wasn't interested in selling. As I passed the property that day, I thought, "You really ought to check it out just one more time." The thought receded, but as I passed the site again and again over the next few weeks, the voice inside became more and more insistent. "Check it out one more time." What happened thereafter can only be ascribed to the workings of the Lord.

I stopped at the developer's office near the parcel. Strangely, from the moment I walked in, even before anyone spoke, I knew we had found our new church home. I could feel it, and I was excited!

"Yes, we might like to have a church at the entrance to our community," the owner said. "We'll rethink our plans and get back to you."

During the months of talking and negotiating that followed, through all the ins and outs and ups and downs of working out a purchase contract, I never doubted the site would be ours. The land—five acres with an option to buy another five acres alongside it—was perfect for our church's future growth. It was more sensible than the three-and-a-half-acre deal that had fallen through. It was more practical than going deep into debt to finance the massive 183-acre location. The new site was something we could manage with a $500,000 loan from the UCC and still realize our dreams in years to come.

The irony, and the blessing, was that the new parcel was smack in the middle of another booming, high-density development planned by the same real estate company to which we had "lost" those 183 acres months before!

We gathered for a ground-breaking ceremony on our fifth anniversary. The March weather was overcast and rainy, but the spirits of the 350 people who turned out couldn't have been brighter or more festive. Everyone wore bright yellow construction worker's "hard hats" and brought a shovel. We rented a large tent, served lunch, hired a band, and released five hundred helium balloons.

The actual church site on the property was outlined with ribbon, and hand-painted signs marked the exact location of the sanctuary, choir loft, bell tower, kitchen, and offices. After the brief dedication ceremonies, adults and children alike marched in procession onto the site singing "The Church's One Foundation." They broke ground together with shouts of joy!

Our New Home

We had very special ideas about our new church building. Indeed, we were so demanding that we gave the architect fits. We wanted something that was uniquely ours, that expressed what we are and what we believe. To begin with, because we had started in the glass room on the ocean, and because we believe in a God of creation, we want to be able to be in touch with that God in our sanctuary and to worship out in the middle of God's creation, not enclosed in a building. We explained to the architect that outdoors is indoors and indoors is outdoors, so he designed a sanctuary with sheets of glass that rise thirty-five feet in the air. We can sit in the chairs and look out on trees and blue sky and clouds going by. The corners of the building are of glass designed to look as if the building were wide open, and there are little fountains inside and outside and a baptismal pool that comes in from the outside. It's a wonderful feeling of being outdoors and indoors at the same time.

Second, although we live in Florida, we wanted to preserve our New England heritage. So we asked the architect to design a building that combined the traditional white clapboard New England church on the green with modern Florida design. Then I asked for two more things. I told the architect that I wanted everybody who drives by our church for the first time to want to

21

stop and go inside. And I wanted everybody who goes inside, the first time or the hundredth time, to have a sense of being in a sacred place. The poor architect went back to the drawing board again and again, trying to piece all these demands together. Eventually he produced a white clapboard church with lots of exterior glass and interior sweeping blue laminated beams that is open and modern and gives a feeling of the sacred. When you walk in, you enter a huge open patio. The idea was that you should get out of the car and have some time to make a transition before you enter into the presence of God. We station greeters in the patio on Sunday morning to welcome people.

We pushed and pushed to have the building finished by December. When the blue laminated beams that were being specially made in Georgia fell off the train and were damaged beyond repair, we had to wait four weeks for a new set. One of our members, Harrison Castle, was a retired engineer; he went every day to check with the contractor. He had his sons, who owned a steel plant in Pennsylvania, make the structural steel that we needed, and he saw that it was delivered on time and put in place. Every Sunday the building committee took people on tours of the site and pointed out all that had been done the previous week.

The building became a sanctuary long before it was even open. I used to drive by all the time. One Sunday I noticed a car in the lot, so I stopped to see who was there. Inside was a woman all alone leaning against the wall. She was in tears. I spoke to her and discovered she had been coming to church for two or three weeks and was in the midst of a very difficult divorce. She said, "I just needed to come here to be by myself." There was a certain sense of God's presence in that place even before the roof went on.

We had a leadership retreat that fall, as we did every year. After our business was done at four in the afternoon, about fifteen of us drove down to the still unfinished building and celebrated the first worship service in our new church. There was no carpeting or chairs, and there was scaffolding and sawdust and debris all over the place. We put a builder's workbench in front of where the chancel was to be below a huge wood cross hanging on the front wall. We sang, and we held hands, and we celebrated communion right there at the workbench. It was the first service in our new church, and it was a very, very moving time for all of us to feel that we as a congregation had finally arrived home.

Celebration

If you don't set a completion date, the building process can drag on and on. We set the opening date for our new church on the Sunday before Christmas 1988. We resisted pressure to postpone the date, and we spent a frantic last week trying to get everything organized. We had no idea whether everything would be ready. They were laying carpet the last week. The fire marshall did not arrive till Friday. Nevertheless, we went right ahead and advertised in the paper and sent out invitation cards. Excitement mounted.

On Thursday night I couldn't stand it any more. I managed to get myself a key, and I went down there. I went into the building and turned on the lights. I was just walking around feeling so happy and so excited when a car drove in the driveway. It contained some church people who had seen the lights and stopped. They said, "We knew you were in here looking around, and we had to come in and be part of this too." So I opened the door and in they came. Pretty soon another family arrived and another one and another one. Before long there were about twenty to twenty-five people who had driven by who just couldn't stand it. We brought out all the chairs and began to set things up in sense of anticipation.

On the first Sunday we opened to a full house. The four hundred seats were filled immediately and people were standing all around the walls in great excitement. After the hymn and the invocation, I came down out of the pulpit and stood in the center aisle in the middle of the congregation and asked, "What do you think of this?" The congregation broke into spontaneous applause and everybody cheered and shouted with joy at being in our new church home.

We anticipated a big crowd for Christmas Eve. We sent out a brochure to ten thousand people in the community inviting them to come to our church service. We put up five hundred chairs and rented an extra five hundred. We opened the front doors and put loud speakers and another hundred chairs in the front patio so that more people could hear the service and look in. People came and brought their children. The building was mobbed with 810 people, and the best seats turned out to be on the patio. People sat out there on a warm, balmy, starry night, and in the middle of our candle-light service, as the choir was singing, a breathtaking full moon came up and shone right in the window over the choir's head. It was a fantastic way to start our new church life.

For the first Easter in our new church, again we set up chairs all over the place, and we had more than twelve hundred people for two services. To symbolize new life, I brought in a cardboard box of six or eight newly hatched ducklings for the children's sermon. I invited the children, tons of them in all their finery, to the front of the church and took out two quacking ducklings to show them. In no time the excited children were reaching into the box, and the ducklings were coming out. Before I knew it, two had jumped out of my hands and run and disappeared under the chairs. We caught one but not the other, although the full congregation was in pursuit. We could hear him squawking under the chairs and people's feet as they tried to grab him; he squawked even during the silent prayer. Finally, as he headed down a side corridor, two men threw their jackets over him and captured him. That duckling stole Easter, but we had a wonderful time. That's the tone of the whole church.

Money Doesn't Matter

It may sound surprising, but when it comes to money, we have a unique attitude for a growing church. We believe that money doesn't matter. There are greater priorities than how much a member puts in the plate on Sunday. For us, love matters more than money. Caring for people matters more than money. Faith in Jesus Christ matters more than money.

Yet the money comes. In our first building-fund campaign we raised more than $410,000 in two-year pledges. Just before the pledges were made, I was driving alone in the car, feeling anxious and worried. What if we don't make our goal? What if no one comes through? All of a sudden, at that low point, I could feel welling up inside me an incredible sense of warmth and assurance. "Have you ever in your life found love and commitment like those you find in this church?" I asked myself.

"No, never."

"And have you ever experienced support, enthusiasm, and the Spirit of Christ the way you experience it here?"

"No," I thought, "I never have."

"Well, then, what are you worrying about?" I heard myself saying aloud. "Don't you understand, you already have what's important? Don't you realize that people will give all they can, that God will be with you, that whatever you raise will be more than you need?"

Reflecting that outlook, in 1990 we passed a $440,000 budget that was $135,000 more than our pledges. That budget includes mortgage payments to the UCC for the loan to build our church, for which we are grateful. After a little discussion, about four hundred members voted unanimously to accept it. Some people might think that deficit budget is outrageous, but I think it shows the faith, enthusiasm, and hope with which we approach the future.

Another example of that faith is our purchase in May 1990 of an additional five acres adjoining our present property. We couldn't afford them in 1987, but we put down a nonrefundable deposit as an act of faith and said, "Somehow in three years we are going to have that money in hand. We're not going to borrow it; we're going to raise it." And we have.

Sometimes the process of giving occurs in a very human, unselfish, and caring way. For a high school student in Jupiter, one of the biggest graduation events is the senior cruise out of Miami. The class takes over an ocean liner for three days, and everyone has a wonderful time. It costs a lot of money, so students begin working and saving months beforehand.

One of the graduating seniors in our congregation heard us talking one Sunday morning about what this church would do in our community when we had our new building. The next day, as the girl's mother was driving her home from school, the two talked about graduation and the big events coming up.

"How are you doing on saving for the senior cruise?" her mother asked. She knew her daughter had been working hard.

"I don't think I'm going on the cruise," said the girl.

"Why not?" asked her mother. "I thought you wanted to go."

"I don't have the money just now," she said.

"What do you mean? I saw money in your pocketbook this weekend."

"Yes I know, but . . ."

"But what?" asked her mother.

"Well, I was in church yesterday, and I heard about everything that was happening, and I decided to put it all in the offering. It's a more important thing to do."

That kind of loving and caring makes any church grow. With the girl's permission, I told her story in a stewardship sermon. Afterward, four church members approached me separately offering to pay the cost of her trip.

Another unselfish gift came from Mary Schmidt, who was inspired by the kinds of things that were going on in our church. She said to me, "I have always wanted to do something in memory of my father and now that I see your church going up, I really would like to make a donation, to do something lasting in his name. As we talked about possibilities, she said he always loved music. I suggested that it would be so nice to have a carillon in our church. Although we had a million other things to spend money on, Mary and I thought that was a wonderful idea, so she donated all the money it took to buy a very nice carillon with loud speakers and tapes, which we put into the church bell tower. On the very first Sunday, we opened the building with music playing to the entire community.

In our congregation, people give in different ways, which is one of the things that makes our church such an exciting place to be. Five of our members are professional golf players who belong to various golf clubs in the area. They came to me one day and said, "You know we would like to do something special for this church and we would be willing, because we're so close to the P. J. National Golf Club down in Palm Beach Gardens, to ask them to donate their space to our church. We would put on a day-long golf clinic there and all the proceeds we would give to the building fund." I thought that was wonderful idea, so for the last three years on a Saturday morning in early spring we invite everyone in the community to the P. J. National Golf Course driving range. Then our five professionals work all day long with the people who come. A super teaching pro takes special groups in the afternoon to play nine holes; their donation for being taught by this outstanding pro is also forwarded to the building fund.

Focus on Youth

In Jupiter, we've discovered not only that parents bring their children to church, but also that children bring their parents. So we pay special attention to young people.

I know a family with three children that moves around the country so often that they are always looking for a church home. It was such a long, difficult process every time—visiting a different church every Sunday, meeting new people, sitting through boring sermons, holding family conferences to evaluate each visit—that finally, the family devised a less complicated system. Now, when the family comes to a new town, they sleep late on Sunday mornings. About 11:15 A.M., wearing old clothes, they pile in the car, drive up to the front of a nearby church, and watch the people on their way out of the service. If the worshipers are quiet and somber, if no one is talking or smiling, if individuals leave by themselves and head straight for their cars, the family doesn't bother with that church. But if the people pour out the doors laughing and talking, if the youngsters run outside with some life and energy, if worshipers don't hurry away but take time to visit together, the next week the family attends that service to check it out for themselves.

I often think people would be envious if they drove up to our church after the service and saw the enthusiasm we show. We have parties on the front lawn with punch and cake. Every week, people stand in the parking lot long after the service enjoying one another's company. Our children come bounding outdoors with Sunday school projects in hand. Our teenagers bring their skateboards and cruise around the building grounds until their parents are ready to go. Our church overflows with a spirit that shouts, "Come join this happy celebration!"

On Sunday, two youngsters were crying as they waited in line with their parents to leave the sanctuary. They had seemed all right during the service and Sunday school, but now they were clearly upset.

"What's the matter?" I asked gently. "Did something happen?"

"Oh, no!" laughed their mother. "They've been having so much fun today. They're crying because they don't want to go home."

"That's great," I thought to myself. "Usually parents drag their children to church on Sundays. Here, they have to drag them away."

Last fall, I was happy to see a teenager return with his parents to our church for the third week in a row. His family was new in the area, so I called to welcome them to their new home. "It's the most wonderful thing," his mother told me. "We could never interest Brad in coming to church before we attended your services. Now he talks about the sermon during the week and wakes us up so we won't be late on Sunday morning."

In our church we begin paying attention to children when they are babies. We baptize maybe four or five children a month in our baptismal pool, which comes in from outside. I and all the children gather around this little pool up in front of the sanctuary. I sit right by the water and baptize the baby. Then we and the congregation sing a song and all welcome this little child into our midst. There's a very real sense that this is a family church indeed.

We make children the initial focus of every one of our Sunday services. They sit in front of the sanctuary for the children's sermon. I wrack my brain all week long for an idea that is both religious and entertaining. I use every appealing device I can think of—hats, masks, skateboards, kites, balloons—all designed to make Christian faith come alive in the children's minds.

From the very beginning we made a commitment to young people. Ever since our opening Sunday we have held weekly church-school classes throughout the year, even though at first we never knew how many children would come from Sunday to Sunday. We were determined to make church school a priority and offer a program even if no youngsters showed up.

Now we have close to two hundred children in church school every week, including two nurseries. They meet inside and outside in every available space. Our part-time minister of education works very hard running a fantastic program, really two full church-school programs. The children and the curriculum are no problem, but finding volunteer staff, for church school or for youth programs, is very difficult.

Therefore, we hired two part-time youth directors, one for middle school and one for high school. They have done fine work so that we are attracting large numbers of young people. We started one year with a "lock-in," in which ninety-some teenagers spent the night in our church building. They ate pizza, watched rented videotapes, had special programs, and played volleyball at three o'clock in the morning. Out of that gathering we developed our senior high and middle-school youth programs. The middle school had thirty-five people on their canoe trip.

We also run a vacation Bible school. For our first six years we had no place to run it, but we didn't let that stop us. We asked the Palm Beach County Parks and Recreation Department to let us use a county park on the beach every summer. Children came from all over to be part of a Bible school on the beach. Since 1989 we have been in our building, which is a relief because it has air conditioning and we do not have to cart everything to the beach every day.

Numerical Growth

Our growth has been phenomenal. We are averaging more than 140 visitors in church each week, sometimes 250. Our goal in 1983 was a thousand members by 1990, and we are now close to that. Our new four-hundred-seat sanctuary is already too small. No sooner were we in it than we decided to have two Sunday services, a smaller one at 8:30 and a larger one at 10:30, but 10:30 was also the time for church school. So in January 1990 we scheduled two

28

identical services at 9:00 and 11:00 with two choirs and two full coffee hours and two church schools. That has worked very well. A lot of people stay for both services.

Such rapid growth has created problems of staffing. We had our regular part-time staff—a minister of Christian education, a building manager, an organist, and a director of music. But the work load for one minister was still staggering, so we hired a part-time program director, who has helped us develop a full range of lenten programs and community programs as well as helping with administration. We also hired two part-time youth directors, as I mentioned earlier. Finally we have hired three secretary-receptionists. They are helped by two computers and a huge copying machine.

Another problem with rapid growth is that as the church family becomes bigger, it is harder for the staff and for members to keep track of one another. So we have a committee that has divided all our 850 people into sixty different groups according to a geographical area. They will be care groups and will meet regularly. Each group will have a team captain to look out for the people in his or her area. The person will call them and bring them together and let the church staff know if there's any way we can help with any of their needs.

A Church That Loves and Cares

Some years ago, the Institute for American Church Growth in Pasadena, California, conducted a study. More than 86,000 people in thirty-nine denominations were interviewed. The finding was simple and clear: churches that grow are more loving than churches that don't grow. Regardless of theology, denomination, or location, churches that grow are churches that love.

A good example of a loving church is the story of a middle-aged woman who finally joined our church after two years of attending. She belonged to a neighboring church in town and just couldn't make the break, she said, although she had joined our choir and was active in our women's fellowship. After she joined, I asked her why. "Your people loved me into it," she replied.

When we started, we had trouble finding an organist. There was a small organ but no one to play it. Finally we found eighty-year-old Minna Higbee, who was willing to come out of retirement. Minna had more enthusiasm than the New York Yankees. We loved her and never minded her occasional musical mistakes. She played the small organ until someone gave us a new and bigger

one. It was one of those home models that had all the fancy
gadgets—rhythm section, drums, boogie woogie, bossa nova, all
the chords. The first Sunday Minna tried to play the new instrument, the tremolo button was on. We didn't know how to turn it
off, but Minna, good sport that she was, simply sat down and
played "Onward, Christian Soldiers," tremolo and all.

Then one day just before Easter, Minna went for a routine physical. The doctor found she had an aneurism and ordered her into
the hospital immediately. Minna said, "I'm sorry, Doctor, but I
can't go today. This Sunday, I have the Lord's work to do. I'll go
after our church service is over." So Minna Higbee checked into the
hospital on Sunday after church. On Monday morning she went
for surgery and on Monday evening she died. Never in my life
have I seen such an outpouring of love, concern, and affection as I
discovered in our new congregation. We were in shock together;
we reached out to her family together. From that experience, we
drew closer as a church and we found new meaning in the Lord
whose Spirit binds us in love.

In our church, we also grow because we care about our community. In London during the bombings in World War II, a retired
Salvation Army leader wanted to do something for the war effort.
She took her savings, bought first-aid supplies, and made up
simple first-aid kits. Then she hung a sign on her front door that
said, "If you need help, knock here." Our new building has a door
on which to hang such a sign, but the community has long known
the message we offer: "If you need help, knock here."

When the West Jupiter Community Center, a relief agency in our
area, has a need, they call on us. We have a direct line to their
director and respond immediately through our volunteer program
called Christians in Action (CIA). Last year we gave more than
$18,000 in supplies and relief through this agency, as well as count-
less hours of volunteer help.

We found that when we moved into our church we had no space
to store items that we had collected for Christians in Action, so we
have maintained, in addition to our own building, space in a local
storage unit. And we continue to collect items that are donated and
then distribute them through our local community center to people
in need. We also work with migrant laborers and try and reach out
in every way we can to try and help people in our community.

We decided that as soon as we had our building we would open
it to the community and use it for the community in every way we
could. We found that we have so many church activities going on
here that it's hard to find time for other groups, but we are com-

mitted to Alateen. A group of teenagers who are in families affected by alcoholism come here every Monday evening to support one another as they try to deal with that very destructive force. We face a lot of that here in Florida. In summer we give our space to the YMCA for their summer day camp, so the building is being used five days a week as well as Sunday.

When it comes to mission and outreach, we have made a decision to become a tithing church. That means that for every $10 we receive in offerings, we give $1 to the work of our church in the state, the country, and the world. We plan to continue that tithing as our budget increases.

An Inclusive Church

Another early decision we took was to be an inclusive church. One aspect of that was to be a family church. By "family" we don't mean just little nuclear families of young parents with young children. We mean we want to be a church family that includes a full range of people of all ages. Often we have as many as twenty to twenty-five children in our nursery on a Sunday morning as well as a large number of senior citizens in church. It is especially good to be a family church in Florida, where many people have relatives up north but not near by. The church has managed to provide for such people. A lot of members have become friends and do things together outside the church.

Another aspect of being inclusive is that we welcome people where they are in their faith. We always say to people when they come to membership-orientation classes that we are an open congregation, not an exclusive one. We do not have a whole list of rules and regulations that you must subscribe to in order to join this church. When a person comes to join us we ask two questions: Do you believe in God and accept Jesus Christ as Lord and Savior? Do you want to make this your Christian home as you live out your Christian faith? If the person says yes to those two questions, then we invite him or her to come and join us on a personal spiritual pilgrimage and to join us in ours as we learn and grow and do our best to live out our faith together. I see my role as pastor as helping to create an atmosphere of love in which we can all grow in faith.

Such an atmosphere means we can share our differences, we can agree to disagree on things, and we can care for one another even if we don't all like the way we stand on certain issues. One of the reasons this has become a lively, upbeat, love-filled congregation is that we do not all think the same on every issue. You can pick any

31

issue from abortion to bussing and you can find people in our church who are on all sides of it. We cover the spectrum here. We are not liberals, we are not conservatives, we are a mixture. In that we find a strength because we feel free to express ourselves and to care for one another.

Last summer at a meeting with the ministers I shocked them all when I said, "You know, in the seven years of our church's life, I cannot remember a major decision of our church that was not unanimous." They all thought a church had to have major disagreements. In this church, while we don't all agree, there is such a spirit of unanimity and a willingness to work together that after the discussion is over and it's clear how we seem to be moving (and it's not always in a direction I would choose), we throw ourselves in together. So everything we've done, from adopting our budget to deciding what kind of building to have, has been done in a spirit of anticipation, celebration, and joy rather than controversy and division. That spirit has made us strong, and I think a lot of people who visit us sense that spirit in our congregation.

Spiritual Growth

It's important to note that growth in our church has not been only physical. It has also been spiritual. We have found that major, sometimes miraculous, changes take place in our lives as we work to build this church we love. One such change took place at our first evening service June 1988. We sang and prayed and shared, and then at the end we tried something we had not done in the history of this church. I asked people who wanted to rededicate their lives to Christ or who wanted to make a commitment to Christ for the first time or who felt the need to come forward to do that and to kneel at the foot of the cross before the windows. I was a little nervous about doing this because our congregation comes from a tradition where people are not used to coming forward in public display of their faith. But I made the invitation and then I stepped back and closed my eyes and said a prayer. There must have been about seventy-five people there that evening, and when I opened my eyes about fifty of them had come forward and they were kneeling down on the step of the chancel. I laid my hands on them and anointed them with oil. It was a very moving time when the spirit of God was real in our midst.

Another kind of change began with just one person. At one Easter Sunday service when we were still at the Hilton, I was surprised to see an old friend of mine, from my former church in

Connecticut, seated in the congregation. His wife had died earlier that year and he was visiting Florida trying to recover from his loss. After the service, my wife and I invited him to our home for lunch, and he shared his deep grief and sadness. Preparing to leave, he said passing, "I had a strange experience this morning. Sitting in church, I thought I saw a woman who used to live near me in Connecticut when I was young. Could she be that same person?"

"Why, yes, I said. "She spends her winters in Jupiter and comes to our church regularly." I didn't think any more about our brief exchange, and my friend returned to his Connecticut home. A few weeks later, the woman he had noticed also headed back to Connecticut.

That spring, I heard via the grapevine that the two of them had made contact. I also learned that my friend would be returning to Jupiter the next winter. He had rented a condominium for the season, and, as I suspected, it wasn't just so he could be near his former pastor. When he arrived in Jupiter, I could see light in his eyes. Soon the couple announced they would be married. One glorious Sunday in springtime, our congregation celebrated the wedding of those two very special people. I can't remember when I had been so deeply moved by a marriage ceremony. Their wedding was not only a sign of their new beginning but of the new life in our church.

Our church suffered a great tragedy, but that too was an occasion for spiritual growth. In March 1990 Rachel Hurley, a fourteen-year-old girl who belonged to our confirmation class, was raped and murdered at the local beach. It is the custom in Florida for parents to drive teenagers to the beach on Saturday to be with their friends for a couple of hours and then return to collect them. Rachel's mother, a good friend of ours, was doing that, and Rachel was walking to meet her, but as she passed through some woods, somebody grabbed her and dragged her off and killed her. That horrible death in a small close-knit community like Jupiter sent shock waves through the whole town. I was with them when they found her body, and I tried to support the family, but there is very little you can do other than just be there. Rachel was widely liked, and about four thousand people came to the local funeral home during calling hours. They had to keep the doors open till 10:30, till the last person was able to go by. The church family rallied to support the Hurley family. Several of us spent the whole time at the funeral home talking to individuals and sitting with groups. The children especially had never before encountered such an upsetting situation. The grief-filled atmosphere was so draining that I felt we had to bring everyone to our church, because a church is a place of hope and new life even in the most difficult times. So we scrambled fast and scheduled a funeral service for the next morning.

The children took the day off from school and walked to the church. About twelve hundred people came plus people from the newspapers and television stations. We talked about the good memories of Rachel and the fact that life does not end when we die and that God in his mercy is good. The children relaxed a little, and I invited everyone to go to the cemetery and then come back to the church for lunch. Everyone did, and as people sat and ate and talked to their friends, there was a genuine sense of healing, and the spirit of God was very real.

The church continued to support the Hurley family. Members called on them and took them meals for weeks. I told the congregation that if someone looked back two hundred years from now and picked one of the most important days in the life of our church, the day of Rachel's funeral would be that day. It was the day when in a time of no hope we were able to surround the Hurley family and the community with the warmth and support of God's love.

Our Twenty-Year Plan

There is a general sense in our church that while such wonderful things have been happening in the last seven years, all that has really just been prelude to the adventure and the journey that we are about to begin. Let me explain a little about it. When we bought our first five acres and agreed to buy the adjacent five, we were in a rather remote area with lots of undeveloped land around us. As we were building, a developer came in and built and sold four hundred single-family homes literally in our back yard. We now have four hundred new families within walking distance. They all hear our bells and know what this church is doing because they sense all the activity. More recently land across the street has been approved for 650 new family homes, and they too will be within walking distance. Ninety homes are going up a quarter-mile up the street. And within a radius of two miles, I'm sure there are several thousand homes, from which we hope to draw in the years ahead, as well as from the wider community. We are confident that we are going to grow and we are going to be able to touch many, many people lives in many, many different ways. That is why we can pass deficit budgets and why we can develop our twenty-year plan.

Our ten acres will be the site of a whole complex. Our first project will be a Family Life Center, right across from the main sanctuary. It will have office space and meeting rooms and space for Christian education and a small auditorium and a kitchen. Our next project will be to expand the sanctuary. We designed it so that the seating space for four hundred could be doubled, and we need that space because we are averaging five hundred to six hundred every Sunday, and last Easter we had more than fifteen hundred people in the building for two services. Then we'll look at the Family Life Center again. We have plans for an addition that will give us a larger auditorium and a lot more space for Christian education.

Looking farther down the road, which is certainly a matter for speculation, we would like to build an adult day-care center and a nursery school building for our nursery school, which started in 1990. Then we could work with the older generation and the younger generation at the same time.

As the days, months, and years pass, when I am alone I think about the people to whom I owe so much. Scores of names and faces come to mind. I think of the dozens of committee meetings, the long hours, the struggles in our day-to-day planning to realize our dreams.

As a pastor I have been blessed beyond words by a congregation that responds in faith and joy to this great Christian challenge. One story is very special. As we planned a party in church to celebrate my wife's fortieth birthday, we teased her unmercifully but in a good-natured way. She had been a good sport about it. One the morning of her birthday, Lynn came to the breakfast table with tears in her eyes. "Uh-oh," I thought to myself, "it's going to be a rough day."

"Are you okay?" I asked.

"Yes, I'm fine," she said. "It's just that I was in the bedroom getting ready for work, and I started thinking about my life and all that I have—all of you and our church. And all of a sudden I got this warm, tingling feeling all over, and I want you to know this morning, I wouldn't want to be anyone else in the world other than who I am right now."

That is the way I feel about this church of Jesus Christ. In this loving congregation, with God's spirit so real, and with so many incredible things happening, I am indeed blessed to be part of it all.

35

A Black Congregation in a White Church

Trinity United Church of Christ, Chicago

JEREMIAH A. WRIGHT JR.

> If the history of the Black church in America is a gener-
> ally neglected area of study, the history of the Black
> churches of predominantly white denominations is es-
> pecially neglected.
>
> —A. Knighton Stanley

T rinity United Church of Christ of Chicago sits squarely within
the black church tradition in North America and has done so
(both uncomfortably and radically) over its short yet fascinat-
ing history. The United Church of Christ is a predominantly white
denomination that is not widely known among African Americans
by that name. The name has only been around since 1957, when
the Evangelical and Reformed Church and the Congregational
Christian Churches merged.[1]

The components of the Evangelical and Reformed Church originated in Germany and Switzerland and never made any efforts to
start black congregations in North America. It is from the Congregational Christian side of the UCC merger that the largest number

---

Jeremiah A. Wright Jr. is the pastor of Trinity United Church of Christ,
Chicago, which is the largest congregation in the denomination. Since
Wright's arrival in 1972, Trinity has grown from fewer than a hundred
members to more than five thousand. This phenomenal growth he at-
tributes to a primary focus on preaching, Bible study, and social action.

of blacks came into the United Church of Christ, both before and after 1957. The Congregational Church of New England, primarily through its American Missionary Association, worked diligently before, during, and after the Civil War among Americans of African descent.[2] The association was chartered in 1849, but two things must be kept in mind: First, there were black Congregational churches prior to 1849—such as the Second Congregational Church of Pittsfield, Massachusetts, founded in 1843,[3] and second, the Congregational Church had long since been an advocate for the Africans through its active involvement in the abolition movement, its support of the famous *Amistad* court case,[4] and its participation, both ministers and lay people, in the Underground Railroad.

The Black Church Tradition

Hundreds of blacks joined the Congregational Church because that was the church that had helped them get out of slavery and because that was the church where (after 1849) the missionaries poured out their life's blood among the Africans. The work of the American Missionary Association cannot be described adequately in just a few short sentences. Suffice it to say that these AMA missionaries established more than five hundred academies in the South, most of them after the Civil War. These academies, normal schools, and institutes not only were responsible for the entrance of hundreds of thousands of blacks into the Congregational Church (and its successors), but they were also the historical antecedents of member schools of the United Negro College Fund today.

Of the five hundred odd schools, academies, and institutes set up by the missionaries in the years immediately following the Civil War, six remain in 1990: Fisk, Talladega, Tougaloo, LeMoyne-Owen, Huston-Tillotson, and Dillard. From humble beginnings these "academies" have developed into colleges and universities, which also are responsible for many of the blacks who now belong to the United Church of Christ.

A. Knighton Stanley says, "If the history of the Black Church in America is a generally neglected area of study, the history of the Black churches of predominantly white denominations is especially neglected."[5] This is doubly true when it comes to the even lesser known Christian side of the United Church of Christ family. Most blacks in North America (especially those outside of the North Carolina-Virginia area) have heard of the Congregational Church but not of the Christian Church; and the irony of that fact is that most of the blacks within the UCC come from the Christian side of the merger! Even more neglected (to use Stanley's word) than the "Congregational" black churches in the UCC are the "Christian" black churches; yet the Afro-Christian[6] churches would argue that they are just as much a part of the black church tradition as any congregation in the African Methodist or the National Baptist traditions.

J. T. Stanley makes the case for them:

> With rare exception, the Black Christian churches that are continuing to do notable work . . . were organized in the 19th Century. Most of the organizers of these churches were born slaves and had limited training. Many of them had experienced balcony worship in white Christian churches,[7] from which they received their name and polity, their missionary zeal for church extension and the "saving of souls," and patterns of organizational structures. They were not always certain of their denominational identity.[8]
>
> Infant baptism was rarely practiced; adult baptism was *only* by immersion. Because of a lack of pools the early churches used creeks, rivers, or ponds for this purpose.
>
> Pastoral "appointments" were read out at each annual conference. Elders, councils, presbyteries, and stewards were frequently used designations.[9]
>
> *Apparent in all Black Christian churches and conferences were emotional intensities and styles of preaching, praying, and singing that were inherently African* [10] [Italics added]

It is part of the black church tradition (which almost no outsider knows about) that makes up the majority of the black congregations within the United Church of Christ,[11] and it is these two polarities—the "cold," New England, Eurocentric form of Congregational worship and the "inherently African" Christian side of the UCC family—that are both captured in the short history of Trinity United Church of Christ, Chicago.

Solving a Problem

With the Christian Church being heavily concentrated in North Carolina and Virginia and both the Evangelical and Reformed denominations not being interested in starting any black congregations, the only predecessor denomination in the UCC to do any work in the rest of the country insofar as gathering black congregations was concerned was the Congregational Church. A very interesting problem had been created by the AMA's work among Africans; and the Congregational Church's "solution" to the problem was to gather a congregation for the misfits!

The problem was that after the Civil War the missionaries had taught the freedmen all the things that a liberal arts education is supposed to teach a neophyte—up to and including how to worship like white people! As long as the graduates stayed near (or in the same city with) the campus of such schools as Fisk, Talladega, and Dillard, there was no "problem." On Sundays the graduate simply went back to the campus to "chapel," where he or she worshiped in the best Congregational tradition.

Once the graduates moved north, however, the "problem" arose, for no matter how well trained these graduates were in the ways of white folks, they definitely could not go into the First Congregational Church of Chicago, Oak Park, Winnetka, or anywhere else in Illinois—not in the 1800s! So, to solve this problem for the graduates who no longer fit into black churches because of assimilation and acculturation to white society and who could not possibly fit into white churches because of their color, the Congregational Church started a congregation for *them*—graduates of the AMA schools.

The first effort, Emmanuel Congregational Church, Chicago, formed in the 1890s, was burned to the ground during the race riots in Chicago at the turn of the century. The denomination did not try again until 1909, when Lincoln Memorial Congregational Church was founded, also in Chicago. Lincoln still stands as the oldest black UCC church in the State of Illinois. In the early 1920s, the second black congregation was formed when the Lincoln Church split. Our second "black" church in Illinois, the Church of the Good Shepherd, Congregational, was founded on the same model and principles as Lincoln Church. It was for a "certain class of people" and not for the masses of people who lived in the projects on the South Side of Chicago. The merger of the Congregational and Christian Churches in 1931, since the Christian Church was southern-based, was a merger principally in name for those persons who lived in Illinois.

One of the problems with the Congregational Church (and one of its identifying characteristics that separates it drastically from the Christian Church in terms of ethos and theology) is that it has never been a "whosoever will"-type denomination in Illinois. In contradistinction to some of its stalwart evangelists, who preached on the sawdust trail during both Great Awakenings, "opening the doors of the church" with evangelical fervor to anyone (of any station) who wanted to receive Christ, the Congregational Church in Chicago in the twentieth century has always been an "our kind of people" denomination.

It might seem as if a church or a denomination would see the blatant fallacy in this way of thinking, given the biblical record. A. Knighton Stanley says there is more than a fallacy; there is a fatal flaw leading only to death in this understanding of what the church is.

> It would appear inevitable that the church of the middle class, grounded in the first instance in narrow self interest rather than dynamic, revolutionary principles, is doomed to failure as a Christian institution. Failure is implied in the "bourgeois type of religious faith" because it does not participate significantly in an ethos seething with movement and revolution, an outgrowth of human need to which the Christian Church, in word and work, has been historically a vital and creative response.[12]

What would seem evident, however, and what was actually true are two different things altogether. The Congregational (and then Congregational Christian) Church in Illinois has consistently been middle class, bourgeois, and "our kind of people" in its orientation. Sad to say, too large a segment of the historic black church has fallen into this trap also, as is chronicled by Gayraud Wilmore in his *The Deradicalization of the Black Church*,[13] and in what James Washington describes as the "bourgeoisification of the black church."[14]

The Congregational Christian Churches in 1953 self-consciously started their third black congregation, this time for the single-family homeowners in what was then the upper-middle-class section of the South Side of Chicago. This area is called Park Manor and is the same section of the city that is described in Richard Wright's *Native Son* as a place where Digger Thomas is afraid to be caught after dark. No effort was made to start a church for the blacks who lived in any of Chicago's housing projects, whether those projects were on the South Side, West Side, or North Side! After all, those residents were not "our kind of people."

This third black congregation, the Congregational Church of Park Manor, was intentionally and strategically placed at the corner of Seventieth and South Park Drive in 1953. At the end of the 1950s blacks were starting to move into the "far south corridor" of Chicago's South Side. Several new split-level homes were built and the denomination now saw a new target area—those blacks moving into the new or newly integrated single-family homes. Again, no

41

thought was given to evangelization in the federal housing project that sat two blocks from the church and had been there since World War II, because those residents were *also* . . . not "our kind of people."

It was under those circumstances and with that mentality that the fourth congregation was founded—Trinity United Church of Christ. At first, every effort was made to keep Trinity middle class and bourgeois and as far away from our Christian counterparts with their "inherently African" ways as possible! That tragic tendency put us right in the middle of the trend that both Wilmore and Washington described, where black singing, black preaching, and black praying styles are avoided and eschewed! Negro spirituals that were "concertized" or arranged or treated as anthems, finely honed homilies, and liturgically correct prayers (preferably read from the back of the UCC hymnal) became the order of the day. As one of our senior citizens has described it:

> I came here in the early days of this church . . . before that boy got here! [her current pastor] It was so cold here that if you said "Amen," all the heads would turn to look at you. If you heisted Dr. Watts, you'd be heisting it by yourself. If you shouted, they'd send for an ambulance *and* a straight jacket! I promised the Lord and three other respectable leaders that I wasn't ever coming up in here again. Then that boy came, and praise God! things started to change![15]

Trinity Church limped along with that double consciousness so painfully described by W. E. B. DuBois, undergoing an experience of growth, radical challenges, and near death. From a few couples who covenanted to try a new-church start in December 1961 to the "faithful few" who signed the charter in June 1962, to the three hundred who watched the first unit of their new church home being built and who moved into it triumphantly, the church experienced the joy of growth! In five years they had grown from zero to three hundred.

Then several things happened, almost in rapid-fire succession. Their first pastor left in 1966. Their second pastor came in 1967, and Martin Luther King Jr. was killed in 1968. All over America, Negroes turned black! The black consciousness movement shook the cities, the colleges and universities, and the black and white churches. Black caucuses were formed in predominantly white denominations. Offices and agencies to address the problem of racism were "commissioned" by national bodies.

Crew cuts and Shirley Temple curls were replaced by Afros.

Three-piece suits and A-line dresses were replaced by dashikis and West African garb. Black gospel music began being sung on black and white campuses (and on historic black campuses with "trained" musicians where prior to this point, only arranged or "concertized" spirituals[16] had been permitted). Across denominational lines, young (and old) black churchgoers who had previously been trying assimilation started reclaiming their African heritage from the style of singing to the style of preaching.

Trinity Church was rocked by that cultural revolution. Musicians who refused to give up "serious" music and members who refused to give up Eurocentric ways tried to hold the fort while scores of persons left to go to other churches where they could be sons and daughters of Africa as well as sons and daughters of God! As a result, the second minister left, and the membership dwindled down to eighty-seven.

A Painful Decision

It was at this point in its history (December 1971) when the congregation took a long and serious look at the way they were in the world. They asked themselves this question: Are we going to be a black church in the black community (like our sister congregations in the Christian tradition down in North Carolina and Virginia with their "inherently African" ways)? Or, are we going to continue to try to be a white church in a black face?"

That expression, "white church in a black face" is exactly what we had become! In the best of the Congregationalist tradition, "we could outwhite white people" to use the words of one of our charter members.[17] Back when W. Sterling Cary was the conference minister of the Illinois Conference, at a meeting with the leadership of our church and some conference staff (while trying to raise funds for our new building), he suggested that we take our choir around to the other black churches in the conference and have concerts. The conference treasurer, John Muir, pointed out to Cary that the other churches did not like us precisely because of that choir! He indicated that when whites in the conference wanted to sample the black church experience they would come to Trinity Church, because going to the other black churches in the conference would be going to churches even colder than their own white congregations!

The congregation then made one of the most painful and powerful decisions any black congregation anywhere has ever had to make. It decided to be black and in fact adopted as its motto: "We are a congregation which is unashamedly black and unapologetically Christian!" That phrase, incidentally, was given to me by the interim pastor, Reuben Sheares II, formerly executive director of the UCC Office for Church Life and Leadership, who pointed out me just how difficult and far reaching a decision it actually was. He counseled me never to forget that "some black people join a white denomination to get away from black people!"[18]

That decision to claim our heritage as African Americans has resulted in a change in focus, program, theology, and mission. It has also caused our death-and-dying mode to reverse itself so that we have gone from the eighty-seven members we had in 1972 to more than four thousand today. (I have taken in more than six thousand persons since I started pastoring, but we currently carry only those members who are active.) The way in which Trinity Church has grown over the past eighteen years is a direct result of the congregation's decision to be a black church in the black community and to be a part of the black church tradition with all of its problems and promises. The balance of this essay will focus on what that decision has meant in terms of theology, mission, focus, and program.

Pastoral Perspective and Spiritual Concerns

First, just a word about pastoral perspectives and spiritual concerns! As a "product of the parsonage," the perspective I brought to Trinity Church included at its foundation fervent prayer, Bible study, and spiritual formation. For many urban (Northern) black congregations within the United Church of Christ, those are "alien" topics; but they were fundamental to my approach as pastor. Taking them seriously, then, I found a strong core of members at Trinity Church who also shared these perspectives. What was most helpful was that I found persons in the congregation who took seriously the constitution and bylaws of the church, which recognized the word of God as being the ultimate authority for all the matters of faith and practice that were to govern our congregation. With those as starting parameters, the growth process and the building up of the faith then became a labor of love and joy.

The beginning of a Bible class and the injection of prayer into all of the life and ministry of our congregation were the places where I started. At first the Bible class was considered more or less a joke around Trinity Church. There were only six to eight faithful persons who "hung in there" with me for a couple of years. Eventually, however, that single pastor's Bible class took root, began to spread and grow, and currently boasts of more than fifteen weekly adult Bible classes each trimester of the year.

Prayer meetings and prayer at all of the gatherings of the organizations and boards of our church started rather tenuously at first, but they have since expanded into a devotional period with deacons assigned as chaplains to each of the organizations, auxiliaries, ministries, boards, and councils. Keeping God at the center of our focus and God as our purpose for being together as a people was paramount in enabling us to address the questions of evangelism, church growth, theology, mission, focus, and program.

In dialogue with the older members of the congregation and the charter members, I learned that lack of such focus and purpose was one of the reasons why the adoption of a European style, denial of our selfhood, the insidious cancer of self-hatred, and a lack of spirit had caused our membership to drop off so dramatically! Reappropriating those basics of the faith and relaying the foundation (spiritually) became the first tasks on our agenda in the early days of 1972–1974. Teaching new members what the UCC is and grafting them into the body of Christ as they accepted membership in our congregation became a part of an ongoing training tool and the vital component of our teaching ministry. A separate section at the end of this essay explains the new-member assimilation follow-up program.

Many persons have been frightened by our slogan "unashamedly black and unapologetically Christian," and many more have misunderstood what it means. I believe that a brief description of what the congregation meant in making that decision through a discussion of our theology, mission, and program will lay to rest many of the fears, misapprehensions, and curiosities concerning this shift in congregational thrust back in 1971–1971.

Theology

As Jim Cone says in his *For My People*, black theology as the members of Trinity have understood it is "an interpretation of the faith in the light of black history and culture and completely separate from white religion." For ten years Trinity Church tried to interpret the faith without separating itself "from white religion," and the result was a church that was unsure of who it was and a community (in which the church sat) even more unsure of who or what that church was. Not only were there no programs related to or directed at the black community in which it sat, but the weekly worship experience (all fifty-eight minutes of it) was as totally removed from "black history and culture" as one can possibly imagine.

The theology of "white religion" is inwardly focused. It is cerebral and apologetic and unconcerned with the "incarnational dimensions of spirituality."[19] In other words, the theology of "white religion" can discuss the death of God and ignore the suffering of blacks right in their own midst; in fact it can ignore its own participation in their suffering and oppression! Black theology, by contrast, starts from the premise that not only can those issues *not* be ignored, but God's saving activity has as its starting place these very issues. The Word became flesh in a poor family living under oppression (not in Caesar's palace). The Word becomes flesh in a South African Bantustan (not in Pretoria). The Word becomes flesh in the ghettos and projects of the inner city (not in the rich, white enclaves that surround the city).

Trinity Church's shift to an embracing of black theology caused a concomitant shift in its view of people. No longer were the blacks who live in the project considered as "those people" or "them." No longer was the question What can we do for those people in mission? or What are their needs? With the shift in theological perspective and the mental separation from "white religion" the questions then became What do *our members* need in terms of ministry? What are the needs of *our* community and *our* people? Doing ministry from the perspective of black theology meant an *embracing* of the other (the lowest, the least, the last, the lost, and the left out) and no longer a viewing of them as "objects" of mission! "They" became subjects in mission and partners in mission, no longer persons who lived near or around the church but from then on persons who were members of the church.

Mission

To serve this present age, my calling to fulfill
O may it all my powers engage to do my Master's Will.

Reinterpreting the mission of our church from this theological perspective caused us to start examining the word of God and the will of God from an entirely different vantage point. We began asking different questions: Where, incarnationally, would God be at work in the world today if God were in this community? Since we are God's church, where do we need to be at work in this community? Since God enters into history on the side of the

46

oppressed, since God cares concretely about the downtrodden, and since God is a God who acts on behalf of the helpless, where is (or should be) God (and God's church) at work in this community in this day and age? How *do* we serve this present age?

When one starts asking different questions, then it follows that one starts finding different answers. When Trinity Church started asking this new set of questions (informed by its shift in theological perspective), then a different set of answers emerged—answers that changed our focus and changed our programs. Calvin Butts at the 1988 Mordecai Johnson Institute held at Colgate Rochester quoted Adam Clayton Powell Sr. (of Abyssinian Baptist Church in New York): "When a neighborhood church begins to define its ministry by its members and not its neighbors, then that church has lost its ministry!"[20] That is exactly where the early Trinity Church had been and exactly what we had begun to do. The shift in theological perspective and membership definition—now expanded to include, not exclude, our neighbor—caused us to rethink ministry in the light of God's revelation and to come up with answers to the aforementioned questions which changed both our self-understanding and our programs.

We began to see mission in terms of the black community and our being in the midst of it. Our church moved from a "Sunday-only-from-9:30-to-noon" kind of operation to a seven-day a week (6:00 A.M. until 10:00 P.M.) full-service, holistic ministry, where we attempt to minister to the whole person of all ages, body, mind, and soul. For just about a decade we grew both numerically and spiritually, in terms of new members and in terms of new programs, with our mission being defined almost in a helter-skelter manner. As new members (our neighbors) joined, we attempted to meet their needs, and as they became a part of the church family, new needs were articulated and new ministries were started (and staffed) to address them. This proved to be too scattered an approach to mission, so three things happened to help give our congregation some focus.

Focus

Where there is no vision, the people perish . . .

First, at the end of the 1970s we pulled together a board for long-range planning whose sole purpose was to focus in on what God would have us do in terms of long-range goals and ministries. If we were serious about being a black church institution that would

47

serve our community (and the world) and not just serve our own members, and if we were serious about building an institution based on holy principles and not a human person, then we had to be intentional about sitting down, listening to God, and discovering what vision God would give to the church for the future.

The board was charged with the responsibility of helping us focus as a congregation on being God's church in God's world and helping us become in ministry and program all that God wants us to become. It continues to function and is one of the five major boards of the church on a par with the board of deacons, the board of trustees, the board of Christian education, and the stewardship council. Some of the programs, projects, and ministries it has helped bring into being over the past few years are the federally chartered Credit Union (with assets in excess of $400,000), one new worship center costing $700,000 and a second new worship center presently under construction at a cost of $8 million, the purchase of two parsonages, an insurance endowment program, two $3.5 million senior citizens housing projects (and corporations) that service 120 families, and a for-profit corporation whose net gains are earmarked for ministries that will never be self-supporting.

Second, in addition to the board for long-range planning, I laid before the congregation my Ten-Point Vision for Trinity Church in the 1980s. My vision was that during that decade Trinity Church would become (1) a worshiping church, (2) a spirit-filled church, (3) a praying church, (4) a tithing church, (5) a Bible-based church, (6) a progressive church, (7) a politically aware and active church, (8) a love-centered church, (9) a stronger working church, and (10) a community-conscious and liberation-conscious church. This pastoral focus is used by the executive council and each of the ministries in its annual planning for, and assessment of, the year's work of each ministry. These parameters help to keep our mission focused.

Beyond the board for long-range planning and the pastor's Ten-Point Vision, the third factor that has helped to shape our focus is a self-study (a critique and recommendations) that the congregation commissioned ten years after their momentous decision in 1971 to become "unashamedly black and unapologetically Christian." What they came up with was a black value system that seeks to articulate and clarify both the vision and the focus of a congregation seeking to be faithful to the God of the oppressed. The Black Value System (adopted by the church at a congregational meeting in 1981) reads as follows:

The Black Value System
of Trinity United Church of Christ

These Black Ethics must be taught and exampled in homes, churches, nurseries and schools where Blacks are gathered. They must reflect the following concepts:

Commitment to God—"The God of our weary years" will give us the strength to give up prayerful passivism and become Black Christian activists, soldiers for Black freedom and the dignity of all humankind.

Commitment to the Black community—The highest level of achievement for any Black person must be a contribution to the strength and continuity of the Black community.

Commitment to the Black Family—The Black family circle must generate strength, stability, and love despite the uncertainty of externals, because these characteristics are required if the developing person is to withstand warping by our racist, competitive society. Those Blacks who are blessed with membership in a strong family unit must reach out and extend that blessing to the less fortunate, especially to the children.

Dedication to the pursuit of education—We must forswear anti-intellectualism. Continued survival demands that each Black person be developed to the utmost of his or her mental potential despite the inadequacies of the formal education process. "Real education" fosters understanding of ourselves as well as every aspect of our environment. Also it develops within us the ability to fashion concepts and tools for better utilization of our resources and more effective solutions to our problems. Since the majority of Blacks have been denied such learning, Black education must include elements that produce high school graduates with marketable skills, a trade or qualifications for apprenticeships, or proper preparation for college. Basic education for all Blacks should include mathematics, science, logic, general semantics, participative politics, economics and finance, and the care and nurture of Black minds.

Dedication to the pursuit of excellence—To the extent that we individually reach for, even strain for excellence, we increase, geometrically, the value and resourcefulness of the Black Community. We must recognize the relativity of one's best: this year's best can be bettered next year! Such is the language of growth and development. We must seek to excel in every endeavor.

Adherence to the Black work ethic—"It is becoming harder for Chicago to find qualified people to work in the city." Whether this is true or not, it represents one of the many reasons given by businesses and industries for deserting the Chicago area. We must realize that a location with good facilities, adequate transportation, and a reputation for producing skilled workers will attract industry. We are in competition with other cities, states, and nations for jobs. High productivity must be a goal of the Black work force.

Commitment to self-discipline and self-respect—To accomplish anything worthwhile requires self-discipline. We must be a community of self-disciplined persons, instead of perpetually submitting to exploitation by others. Self-discipline coupled with a respect for self will enable each of us to be an instrument of Black progress and a model for Black youth.

Disavowal of the pursuit of "middleclassness"—Classic methodology on control of captives teaches that captors must keep the captives ignorant educationally but trained sufficiently well to serve the system. Also, the captors must be able to identify the "talented tenth" of those subjugated, especially those who show promise of providing the kind of leadership that might threaten the captors' control. Those so identified are separated from the rest of the people by

- killing them off directly and/or fostering a social system that encourages them to kill off one another
- placing them in concentration camps and/or structuring an economic environment that induces captive youth to fill the jails and prisons
- seducing them into a socioeconomic class system which, while training them to earn more dollars, hypnotizes them into believing they are better than the rest and teaches them to think in terms of "we" and "they" instead of "US"

So while it is permissible to chase "middleincomeness" with all our might, we must avoid the third separation method: the psychological entrapment of Black "middleclassness." If we avoid this snare, we will also diminish our "voluntary" contributions to the first two methods above. More importantly, Black people no longer will be deprived of their birthright: the leadership, resourcefulness, and example of their own talented persons.

Pledge to make the fruits of all developing and acquired skills available to the Black Community.

Pledge to make the fruits of all developing and acquired skills available for strengthening and supporting Black institutions.

Pledge allegiance to all Black leadership who espouse and embrace the Black Value System.

Personal commitment to embracement of the Black Value System—To measure the worth and validity of all activity in terms of positive contributions to the general welfare of the Black Community and the advance of Black people towards freedom (and liberation).[21]

These values, in addition to the pastor's vision and the board for long-range planning, serve as parameters within which to focus our mission and ministry as a black church solidly within the black church tradition and seeking to be faithful to that tradition as we move toward the twenty-first century.

Program

The People had a mind to work.

When the church shifted in 1971 from being a "white church in black face" to being a black church, it approached its task from the perspective of the black theology that (1) had been articulated in the souls, sounds, songs, and sermons of black folk from time immemorial and (2) was being systematized and printed by the black theology movement of the late 1960s and 1970s. The theological assessment behind the shift caused the members of Trinity to begin an engagement with the Bible that they had not previously had. Filtering all one's actions, thoughts, reflections, decisions, programs, and ministries through a study of God's Word was something new for the congregation in 1972. It is now "old hat," yet that filtering process is the foundation for all the theology, mission, focus, and programs of the church.

Bible Study

The Bible Study Development program is a full-scale curriculum of adult Bible study that starts a person off with a definition of "the inspired word of God"—not from the simplistic definitions given by the "Word churches," the "Christian Centers," and the televangelists, but from an engagement with Paul Achtemeier's text, *The Inspiration of Scripture*.[22] Then it builds slowly on that foundation a scientifically informed and spiritually based study of the sacred texts, both Hebrew and Christian.

A recommended sequence of courses is the Inspiration of Scripture course, the Bible Basics course (which does a broad overview of the various genres and groupings of biblical books), and the God's Word and My Salvation course (which answers foundational questions for "new Christians"). These "new Christians" are often under attack in a city such as Chicago from some parts of the Pentecostal family (who consider them not being "saved" if they're UCC), some parts of the Moody Bible-Wheaton Bible College stronghold, some parts of the Black Muslim family, the Black Hebrew family, and the Black Nationalist Community (which is fairly large in our city), and all parts of the Jehovah's Witnesses.

Following the Salvation courses are survey courses (Survey of the Old Testament: Law and History, Survey of the Old Testament: Poetry and Prophecy, and Survey of the New Testament). Then there is the Biblical Faith and the Black American course, which uses Latta Thomas's book by the same name; and that concludes the core courses, or the "required" courses, in the recommended sequence before students are "allowed" (or encouraged) to take the intermediate and advanced courses. The intermediate courses are studies of the individual books of the Bible, the topical courses, and the survey courses in black religious experience. The advanced courses include in-depth examination of different approaches to exegesis and the more technical (or concentrated) courses on some specific aspect of the black church in the Americas.

Each trimester at Trinity Church there are anywhere from fifteen to twenty weekly Bible classes (depending on class size). This study program is the foundational program for all the other forms of ministry in which we engage.

Church-wide Study

The Church-wide Study program is separate and distinct from individual or group Bible study. The congregation engages annually in a church-wide study course. It generally has two foci. The first is on the book that all the organizations of the church are using all year long as the guide to their devotional periods and their group or all-church retreats. Generally, a chapter a month is covered by the "chaplains" assigned to each ministry, who is one of the ordained deacons of the church. The deacons themselves receive training on each month's chapter before going in to the ministry to lead the discussions.

The second focus is on a book that the entire church membership examines during black history month. Each year we study a book by a black person whose author is still alive in order that sometime during the month of February the author can come to the church and engage in conversation with the members. Over the past few years we have read and listened to such authors as Latta Thomas, Clayton Jones, Wallace Charles Smith, Henry Mitchell, Ella

Mitchell, Vincent Harding, Ivan Van Sertima, and Cain Hope Felder.

Separate and distinct from both the month-by-month book and the black history month book, the black liberation bookshelf holds a monthly seminar on some work by or about black people. This group generally invites an outside speaker in to share with members of the congregation; and through their efforts we have hosted such notables as Jacob Carruthers, Bettye Parker, Haki Madhabuti, Bobby Wright, Iva Carruthers, Margaret Burroughs, and Lerone Bennett. These three "church-wide" efforts serve to reinforce the Bible Study Development program and its goals and objectives.

Christian Education from the Black Perspective

Back in 1973, it was those predominantly white denominations with significant numbers of black congregations in them—the United Methodists, the United Presbyterians, the Lutheran Church in America, the American Baptist Church, the Episcopal Church, the Christian Church (Disciples of Christ), and the United Church of Christ—who came together under the auspices of the Joint Educational Development (JED) to put together black-oriented church-school curriculum and materials. They entitled the program "Christian Education from the Black Perspective." It was the collective thinking of these Christian educators that produced vacation Bible school materials and one- or two-year church-school curricula modules from the black perspective. They also provided the understanding that unless black children read and see materials that relate to them and their experience, no matter how well intentioned any presentation may be, all it will do is perpetuate the racism that is already a cancer in the body of the North American populace.

That philosophical commitment has led to many exciting joint ventures between the cooperating denominations; but more important, it has given us at Trinity Church a starting point from which to move in all our educational endeavors. Our youth church, our Saturday church school, our seventeen youth programs, and our adult education courses are all designed with the understanding that all our education at Trinity Church will proceed from "an interpretation of the faith in the light of black history and culture." Unfortunately, many of the "historic black denominations" have not yet made that commitment; our commitment is based not on what others are doing but on what God has already done!

An understanding of who we are and whose we are based on the above "foundational" program issues is found in the more than sixty ministries at Trinity Church. Just a few of them will be cursorily described here to give the reader some idea of the programs that flow from the commitment described above.

Child Care

To meet the need of unemployed and underemployed families in our neighborhood (whether single-parent or two-parent families) we began in 1974 and continue to operate two federally funded Title XX child-care programs. They provide quality child care (with an educational component and a full-time social worker) for needy families, who are required to pay—on a sliding scale—a mere pittance of what child care currently costs in the city. The programs operate from 6:00 A.M. until 6:00 P.M. and provide hot meals to children ages three to five.

After School

Where does a black child going to public school learn who the *real* father of medicine is (Imhotep) and not the one whom the Eurocentric educational system presents. Where does that child learn about Henry Highland Garnett, Bishop Henry McNeal Turner, Jarena Lee, Paul Cuffee, Queen Ann Nzinga, and Marcus Garvey? Based on the model of the synagogue schools in Philadelphia, where little Jewish children learn their history and heritage after school, our Sojourner Truth Cultural Awareness Institute is an after-school program (in two parts), which addresses the same needs in the lives of African American children.

Sojourner I is the program for children in first grade through eighth grade. It runs every week during the forty-week academic year. Sojourner II, for high school age, attempts to give students factual material about black history and culture that they do not learn in the public school curriculum. It also attempts to teach the teenagers values and how to make informed moral judgments when confronted by all the issues facing a black teenager in an inner-city setting.

Official Board and Apprenticeship Training

To be elected to the board of deacons or the board of trustees at Trinity Church now requires that persons be trained as apprentices for these important positions. The class system and the rotation of elected officers used throughout the United Church of Christ is utilized at Trinity, but preparation for ordination and for full-time service as a trustee or deacon is preceded by a full year's apprentice program. The board of deacons starts its apprentice program in the fall of each year at a week-long series of classes run nightly from 7 P.M. until 10 P.M. (Daytime classes are offered for those persons who work in the evenings.)

During that week, the apprentices are given an overview of what it means to be a deacon in the church, starting with being a covenant people from Genesis 12 coming all the way down to the formation of the Christian church in the first century and on to the Reformation in the sixteenth century. They study the development of the historical predecessor denominations of the United Church of Christ, the development of the black church, and changes in the perspectives of the office of deacon across those centuries. The two sacraments of the church, the biblical foundations for them, our Judeo-Christian heritage, and the role of ordained deacons in administering them are also taught in this course.

Following the week's training, the apprentices are assigned to a team of deacons and actually "walk" with them for a full year, visiting the sick, taking communion to the infirm, going to prisons, serving at funerals, preparing the sacraments, and attending monthly meetings wherein there are mini-sessions for training and preparation for service. An additional six-week program (once a week at night) is offered for the apprentices, where they cover in detail and in depth the Statement of Faith of the United Church of Christ, the constitution and bylaws of Trinity UCC, the Black Value System, the pastor's Ten-Point Vision, and the guidelines of the board of deacons. One year's apprenticeship gives the apprentices a broad view of the work of the office of deacon and the board of deacons a chance to look at the sincerity of apprentices to ascertain more judiciously (in accordance with Acts 6) the apprentice's sincerity about seeking the office of deacon.

The board of trustees in similar fashion has an apprenticeship program whereby apprentices are given a full year's training before they are eligible for election to the board of trustees. They are taught the various tasks and responsibilities of being a trustee of Trinity UCC. They actually work with the counting teams on Sundays and are assigned to the personnel committee, the property committee, or another board committee to gain a feel for the work of the trustees before they make that three-year commitment.

55

Tutorial Programs

A black church is a place where people care and where that care is made manifest by "incarnational spirituality," where concrete acts of love demonstrate that God really did give me a "new way of walking and talking." That statement becomes real in Trinity's tutorial programs, where each week more than a hundred children from kindergarten through college are tutored individually in math, reading, and science to improve their skills and their scores.

Actual apprenticeship programs are provided in a few areas, as for example, clerical skills, housing management, and horticulture. In these programs, students are sent to school—with the church paying their tuition—and then employed by the church while they learn their trade. As soon as the new church facilities are completed, both the tutorial and the apprenticeship programs will expand into the computer and computer-literacy fields.

Scholarship Programs

Trinity Church believes firmly in putting its money where its mouth is. We have been pushing excellence in education for so long that some members are probably tired of hearing about it. We do more than push it verbally, however. We back it up with our dollars. On an annual budget that is in the neighborhood of $50,000 or $60,000 the scholarship programs function in four ways:

1. Each year $16,000 to $20,000 worth of scholarships are given away, depending on monthly scholarship offerings. The scholarships are given chiefly to graduating seniors going to college. One or two special awards are given to grammar school graduates and students already in college, seminary, or graduate school. The scholarships are based on three criteria: academic excellence, extracurricular activities at school, and extracurricular activities at church.

2. Each year seminarians who are members of Trinity can be reimbursed for tuition and books up to $3,000 per student, as long as they are actually working in their home church, are enrolled in an accredited seminary, and maintain an overall "B" average. We currently have eighteen such members.

3. Emergency scholarship aid is given to individual students on an "at need" basis. This practice is kept to a minimum and is utilized only when a person might have to drop out of school.

56

4. At an Annual Scholarship Oratorical Contest in black history month, children from first grade through high school compete—in their age groups—before the entire congregation.

Abuse-Recovery Ministry

Substance abuse is a well-known problem in the black community. How to help individuals and families, however, is often a task that is left up to secular social service agencies and counselors. Persons are referred to Alcoholics Anonymous and Narcotics Anonymous; but far too many of these programs do not ground a person in the faith of our ancestors, while others act as if the person's spiritual dimension does not exist beyond the capacity for self-help. Our church, however, seeks to help those persons, starting from biblical, spiritual, and experiential bases. Our counselors are themselves former substance abusers who can now "witness" from personal experience to those who need a word of hope.

Counseling Ministry

Closely related to the above mentioned program is the vast area of pastoral counseling, pastoral psychotherapy, and individual, family, and crisis counseling. Assisting the five staff ministers and the seven volunteer ministers[23] at our church are a cadre of trained therapists who volunteer their time and expertise in handling the heavy case load of counseling at Trinity UCC. This ministry, incidentally, was one of the many that was started by the laity themselves, who "caught the vision" after a Bible study on tithing one's time and talent (in addition to one's money).

Legal-Counseling Ministry

Yet another example of how persons "catch the vision" is the way our attorneys banded together to provide free legal services to senior citizens and free legal counseling to members of the church, after hearing how the social workers were committed to giving back to God because of God's having blessed them. In addition to providing their skill, the lawyers also provide nurture and support for members of the church who are already in (or are headed for) law school and members studying for the bar exams.

Prison Ministry

Providing support to the families of those who are incarcerated, as well as actually visiting prisons, is the focus of the prison ministry, which seeks to take seriously the Lord's words "when I was in prison, you visited me." So often in a city like Chicago, churches carry choirs out to the prison, offer a worship experience, and go back home, leaving the prisoners high and dry. Our program seeks to provide for educational and spiritual needs long after the benediction has been given.

Single-Adult Ministry

One of the historic, and still continuing, trends of the black church has been its role as the extended family for so many who were "motherless" or "fatherless." The fact that on any given Sunday in almost every black church population at least 50 percent of those sitting in the pews are single is appalling, when you consider how few of our churches have moved from the Stone Age in their understanding of, and ministry with, singles. The single-adult ministry of Trinity Church seeks to take seriously the three categories of singles (never married, widowed, and divorced) and to provide a wide range of programs addressed to their specific needs as black Christian men and women.

Church in Society

That the black church has long since been at the forefront of the struggles for liberation both politically and economically is almost an overdocumented fact. To continue in this sterling tradition and to keep our congregation from developing an other-worldly spirituality or piety that divorces itself from the concerns of this world, our Church in Society program was developed. Its purpose is to keep us engaged with the society in which we live, locally, city-wide, statewide, and nationally.

"Engagement" can and does mean anything and everything from signing petitions to letter-writing campaigns; voter-registration drives; political and educational forums, workshops, and seminars; Operation PUSH membership drives; dialogue with officials in the criminal justice system; disseminating literature; up to and including running for political office. This "cutting edge" of ministry has a tendency to keep the congregation always in a dialectic tension between reflection and action.

Ministerial Training

"Equipping the saints" takes on many faces at Trinity Church, from deacon and trustee apprenticeship programs to in-service workshops for the Bible Study Development teachers and church-school teachers, weekly staff meetings, programs to visit the sick taught by instructors from the local seminaries, leadership-development classes for the officers of the church, up to and including monthly training sessions for the eighteen seminarians. Our seminarians (unfortunately) are all going to white seminaries, where they receive little or no training in the history, development, or theology of the black church. These monthly meetings with them are designed to give them some exposure to the rich diversity and history that is ours. Each month they have to read and grapple with some author who is black or who has written about the black experience in religion.

Special Worship Services

In addition to worshiping each Sunday in the black religious tradition and having two Wednesday prayer preaching services (Remember! That was a radical break with the way we had been from 1961 to 1971.), several times each year African and African American observances are celebrated by the entire church family. Two of those "special" services are *Umoja Karamu* and *Kwanzaa*.

Each year at Thanksgiving, the congregation gathers to celebrate the *Umoja Karamu* (Swahili for "feat of Unity"). The choir, the ministers, the deacons, and all the liturgists dress in African garb, and our pilgrimage as African Americans is celebrated by songs, dances, stories, and ritual foods as we reflect on the way over which God has brought us—from tribal life in Africa to presidential candidates in North America! The *Umoja Karamu* was written as an African American ceremony by Dr. Edward Sims of Montgomery Junior College in Pennsylvania. The funding for it came from the UCC Board for Homeland Ministries.

Kwanzaa, the African American ritual developed by Maulana Karenga, is celebrated each night at Trinity Church between December 26 and December 31. The ministries are grouped together (seven or eight each night), and each night one of the principles of the *Nguza Saba* is lifted up, with the ministries explaining (or demonstrating) how they best exemplify that particular principle in their ministry. On the last night of *Kwanzaa* we end with a potluck supper and go right into the traditional black church watch meeting service, complete with testimonies and getting down on our knees at 11:57 to "pray out the old year and pray in the new."

New-Member Follow-up

On the Sunday that a person "walks the aisle" to express publicly his or her desire to become a member of the church, one of the ministers of the newness-of-life ministry along with the church clerk accompanies the person to an anteroom to begin to explain the new-member process and to "walk" with the candidate as he or she is taken into the church family. The candidate is given information as to when the new-member classes will be held and which class he or she will attend, depending upon whether the person is joining by Christian experience (meaning that the person has been baptized and belonged to another church before Trinity) or whether he or she is joining as a candidate for baptism. The candidate is given printed resources about the UCC, Trinity Church, the class, and some devotional material.

The newness-of-life minister exchanges telephone numbers with the new members and then begins the process of staying in touch until they have completed their classes and are "fellowshiped" into the church family. This contact includes periodic telephone calls, checking up on them— especially if they don't make their assigned classes—and encouragement in terms of Bible study and their use of the devotional materials. If new members are candidates for baptism, a lot of explaining goes on about the vocabulary used by the Christian church, the Christian family, the Trinity Church family, and this whole new way of being for those who have expressed faith in Christ Jesus.

During the last hour of the new-member classes—both Christian experience and baptismal—each of the ministries of the church is explained and questions arising from the annual reports are answered. We take time for this information because members are expected to indicate on the Sunday they join where they intend to work in the life of the church. The new members make a commitment in terms of their financial resources and their time and expertise or interest in a particular area.

On the Sunday of the right hand of fellowship, new members' names are called out along with the ministries with which they intend to work. Their name tags include both their own name and their chosen ministry. Following the benediction, the congregation comes around to shake hands with each new member, and members of the various ministries make themselves known to the new members who have chosen them. Greetings, names, and addresses are exchanged, and the new members are reminded that they are expected at the various ministry meetings.

On the Monday following the first Sunday of the month when new members are received, the membership clerk of the church sends to the various ministries (both to their presidents and their membership secretaries) the names of the new members and their addresses and work and home telephone numbers. The stewardship council follows up one month after the fellowship Sunday by checking with the various ministries to see if that new member has in fact been to the meeting. If he or she has, then the follow-up is left to the ministry itself. If the person has not, the stewardship council calls that new member to find out if there has been some change in his or her desire to work with a particular ministry, if there has been a transportation problem, a work-scheduling problem, or whatever it was that prevented that member from following through on the commitment to serve. Most of the time it is simply a matter of scheduling, and that prompting call from the stewardship council reminds the new member that he or she is cared for, cared about, and being counted on to work.

The newness-of-life ministry encourages the new member to enroll in Bible class and to attend the midweek prayer services of the church, in addition to whatever ministry he or she has selected. Once the new member is actively involved in his or her ministry, the newness-of-life ministry closes the file on that new member.

Trinity in the Black Church Tradition

How and where we fit in the black church tradition is best exemplified in two ways: the preachers who come here and where (and why) our members go when they leave.

Over the past eighteen years we have had a great variety of outstanding black preachers at Trinity. Our members don't care what denomination these preachers are, just so long as they give the congregation something for their heads *and* their hearts.

Persons who have preached at Trinity Church since 1971 include the following: Samuel McKinney (Baptist), Charles Cobb (UCC), Clarence H. Cobb (Spiritual), Clay Evans (Baptist), Jeremiah A. Wright Sr. (Baptist), McKinley Young (AME), Bishop Louis H. Ford (COGIC), Mary H. Wright (Baptist), Morris Lee (Baptist), Nathaniel Jarrett (AMEZ), T. Garrott Benjamin (Disciples of Christ), Jessica

Ingram (AME), Cecilia Bryant (AME), Brenda Little (Baptist), Hycel Taylor (Baptist), Gardner Taylor (Baptist), Frederick G. Sampson (Baptist), Charles G. Adams (Baptist), Bishop H. H. Brookins (AME), Charles Spivey (AME), James A. Forbes Jr. (United Holy Church/UCC/Baptist), W. Sterling Cary (UCC), Yvonne Delk (UCC), Kenneth T. Whalum (Baptist), Harold Carter (Baptist), William A. Jones (Baptist), Charles Booth (Baptist), Bishop John Bryant (AME), Henry Mitchell (Baptist), Carolyn Knight (Baptist), Frank Madison Reid III (AME), Cynthia Hale (Disciples of Christ), Prathia Wynn (Baptist), and Robert Franklin (COGIC).

When members of Trinity leave Chicago, they ask for a referral to any black church where the word of God is preached with power, where the members are politically active in the liberation process, where the music is in the black church tradition, and where the educational ministries are comparable to those in their home church. They also ask for a church that takes seriously value number 8 in the Black Value System, because one of the things we teach and preach the hardest is that the black church must never become a "silk stocking" church for "them that's got." It must always be a church that cuts across all socioeconomic and educational levels. Otherwise, it becomes guilty of the same sin and heresy as its white counterparts.

NOTES

1. *History and Program of the United Church of Christ* (New York: United Church Press, 1986).

2. J. Taylor Stanley, *A History of Black Congregational Christian Churches of the South.* (New York: United Church Press, 1978), p. 9.

3. This church, incidentally, was founded when the new pastor's wife came to Christ Church, Pittsfield, where blacks and whites had been worshiping together. When she saw that the Africans were drinking from the same communion cup, she said, "This will never do!" and subsequently persuaded her husband and the officers to set aside funds and materials for building a house of worship for the blacks!

4. The *Amistad* was the name of a slave ship that was taken over by mutinous African slaves and sailed into Boston Harbor. Once in United States territory they demanded their freedom and repatriation to West Africa. The Congregational Church paid for and successfully defended their case in court.

5. A. Knighton Stanley, *The Children Is Crying: Congregationalism Among Black People* (Philadelphia: Pilgrim Press, 1979), p. 10.

6. This is a term that the churches chose for themselves in the nineteenth century. J. Taylor Stanley, *A History*, p. 54.

7. Reminiscent of Richard Allen and Absalom Jones.

8. Nor did it matter!

9. While baptism by immersion makes these Christian churches seem Baptist, the titles and polity seem more in line with their African Methodist brothers and sisters.

10. J. Taylor Stanley, *A History*, p. 55.

11. Of the 288 black churches within the 6,500 congregations of the UCC, 200 of them are from the Christian tradition!

12. A. Knighton Stanley, *The Children Is Crying*, p. 2.

13. Gayraud Wilmore, *Black Religion and Black Radicalism: An Interpretation of the Religious History of Afro-American people*, 2nd ed. (Maryknoll, N.Y.: Orbis Books, 1983), pp. 135–166.

14. James Washington, "Kingdom Building: Tools for the Task, The Aristocracy of Faith (Vocation and Method)," Hildebrand-Robinson Lectures of the AME Church, Philadelphia, September 1987.

15. Testimony of Mrs. Sadie Triplett, Watch Meeting Service, Trinity UCC, December 31, 1978.

16. Wyatt Tee Walker, *Somebody's Calling My Name: Black Sacred Music and Social Change* (Valley Forge, Pa.: Judson Press, 1979), p. 62.

17. A term coined by Mildred Chapman, charter member of Trinity UCC.

18. Interview with Reuben Sheares II, March 1972.

19. This term is used by John McKinney in his lecture "Creation-Centered Spirituality" at the Hampton University Ministers Conference, June 4, 1987.

20. Calvin Butts, "Pastoral Perspectives on Political Activism," Twelfth Annual Mordecai Wyatt Johnson Institute on Religion and Politics, Colgate Rochester Divinity School, March 1988.

21. Jeremiah A. Wright, *The Twenty-Fifth Year of Ministry*, Chicago: Trinity United Church of Christ, 1986), pp. 3–5.

22. Paul J. Achtemeier, *The Inspiration of Scripture*, (Philadelphia: Westminster Press, 1980).

23. Volunteer ministers are ordained clergy who work somewhere other than Trinity Church (such as denominational staff, hospital chaplaincy, or private pastoral counseling), while maintaining their membership at Trinity and volunteering their time there.

By Faith . . .
Together!

First Community Church, Columbus, Ohio

BARRY L. JOHNSON

This is the story of a dream, a vision, a failure, and a triumph. First Community Church was enjoying one of its most prosperous eras. Over the last seven years, worship attendance had increased 25 percent, attendance at the church's summer camps had tripled, a successful television ministry reaching more than 2 million people had been established, missions contributions had doubled, and both the church budget and operating funds contributions had increased by 50 percent. During this time period, physical improvements had abounded at the church, Camp Akita, and First Community Village. Still, the long overdue project of extending the ministry of the church to a new location needed to be addressed.

It's a stately old building, the one housing First Community Church at 1320 Cambridge Boulevard, Columbus, Ohio. Stately and inadequate. I first saw it on a brisk fall evening in 1976, when I was there to hear a lecture. At the time, I was the senior minister of Shiloh Church (UCC) in Dayton and had no idea that one day I would hold that office at FCC. "Is this all there is?" I asked my associate, Gary Hogue, who had made the trip to Columbus with

Barry L. Johnson has been senior minister of First Community Church, Columbus, Ohio, since 1983. Previously he was senior minister of Shiloh United Church of Christ, Dayton. He has been the pioneer in local-church television ministry in the UCC.

me. "Surely, this renowned hotbed of innovation and cutting-edge ministry has better facilities than this."

"No way," he responded. "I've been here before. This is all there is. What you see is what you get."

Lyle Schaller has noted that there is nothing more potentially destructive or delightful to a church then the challenge of relocation. Twelve years after my first visit to FCC I found myself leading this storied congregation as it confronted, for the second time, the issue of relocation. Now, having struggled through the tedium of long-range planning, the hassle of reviving the issue of relocation, the pain of a negative vote, and a subsequent year of picking up the pieces and developing a fresh approach, which succeeded only in raising the funds to build a Center for Extended Ministry and to renovate the current building, I can only say that, once again, Schaller was right. I hope this synopsis of an extraordinary journey is helpful to every leader confronted by a similar opportunity.

The Setting

Before I recount the relocation saga at First Community Church, I want to offer a brief overview of the ambience of the church. FCC is intentionally diverse, inclusive, and, as an institution, willing to put up with almost all forms of behavior. Consequently, an enormous amount of energy is invested in honoring minority positions and opinions. Ironic though it may seem, FCC's preoccupation with tolerance lends itself to perpetual conflict. Of course, the conflict ratio increases in direct proportion to the aggressiveness of the programs and policies of the church. Action prompts reaction, and since it is the nature of this church to "make space for the individual," nearly all actions are deemed acceptable no matter how disruptive they may be. Hence, when folk are unhappy with the direction of the church they are given plenty of space to voice their concerns. The stronger the leadership, the stronger the opposition.

I would be less than candid if I did not admit that my tenure at First Community has been marked by lots of action and lots of conflict. From the beginning, there has been a small but persistent group of individuals more than willing to oppose my leadership. At first, this opposition tended to focus on theology and administration. As the years passed, it became increasingly personal.

All of which is simply to explain that a key portion of the most ardent opposition to the relocation of First Community Church was little more than opposition to the ministry of Barry Johnson.

The Challenge

First Community Church is a mini-denomination. With nearly four thousand members, ten professionals on the program staff, forty full-time employees, a thirteen hundred-acre campground, a retirement village housing more than four hundred people, a complete television production studio, and a $2 million operating budget (excluding the retirement village), FCC is a multi-layered institution marked by a rich history, an enormous program, a demanding congregation, and a building that is simply insufficient.

The sanctuary seats a maximum of twelve hundred people; seven hundred are unable to see 80 percent of the chancel because they are seated at right angles to it.

The church parking lot accommodates eighty-five cars. That's it. No more. Those unable to find a spot in the lot are relegated to street parking in a neighborhood that is less than pleased to have "all those church folk" blocking their driveways and using up every foot of available curbside space.

The roof leaks. The offices are too small. There is no room except the sanctuary where more than two hundred people can gather. There are only two rooms available for adult education on Sunday morning. The youth are forced to meet in the musty balcony of an eighty-year-old heirloom, the oldest section of the church, built in 1910. Babies must be left in a poorly constructed brick structure across an alley from the main building. The rest rooms are too small, improperly located, and predictably depressing. The news office floor features flowing water at least ten times a year.

Yet a lot of people love the old place. This is not a good situation. Without a shadow of a doubt, First Community Church needs a new building. But need and want are two different issues, and never has that been more clearly demonstrated than here in Columbus during the last four years.

A Sense of Déjà Vu

Relocation is not a new subject at First Community Church. Roy Burkhart, who served FCC for twenty-six years, perceived the need to relocate before he retired in 1958. Doing his best to lay the groundwork for such a move, Burkie, as he is affectionately remembered, secured a twenty-acre piece of land ideally located in what was then the fastest-growing zone in northwest Columbus. At the same time, he was formulating a dream to build a complex where people could spend the December years of their lives provided with maximum care and needing to expend minimum effort. This was at a time when retirement homes were virtually unheard of. But Burkhart persisted, and when he retired, he had set the stage for both the relocation of the church and the construction of First Community Village. Or almost. That's where the rub comes. When the new senior minister, Otis Maxfield, arrived on the scene, he found himself confronted with two major projects and no major money. He chose to pursue the retirement center concept and, with the help of a few influential lay people who signed mortgages, succeeded in constructing First Community Village. The congregation didn't vote on this venture. It was simply done.

In the meantime, the relocation issue was put on hold. It stayed that way until the first phase of the village was nearly completed. At that time, relocation was again placed on the table and met with a positive response. Of course, the predictable naysayers did emerge, but in a gala all-church event at Veteran's Memorial Auditorium in downtown Columbus (one of the few places where the congregation could gather as a whole) the congregation voted by a two-to-one margin to relocate FCC to the corner of Reed and McCoy, some six miles north of Cambridge Boulevard. Architects were designated and plans for a $3 million church were conceived. With a little diligence one can still turn up a few copies of those drawings.

The problem was money. When Maxfield began to canvass the congregation in search of support, he discovered that many of the key contributors were already obligated to First Community Village, and those who were not obligated just plain did not want to participate in the relocation of the church. There was a lot of talk about "the new church," but it was really placed on a back burner. There, it fizzled.

A few years passed and Otis Maxfield chose to leave First Community. With him went the major incentive for building a new church. FCC held on to that twenty-acre plot for more than ten years before selling it in order to pay for expenses incurred when a capital-funds campaign failed to generate enough income to pay for badly needed remodeling that had already been completed. I've heard this problem is relatively common in churches wrestling with the question of relocation. There is enough sentiment to stymie a move but not enough financial support to maintain the old building.

Leadership, Vision, and Planning

The failure to build at Reed and McCoy made a serious dent in the confidence of First Community Church. It was a bitter pill for the leaders of the church, who were all relatively young. The chairman of the governing board at the time of the vote was only thirty-two. Several of the various committee chairs were also in their thirties. Forced to let go of the task, they never surrendered the vision. Two decades later, some of the same people would be back on the line, doing their best to assure the future of the church they loved.

Here I want to say a word about the role of the senior minister. It is my opinion that major projects must have major champions, lay as well as clergy. One of these must be the senior minister. I was once told that it is the duty of the senior minister to paint the vision by which the church is drawn into the future. I believe that. Thus, without the full commitment of the senior minister to the concept of relocation, every effort is destined to fail. As I reflect on the history of FCC, it seems to me as though once Otis Maxfield stepped back from the relocation challenge, none of his successors chose to pick up the gauntlet. I suspect all of them thought about it, and there are stories that a few investigated the possibilities, but none appeared willing to reclaim the dream.

I came to First Community Church with the conviction that this was one of the last of the large, prosperous, liberal churches in the nation. The heritage of innovation amid diversity laid claim to my heart early in my conversations with the search committee. Nonetheless, I knew that the relocation issue had to be addressed if the future of this unique institution was to be preserved. I also sensed that it would not be an easy issue to resurrect. During my early days in Columbus, several people spoke to me about relocation. "Do you think we'll ever build a new church?" "How do you plan to overcome the parking problem?" And most ominous, "They tried to move this church once, but we stopped 'em and we'll do it again."

At the same time I was hearing such feedback from the congregation, the staff made no bones about informing me of the inadequacies of the building. They pointed out the cramped offices, leaking roof, despicable rest rooms, and poor meeting spaces. Within a few months I had experienced the failure of the infrastructure. The temperature in most of the classrooms was totally unpredictable. It was not at all unusual for children to wear coats in class because there was not enough heat. Almost all the offices were equipped with portable space heaters glowing red with the announcement that the heating system was woefully inadequate. What about the sanctuary? Well, it's the fooler. It had a homey charm about it that denied practical reality. Since the majority of the congregation rarely used the remainder of the building, I knew the sanctuary was the key to increasing awareness of the building's inadequacies.

Two circumstances added to the challenge. First, FCC had done a major renovation in 1978 that, at least on the surface, made the sanctuary feel acceptable . . . particularly to those who had been living with it for years. New carpet, a new sound system, and a redesigned chancel made the worship space feel new to most of the old-timers. Of course, acoustics were still miserable, and owing to the cross-shaped floorplan, only those directly in front of the altar could actually see all the participants in the service. Still, it felt "fixed" even if it wasn't. The second circumstance was the result of my own efforts. One year after I arrived at FCC, we conducted a successful capital-funds campaign to air-condition the sanctuary and install a complete broadcast-quality television system. This meant that the comfort level in the sanctuary increased at the same time the chancel was being brilliantly illuminated by eighty new television lights. The result was a feeling of bright new life. I could hear people thinking, "This is just fine!"

It was not. The television ministry did result in a new flow of visitors and extensive impact on the central Ohio area through our weekly telecast on CBS, but it did not and could not solve the building problems at 1320 Cambridge Boulevard. Somehow, we had to come up with a way to communicate to the whole congregation how frustrating it was to try and conduct ministries in such an inadequate building. The opportunity arrived through the efforts of a consultant in 1987.

In 1987 First Community contracted with Speed Leas of the Alban Institute to conduct a long-range-planning process that would encourage the congregation to look twenty-five years into the future. It took six months and an enormous amount of research, but the final report listed four priorities for First Community Church: (1) the *Spiritual Searcher*, a plan to enlist theologians and philosophers to visit FCC regularly and expose the congregation to new systems of spiritual and theological thought; (2) an *Older Persons Ministry*, which would respond to our aging community with freshly evolved programs specifically for older

70

adults; (3) *Akita*, a commitment to renovate and expand the resources at our thirteen-hundred-acre campground located some fifty miles southeast of Columbus; (4) the *building*, a commitment to study the current building with a concern for whether or not it would be adequate to meet our needs twenty-five years in the future.

Here, I need to be frank. The building issue originated with the staff and was largely fueled by staff energy. As far as the lay people were concerned, they were mostly unaware of the problems the building presented. They also suffered from what I see as a special dimension of the large church; they thought that because FCC was then, it always would be, a large church! Growth was not a concern to them. They were much more interested in developing programs for personal purposes than in positioning the church for maximum growth. When the staff began to articulate the problems, however, their concerns found ready ears among the long-range planners, and the building issue showed up on the chart of every planning group. It was time for the governing board to act.

Of all the lay people who had an important impact on the relocation issue at FCC, none proved more significant than Jeff Keeler. Keeler, who assumed the chair of our governing board in February 1988, is a gifted businessman, a faithful churchman, and an extraordinary human being. He caught the vision of a new building early and never lost it. I would say he is a conservative man, but I don't want to mislead you. Mort Sahl once observed, "A conservative is someone who believes nothing should be done for the first time!" That's not Jeff Keeler's kind of conservative. Keeler does believe things should be done for the first time, but only after adequate homework and always with respect for the past. Knee-jerk responses run against his grain; well-planned excursions into unknown territory capture his fancy. He was the perfect leader to join hands with me in spearheading the campaign for the new building.

Jeff named four task forces to prepare action plans for each of the priorities presented by the long-range-planning committee. The facility task force was headed by a much respected former chair of the governing board, Don Gardiner. An attorney, Gardiner is a stickler for detail and simply will not accept sloppy work. The task force studied demographics, interviewed church-growth consultants, conducted surveys, visited other churches that had relocated, and studied possible sites where FCC might build. It deliberated for eight months before unanimously recommending that the church consider building new premises as soon as possible.

Meanwhile, Jeff Keeler named three more task forces to take us even farther down the relocation road. The site-acquisition task force had the charge of finding the best possible location for a new church. The financial-feasibility task force was challenged to bring in consultants to evaluate the financial potential of the congregation to undertake a major building program. The design-concept task force was commissioned to conduct an architectural competition to submit a design for the new building to present to the congregation prior to the vote on relocation announced for Pentecost Sunday, May 14, 1989. Momentum continued to build. Up until this point, I had the feeling that things were going very well. Those working on the various task forces had occasional differences of opinion, but they usually arrived at a point of consensus. As far as the need for a new building was concerned, there was strong agreement among the lay leaders and staff that it was absolutely necessary. Predictably, however, opposition began to form.

Organized Opposition and Democratic Voting

What is the best approach to organized opposition? For years, I had operated under the principle that it is unwise to give a forum to negative forces. Hence, when the editor of the church newsletter told me she had received a letter requesting the announcement of an open meeting to "discuss the direction of the church," I balked. With the leadership of the church unified behind the need to build a new structure, I couldn't imagine using the church newsletter to call a meeting for those opposed. After consultation with Keeler, we determined that we would not use the newsletter to publish announcements and opinions of those opposed to relocation.

That was an unfortunate decision. Within just a few days, the committee for an informed congregation was formed, which produced and distributed their own newsletter. Interestingly, they chose not to list their names in their first publication. Later, after this secrecy was criticized at a congregational meeting, they did accept responsibility by listing their names. Of course, they made an issue out of the lack of cooperation in putting their concerns in the FCC news. They also began to generate as much fear as possible about the whole relocation issue. What would it cost each member? How were we going to dispose of the beloved old building? Why was the governing board spending all this money on research without consulting the congregation? How could the congregation be assured the governing board wouldn't sell Akita or First Community Village to pay for the new building? And how could we be assured that all members would have an equal vote on this issue?

Those of us who had already been working on this project for two years thought that most of the opposition's questions were ill-informed and unnecessary. Nearly all had already been answered in the FCC news. Still, the fact that an ad-hoc group would raise such issues cast a pall of mistrust over the elected leaders of the church. The sad thing was there was no system of accountability in this process. The opposition could terrify others with the idea that church leaders were thinking about selling Akita or the Village, and all the leaders could do was play defense. The committee inflicted substantial damage on First Community Church without ever being called to account for it. As you might guess, most of them were people who made only token financial commitments to the church and made it a point not to attend worship.

If we erred by not being democratic enough with the information and publicity processes, we erred even more dramatically by being overly democratic with the voting process. One of the first issues raised by the committee for an informed congregation was whether absentee ballots would be allowed. The First Community constitution clearly states that decisions may be made only by those present at a congregational meeting. In a special town meeting our legal counsel explained this point to the congregation, indicating that absentee ballots would be in conflict with our constitution.

Then, I asked to speak to the meeting and suggested that in the interest of truly determining "the will of the congregation," we set aside the constitution at this point and allow for absentee ballots. Thinking this to be a noble approach to a ticklish issue, I lived to regret it. We received votes from around the world, some from people who hadn't been in the church for more than twenty years.

Of course, the very concept of the secret ballot is another issue that deserves to be carefully scrutinized. It's too easy to act one way and vote another. Hence, I would not again concur with having a secret ballot. For the health of the church, I believe the best way to vote is on one's feet in a public forum.

That brings me to the last item of overextended democracy that deeply affected the outcome of the relocation vote. Several people were disgruntled that the voting day was on the second Sunday of

May, when they would be out of town for various commence-
ments, weddings, class reunions, and so on. Once again, we
sought to be as fair as possible by making arrangements for voting
on the Wednesday evening prior to Pentecost. Believe me, I saw
people that night that I had never seen before and have never seen
since.

The committee effected one more change in the voting process
that added fuel to the flames of mistrust. Maintaining that the
elected leadership could not be trusted to count the ballots, they
suggested that an independent accounting firm be contracted to do
that task. Again, rather than battle what we considered to be inane
issues, we agreed. Hindsight tells me never again to concur with
any action that affirms the innuendoes of mistrust.

Meanwhile, the extraordinary work of the various task forces
continued. In addition to outstanding leadership, Jeff Keeler provided one more ingredient that enabled FCC to address openly the
issue of relocation. He contributed $100,000 to cover the costs of
research and design. It was one of the most gracious and selfless
gestures I have ever witnessed. Keeler had no more idea than I did
how all this was going evolve; he just wanted to make certain the
issue had the best hearing possible.

The site-acquisition task force succeeded in finding a prime location precisely in the center of one of the fastest-growing areas in
Columbus. Located just five miles northwest of FCC, these eighteen-and-a-half acres were positioned to service the current congregation, take advantage of a booming development area, and
provide access to three major thoroughfares, including I-270,
which virtually circles the city of Columbus. It was almost too good
to be true. Then, when ten members of the church agreed to buy
the land and hold it while the church arrived at a decision, I felt the
spirit of God was really letting loose.

At the same time land was being located and secured, the design-concept task force, thanks to Keeler's generous contribution,
was conducting a nation-wide architectural competition to provide
schematic drawings that could be used to show the congregation
how the new church would appear before asking them to vote.
After interviewing eight firms, we selected four finalists. Final
designs were presented on April 3, and the choice was unanimous.
The firm of our own Bob Wandel, who had been a member of FCC
since he was a child, brought in a design that had people cheering
and weeping at the same time. It was vintage First Community. As
I wrote in the FCC news, "Wandel's design is an answer to prayer."

It was. Stately, stone, innovative, and beautiful, it captured the very spirit of FCC. Even some of those who were adamantly opposed to relocation seemed warmly drawn to this concept.

When the financial-feasibility task force reported there were enough assets in our congregation to construct the proposed building, there was only one thing left to do. Vote.

Wednesday Storm Clouds and Sunday Despair

On May 10, I gained insight into how strong a groundswell of negative forces was moving against relocation. Stopping at the church after a round of golf, I thought I'd make sure the Wednesday voting process was running smoothly. I was met by our executive minister, Jeb Magruder, who was pale and nervous. "Who are these people?" he asked, gesturing toward those going in and out of the booths. I looked—and couldn't answer. The fact that FCC hadn't honestly cleaned her membership rolls for fifteen years now came home to haunt us. I talked with one person who didn't even know who I was. "I was here with Burkie," he explained. "I suppose you remember Otis, then?" I asked. "Sure do." "And what about Dr. Teikmanis?" "Nope. I was gone by then." Arthur Teikmanis came to be the senior minister of First Community Church in 1968.

We learned later that by the time voting ended on Wednesday, negative votes outnumbered positive, four-to-one.

On Sunday morning, those in favor of relocation sensed that we needed a great day to overcome the negative impact of the Wednesday voters. I prayed for good weather and high attendance. We had both. Keeler had ordered a red-and-white striped tent for the front lawn of the church to mark what we were all certain would be a festive, happy occasion. More than twelve hundred people attended worship. Another two hundred dropped by just to vote. One was so bold as to confront Jeb Magruder: "I'm here to vote, where's Brownlee Hall?" I preached a pastoral message about accepting the will of God, and feeling a bit more confident due to the crowds and the weather, we all went home to wait for the tally.

Three months earlier I had made plans to fly to Scotland that Sunday afternoon with a group of golfing friends. As the day of decision drew nearer, I decided I simply couldn't be absent when the vote came in. I changed my plans, scheduled a Monday flight, and made arrangements for the staff and lay leadership to gather for a victory celebration at six o'clock Sunday night. It proved to be one of the wisest, if not most ironic, decisions I ever made.

Shortly after 4 P.M., Joe Yearling, the church treasurer, who had been chosen to oversee the work of the accounting firm, called me. "Barry, it's not good news," he said softly. "The count was 886 positive, 1,109 negative." I felt as if I had been hit with a Sten gun. "Thanks, Joe, I know this was a tough call to make. We'll handle it." I told my family we had failed, sat on the edge of the bed and wept for a few moments, and then got up and took a shower. I had no idea what I was going to say to all the faithful people at the six o'clock meeting who had invested so many hours and so much effort in working for relocation.

I put on a kelly-green jacket over a pair of iridescent checked golf slacks. I was going to do everything in my power to keep the outlook positive. Downstairs, I could hear my son speaking to his sister. "You won't believe it, Tracy, he's up there puttin' on those go-to-hell pants. He's gonna figure out how to do it anyhow!" That boy had a lot more confidence than I did.

Perhaps the most difficult moment came when I met Jeff Keeler in front of the church about thirty minutes later. He did not know the outcome of the vote. When he saw my costume, he started laughing. "That good, is it?" he asked. "No, that bad!" I gave him the count and watched his head drop. He had worked so hard, given so much, taken such risks. It didn't seem fair. In typical, take-charge, Keeler fashion, he leaned into the car and told his wife what had happened. Then he pivoted and headed toward the door of the church. "Let's go to work." That's all he said and I knew he wasn't ready to fold the tents just yet.

At six o'clock the governing board, staff, and planning task forces gathered. Although the room was full, it was hushed. I had no trouble being heard. "I want you to know that I am as pleased to be the senior minister of First Community Church right now as I was at 11 A.M. this morning. I don't know how, but somehow we will turn this pain into new power for First Community. You know, I really do believe in the working of the Holy Spirit. Although it feels terrible, I must accept, and challenge you to accept, this vote as the will of God. We have a lot of work to do and we're going to need each other."

A year later, Ronald Jenkins, the gifted minister of music at FCC, told me how he had felt as he listened to me. "I stood there looking at all those people who had worked so hard for so many years, and at the staff members who knew how badly we needed that new facility, and all I could think about was all those people I had never seen before who were in there voting on Wednesday night. Those people who never come around here had made the decision about the conditions under which those of us who give our lifeblood to this place would have to work. I didn't care what you said about 'the will of God.' I was so angry, all I wanted to do was leave."

Twenty-four hours later I found myself soaring above the Atlantic in a DC-10 contemplating the most devastating loss I had ever experienced. Where would we go from here? Few churches ever needed a new building more than First Community. How could we salvage anything from this vote? Should I stay at FCC, or was this vote a mandate for me to leave?

The Roundabout

Scotland offered me more than a needed escape with some good friends. Playing eleven golf courses in eight days demanded that we move rapidly through the land of heather and sweaters. As we did so, we frequently came to those wonderful traffic circles the Scots call roundabouts. Since we were not always sure exactly where we wanted to go, the roundabouts afforded us an opportunity to recheck the map before whipping off in a chosen direction. The concept captured my imagination.

I sensed that the opposition would want to move quickly to renovate our present site and get rid of the option on the northwest land. I also knew some of them would work hard to tie the negative vote to my leadership in an attempt to effect my resignation. I also knew that the backbone of First Community Church was very much in favor of relocation and willing to work with me if I could come up with some kind of response to the negative vote that would accommodate both positions.

Hence, upon returning to Columbus, I proposed to the governing board and congregation that we take the summer as a "roundabout," a time to slow down, look around, evaluate the circumstances, and choose a new direction. At the first governing board meeting following the vote, I explained my position. "I don't want to make any major decisions until we've had time to digest the vote and determine a creative course of action." I was buying time, measuring options, and using the summer to dull the impact of the negative vote.

A Special Insight

Three or four weeks after the vote I telephoned my old friend Lyle Schaller about another matter. During our conversation, he asked me about the decision of May 14 and chuckled as I explained the voting procedures. "You can't make it so easy for irresponsible people to do irresponsible things," he cautioned. "The healthiest way for a congregation to make big decisions is in an open forum where people have to raise their hands or stand up and be counted." Then he asked an interesting question. "Barry, did you have the money to do the job if the vote had passed?" I told him what the financial consultants had told us about our giving potential. "That's not what I mean. Were the people with money with you or against you?" "They were with us," I answered. "Then your next task is to figure out how to let people vote with their money. Any dormant member can be coaxed into voting no. It takes a little bit more to put your money where your mouth is."

As I hung up, I began to brood about the "window of opportunity" now slipping away from First Community Church. If people were ready to make substantial contributions, we couldn't afford to let that inclination fade. It takes a lot of energy, homework, and courage to get a church even to consider relocation. If we didn't salvage some of that momentum, it would take years to regenerate. We needed to come up with a way to present the relocation issue in an open forum. We needed to let the whole congregation see the depth of commitment behind the relocation effort. And we needed to hold on to that strategically located eighteen-and-a-half acres.

The Pay-Forward Mindset

About this time I started thinking about my legacy to First Community Church. An old quote echoed in my mind. "It was David's to take the city, Solomon's to build the temple!" I knew that I might never see a new First Community Church on that northwest property, but I also knew the decisions I was making would determine whether such a development could ever occur. Suddenly, my perspective shifted from what could be accomplished in the now to what could be enabled in the future.

Woody Hayes, the late, much heralded football coach of the Ohio State Buckeyes, often admonished people to "pay forward." It was Woody's way of keeping an eye to the future, recognizing that what is done in the present often shapes what is possible in the future.

The congregation had voted no on a proposal to relocate the church at a cost of $12 million to $16 million. They had not voted no forever, nor had they voted no to the possibility of keeping the hub of our ministry at 1320 Cambridge Boulevard while establishing a branch on the new property. A new vision was assembling in my mind. Now the question was, How could this be communicated to the whole congregation?

A New Vision

Some people suggested to me that we simply announce a capital-funds campaign to buy the northwest land and renovate the old building. I backed away from that idea, certain that we would receive flak about buying the land after a negative vote and that we would have very little support from our most able contributors for any kind of renovation.

I felt it was time to engage the congregation personally in a dialogue about all these issues. Knowing the people were tired of the struggle and unlikely to attend congregational meetings for this purpose, I proposed to the governing board that the best approach was to use the Sunday morning time slot and create a blend of a congregational forum and a worship experience. First Community is unique in many ways, but when it comes to the worship service, it's just like any other church. That hour is sacred. We try not to mix business with worship. It was no small risk to tamper with the worship experience, but it was the only way gently and openly to confront the building issue again. If we were to hang on to the momentum of the previous three years, it was the only thing to do.

Working Worship Services

So we came out of the roundabout in September by announcing three "working worship services." For these three Sundays we continued to have a regular worship service at 9 A.M. but started the working worship services at 10:30 A.M. instead of the usual 11 A.M. in order to allow more time for the dialogue process. This made it possible for those who wanted only to attend a worship service to do so. Some did just that, but the overwhelming majority came to the working worship sessions. Each began with a call to worship, the usual prayers and announcements, hymns, and even anthems from our choir. Then I presented a brief overview of our experiences during the last year leading to the 55/45 vote, which, in effect, represented a divided congregation. I challenged the people to think in terms of coming together, accepting our differences, and doing what was best for First Community Church. After that, we brought out easels with newsprint, placed microphones in the aisles, and encouraged people to share their feelings. Thereafter, I served as the facilitator, fielding questions and writing suggestions on the newsprint.

Each service centered in a specific question. The first focused on "What can we do at 1320 Cambridge Boulevard?," the second on "What can we do at the new location?," and the last on, "How do we honor long-range planning priorities?"

The working worship services worked beautifully. The people did as we thought they would; they shared openly and clearly, demonstrating there was a lot of sentiment and good horse sense behind both projects—renovating the current building and building something on the new property. Of course, there were some adamant statements made in opposition to both ideas, but such positions were definitely in the minority. When the last working worship service concluded, it was obvious that FCC was ready to move forward.

Two New Task Forces

One of the marks of exceptional leadership is the ability to spot an opening and take advantage of it. Jeff Keeler may be the most natural leader with whom I have ever worked. As soon as the last working worship service was concluded, he named two new task forces, the 1320 task force to pursue the concept of renovation and the extended-ministry task force to draft a proposal for a scaled-down presence on the new land. Recognizing that those who most adamantly opposed relocation were solidly behind the idea of renovating the old building, he recruited several of them to work on the 1320 task force. It was a brilliant piece of statesmanship. Now, instead of standing outside complaining about the process, they were inside faced with the responsibility of doing something creative themselves. Suddenly, some of the very people who had cast shadows of doubt on previous research found themselves repeating the research process only to arrive at the same conclusions of the original building task force. No one had been misled. The leaders who had examined the possibilities of expanding the old building, only to be stymied in every direction and have their work impugned by innuendo and rumor, now found it justified by some of the very people who had called it into question.

During the working worship services it was also suggested that we employ an outside research agency to verify the desirability of the location of the new property. Again, what we were seeing was a not-so-veiled insult of work done by a previous task force. The Polimetrics Research group at Ohio State University was employed to conduct one of the most extensive market research surveys ever done for a local church. Their survey totally confirmed the work done by the building task force two years earlier. In short, it told us the new property was ideally situated for maximum church growth.

Operating-Funds Campaign

In the middle of all this it was necessary to conduct the annual operating-funds campaign for 1989. The naysayers were quite vocal in announcing that this campaign was doomed. "A lot of people are angry that we're still fooling around with that land. They won't support the church." "How can you hope to raise any money when the church is split over relocation?" "I'm not giving a dime until I see some renovation started at 1320."

My frustration level catapulted as I listened to all this nonsense. I was tired, overloaded, and fed up with the ankle-biters, who I felt had been chipping away at me for years. It all came to a head at the October governing board meeting, where some of the most positive, wonderful people in the church got bogged down in a dispute over what kind of building we might suggest for the northwest property. I remember writing the word quit on the yellow pad in front of me. My spirit was broken. I drove home that night composing a letter of resignation in my mind.

The next morning I was still thinking about leaving when I flipped on the "Today" show as I was dressing. Jane Pauley was interviewing the Texas financier H. Ross Perot. "How do you explain your success?" she asked. Perot was quiet for at least five seconds before answering. I stopped tying my tie and waited to see what would come next. Looking straight into the camera, he said, "I won't quit. I can't quit. I'm too dumb to know how to lose!"

I loved it. It was exactly what I needed to hear. I had never quit on anything in my life. This wasn't the time to start. Two days later, I made a special presentation at a dinner for the top twenty contributors to FCC and repeated Perot's words. "I won't quit. I can't quit. I'm too dumb to know how to lose!" Apparently, it was a message for which they had been waiting. Their affirmation with hugs, handshakes, and verbal encouragement was overwhelming. I needed it. It felt wonderful.

Better yet, the spirit of that meeting leaked into the congregation. Not only was I refusing to fold, so were the rest of our leaders. We were not going to quit. We were going to adjust to the circumstance and keep this church moving forward. It was that simple. With that attitude and some superb direction by the lay leaders handling the 1989 operating-funds campaign, we enjoyed one of the most successful campaigns in FCC history. The old horse may have been a bit wobbly after the negative vote, but it was still one of the strongest mainline churches in America.

Firming Up Our New Direction

By the end of the year, the reports from the two new task forces came back to the governing board setting forth the new vision for First Community Church. The 1320 task force reported it would take $3.5 million to spruce up the old building, repair the pipe organ, install a new boiler, refurbish the rest rooms, and patch the roof. Granted, we wouldn't be gaining any new space, but we would be taking care of what was there and making the place a bit more habitable. The extended-ministry task force presented a $3.5 million plan to build a new, multipurpose center on the new property. This center could be used for all-church banquets, conferences, and worship. It would afford FCC a presence in the burgeoning northwest area and alleviate some of the space pressures on the old building. Even more important, this step would secure the land so that the option of development at a later date would remain with First Community Church. From my point of view, we had finally arrived at a workable solution to the building problems I had noted some twelve years earlier.

You may wonder how we could proceed with this new plan without a congregational vote. The First Community constitution indicates that only in a situation involving a mortgage is it necessary to secure congregational approval. It is the prerogative of the governing board to make all other decisions. The truth is, we weren't required to vote on the relocation issue. We did so because we knew the chances of raising $16 million without a groundswell of support from the congregation were very small.

Hence, a pivotal question remained. Less than one year after rejecting a proposal for relocation, would the congregation underwrite a two-pronged capital-funds campaign aimed at renovating the old building and constructing a new Center for Extended Ministry on the north property? There was only one way to find out. It was time to conduct the campaign.

Professional Fund Raisers—Good or Bad?

For some reason, churches tend toward debates about the whole idea of hiring outside agencies to assist with fund raising. It's as if we are too proud to seek expert counsel, even though it significantly increases the probability of success. Thirty years earlier, the first time FCC seriously considered relocation, the congregation passed a resolution against using professional fund raisers. Consequently, that effort failed for a lack of funds. Aware of this history, the governing board unhesitatingly signed a contract with Resource Services, Incorporated of Dallas, Texas. It was one of the more prudent steps in our road to recovery. The RSI people provided a superb program, sage and sensitive counsel, and a spiritual perspective that was much needed if our efforts were to succeed.

One of my first responsibilities was to develop a theme for the campaign. While sitting in a hotel room in Fort Lauderdale, Florida, I found myself focusing on the two elements that I felt were most essential to our success. First came faith. Unless we believed God would bless our efforts and unless we also believed that what we were doing was to the ultimate glory of God, the campaign didn't have a chance. Second came a need for unity. FCC had been badly wounded by the conflict over relocation. Our leaders had been unfairly shrouded with clouds of distrust. If we were to gather serious financial support for the two-pronged project at hand, we could only do so together. Instantly, I knew this would be our theme, "By Faith . . . Together."

The RSI model is a treasure. It is based on involving as many people as possible in the campaign. By the time we reached the celebrative banquet at the end of our campaign, more than seven hundred people had accepted and carried out specific jobs for "By Faith . . . Together." Again, we made it a point to enlist the support of persons who had opposed the relocation effort. Almost every committee in the process had a bipartisan dimension. But there were still a couple of hurdles to overcome.

Same Game—Wiser Responses

Some people just would not climb off the negative bandwagon. Refusing to serve on campaign committees, they chose to sit outside and carp at the proceedings. By now, we were no longer surprised at their tactics. Two issues emerged. First, they wanted to make certain that people would be allowed to designate where their contributions would be used, for 1320 or for the Center for Extended Ministry. Second, they suggested that we employ an outside accounting agency to manage the capital resources and provide audited reports.

By now, my patience, which has never been a strong point, had really worn thin. My experience had always been that designated pledges were not in the best interests of the church. Therefore I endorsed the single-commitment idea, meaning that all gifts would be split equally between the two projects. Our governing board and the people from RSI convinced me to the contrary. In the end, we provided a pledge card on which a donor could commit his or her total gift to one or the other of the projects, divide the gift between the two, or simply mark the commitment, "undesignated." In the last case, we announced that all "undesignated" gifts would be divided equally between the projects. My wife and I set the pace for the campaign by publicly announcing our pledge to be divided 50/50 between 1320 and the Center for Extended Ministry.

As to the call for an outside accounting firm, we discreetly informed those making the suggestion that if they were that untrusting of their elected representatives, it might be better for them to refrain from making any commitment at all.

The Thrill of Victory

As we started the "By Faith . . . Together" campaign, I made a silent pledge to myself. I knew I didn't have any arrows left in my quiver. There was no more for me to give. If we did not succeed in reaching the $3.5 million goal for the Center for Extended Ministry, I had made up my mind to leave First Community. It's not that FCC is not an exciting place to serve. It is. But it had been through several senior ministers in a short time, and without the success of the northwest project, I didn't think I would have the mandate to continue leading the church. There was no way I wanted to preside over the inevitable slow demise of such a well-known church if we failed to secure the land and put something on it. I knew we could remodel 1320 until the moon turned to green cheese and it still wouldn't solve the location and parking problems. I also knew, as did many of the long-time members, that buying the land wasn't good enough. We had to put something on it. If not, it could quite likely be sold like the Reed and McCoy location in the 1960s. History is a trusted teacher.

I told Jeff Keeler about my personal $3.5 goal and he just smiled. "If you get $3 million for the center, you'll go for it." "Not this time," I responded. "I need a clear signal."

There were actually three goals for the campaign. The leadership goal of $3 million in total contributions to both projects represented the minimum necessary just to purchase the land and make some modest changes in the present building. The victory goal of $5 million in total contributions would allow us to put some kind of structure on the northwest property and make some structural changes at 1320. The miracle goal of $7 million, which all of us felt was basically out of reach, would mean the building of the Center for Extended Ministry and a complete renovation of the present church.

Contributions began slowly. Early indications were that we would be lucky to make the leadership goal. Then, a strange phenomenon developed. We didn't receive the $1 million gift that was supposedly necessary for the campaign to succeed. Rather, we started to receive a number of $100,000 and $50,000 commitments. We had hoped to have $3 million in total contributions by the all-church banquet scheduled for May 22. On May 14 we had already broken that goal. And one of the special thrills of my ministry was the privilege of announcing at the banquet that advance commitments exceeded $4 million. Victory Sunday was set for June 3.

All this time I was keeping a close eye on the split between the projects. That $3.5 goal for the northwest project burned in my mind. On June 1, we had $3,410,000 pledged to the Center for Extended Ministry and $1,885,000 for the building at 1320. Jeff Keeler called to see how we were doing, and when I told him he inquired, "What do you think? Close enough?" "Nope," I answered. "Well, get on the phone," he directed. "I'm sure you can find $90,000." I laughed and started to make a list of people who might make that kind of additional contribution. Then I stopped. "Not this time," I thought. "If this thing is going to fly, it has to crack that barrier on its own." I know that may appear irrational to anyone reading these words. After all I had invested in making this thing fly, why should I grow timid in the final forty-eight hours? To me, it made sense. I was looking for a signal, a personal checkpoint, a sign of the Spirit.

On Saturday morning, as I was putting the finishing touches on Sunday's victory message, my telephone rang. A man who hasn't been terribly active around the church said that he and his wife were reconsidering their pledge. He explained that he was excited about the vision involved with the Center for Extended Ministry, and the more he thought about it, the more he wanted to do. Hence, he pledged an additional $100,000 for the northwest project. He couldn't see the tears in my eyes or feel the lump in my throat. I hung up the telephone and sat there remembering the pain on the day of the vote. I saw Jeff Keeler turning to walk into the church. I recalled the waiting staff, shocked by what felt like a personal rejection of their efforts. The words I had so often shared in grief situations echoed in my mind, "I will not leave you desolate." I chuckled to myself, recalling my son's ragged-edged assessment of my checked pants on the day of the negative vote. Then, all alone in my study, I began to mouth the words of a great hymn my grandmother used to sing while puttering around her yard in central Illinois.

> Great is Thy faithfulness! Great is Thy
> Faithfulness!
> Morning by morning new mercies I see;
> All I have needed Thy hand hath provided,
> Great is Thy faithfulness, Lord unto me!

One year after the negative vote on Pentecost 1989, the people of First Community Church gathered for Victory Sunday on Pentecost 1990. We had raised $3.6 million to build the Center for Extended Ministry and nearly $2 million to refurbish the old building. We were not relocating the church, but we were taking a giant stride into a flexible future for First Community. For those who had stayed the struggle, it was a day of triumph, beauty, and gratitude.

The Keys to Success

Why did "By Faith . . . Together" succeed? I believe there are several valid reasons.

First, the practice of involving dissidents in the planning process was extremely effective. It took the edge off the opposition. Some of these people never did come around to embracing the two-pronged project, but because they were part of the planning, they chose not to attack it.

Second, the negative vote provided incentive for success. No organization likes to fail, certainly not a place like First Community Church so loaded with people for whom success is a way of life. Therefore, so long as the next proposal made a modicum of sense, it was sure to gain support from the folk who really did love the church and want it to be strong and healthy.

Third, I am convinced the tenacity of lay people to stay with the cause, to change course willingly without surrendering vision, to make the effort of a creative approach, and to commit both hours and dollars to a successful venture is essential to victory.

Fourth, the verification of previous research both by new church task forces and by outside agencies affirmed the integrity of the original proposal. When that Polimetrics report came in with virtually the same conclusions that had been reached by the building task force, it was a great day for First Community Church.

Fifth, I need to doff my hat to the people at RSI, their model for fund raising, and the "By Faith . . . Together" campaign directors. The wisdom and guidance of Bill Wilson and Earl Craig from RSI were particularly effective in keeping us all open to contrary points of view. The RSI model fosters a form of interdependence that smothers differences. And when it came time to select campaign directors, we were fortunate that five of the most respected members of both the church and the community agreed to serve. Their names brought instant credibility to the project.

And finally, I stayed. The pattern at First Community since Roy Burkhart retired in 1958 had been for senior ministers to remain until they were neutralized or defeated by the multi-layered political processes of the church. I am certain many members expected me to leave after the negative vote in 1989. Some of my professional friends encouraged me to do just that. If I had to put my finger on the turning point in this adventure, I would say it was the night when I quoted H. Ross Perot to some of our leading supporters: "I won't quit. I can't quit. I'm too dumb to know how to lose!"

The triumph at FCC is not in the relocation of the church. That didn't happen. The triumph is in overcoming a negative vote with a positive solution. The triumph is in returning the destiny of First Community Church to the people who really make it run. And the triumph is in successfully focusing the energy of the church on the future. We will renovate the old building. The chances are that 1320 Cambridge Boulevard will remain the hub of FCC's ministry for years to come. I don't know that I will ever see a completely new First Community Church on that new land. But I do know this—it will always be an option.

God Will Not Fail

South Haven United Church of Christ, Bedford, Ohio

MARTHA SWAN

E arly in my ministry at South Haven Church, Bedford, Ohio, I had a most unusual experience. On a Friday that I had declared a day of prayer for the church, I asked God for a word of direction—something to provide vision and hope for our journey. I decided to turn to the Old Testament lectionary reading for the approaching Sunday, which was in Zechariah 9. In order to have a feeling for the passage, I started reading at the eighth chapter, and the words leapt out at me.

> Thus says the LORD: I will return to Zion, and will dwell in the midst of Jerusalem; Jerusalem shall be called the faithful city, and the mountain of the LORD of hosts shall be called the holy mountain . . . old men and women shall again sit in the streets of Jerusalem . . . the streets of the city shall be full of boys and girls playing in its streets. . . . But now I will not deal with the remnant of this people as in the former days. . . . For there shall be a sowing of peace; the vine shall yield its fruit, the ground shall give its produce, and the skies shall give their dew; and I will cause the remnant of this people to possess all these things. Just as you have been a cursing among

Martha Swan led a struggling congregation at South Haven United Church of Christ in Bedford, Ohio, to new life and mission, which resulted in the church's receiving a Membership Growth Award at General Synod XVI. Now secretary for evangelism and membership growth for the United Church Board for Homeland Ministries, Swan travels throughout the United States preaching, teaching, and leading workshops and seminars on evangelism, worship, and renewal of faith. She writes for *Growingplans* and has published an original songbook and recorded an album.

the nations, O house of Judah and house of Israel, so I will save you
and you shall be a blessing. Do not be afraid, but let your hands be
strong.

—Zechariah 8:3-13

It is hard to describe the feelings that I had, but it was as if God
were actually speaking to me through the scriptures, saying, "This
passage, which once described my promise to Israel, I now give to
you as a promise." I could not believe it. I read it over again, trying
to grasp if it really could have been "a word from the Lord." For the
next day I lived with the passage in my mind, turning to it again
and again, pondering its meaning. Finally, on Sunday morning, I
stepped out on faith and shared the passage with the congregation
as a vision for the restoration of South Haven. I was not sure how
any of this was going to come to pass, nor was I sure what it all
meant. I had decided to believe that it was indeed a promise made
by God, and I would try to trust God to bring it about. Taking that
decision was the most frightening thing I had ever done in my
ministry.

The most astonishing thing is that now, four years later, all the
promises in this passage have been fulfilled. The congregation has
quadrupled in size, from 35 members to 140. There were only two
families with small children four years ago; now there are eighteen
such families. Where there used to be conflict, there is now genuine cooperation. Even the "ground has yielded its increase," as we
have sold a part of our property and are in the midst of developing
a housing facility for low-income elderly and the handicapped.
Whereas five years ago South Haven was known as a "problem
church" by the denomination, the church is now considered a
"blessing," even having been awarded one of the Milestone
Growth Awards for 1987 by the Board for Homeland Ministries.
Even the final word of this promise has come true—the one part I
never would have imagined possible. South Haven's inhabitants do
come from "many cities"; our membership now includes people
from twenty-one different communities!

In the pages that follow I will attempt to describe some of what
we, as a small discouraged church, have experienced as we have
tried to claim the promise made by God. Again and again over the
years I have gone back to the Zechariah passage to remind myself
and the people that it is *God* "who will cause the remnant of this
people to possess all these things." We have tried not to fear, and to
let our hands be strong. Some of what we have tried to do in our
ministry over these five years may give rise to ideas that other

churches may find helpful, but there is an underlying truth that I think is more helpful than anything else. The truth is that we are called to celebrate our uniqueness—as individuals and as congregations.

A tendency I think we all have is to desire what others have. We tend to put down our own specialness in favor of wishing we were like someone else. We do it as individuals and we do it as churches. I feel privileged to share some of our story with you; if it helps at all, praise be to God! But the most important thing is not what we have done but what God is doing with *all* of us. Don't be afraid to claim your own unique giftedness and step out on God's word, believing that you too have a vision and a promise from God. "Do not be afraid; but let your hands be strong!"

Believing That God Does Not Fail

When I first spoke to the associate association minister about the burden God had placed on my heart for South Haven church, inquiring whether he thought the congregation might consider me for their pastor, his reply was, "How do you feel about failure?" That caught me by surprise, and after taking a few minutes to think about the implications of what he was asking, I found myself answering, "I do not believe that God is in the business of failing. If it is God who calls me to this place, God will not fail."

I did not know it at the time, but those words would come back to me again and again over the next few years, as words of encouragement from the Spirit of God, strengthening and sustaining me whenever I questioned whether or not South Haven Church would be renewed. "God is not in the business of failing. God will not fail."

There is no question that my sense of "call" to this church was very deep and very real. As a student in seminary with a year of course work still to go, I was not looking for a church. I was not even sure I wanted to be a parish minister, but while I was working at the association office I began to hear stories about this discouraged little church that was having difficulty finding a minister. Its financial situation looked dismal—only $1,200 had been pledged for the previous year, and the existing mortgage of nearly $8,000 per year plus high utility bills were enough to discourage most prospective ministers from applying.

At one point the worshiping congregation had dwindled to a dozen faithful, and though one of the interim pastors had had some success in building up the enthusiasm and attendance during the fall months, by the time Lent of 1982 appeared, the worshipers were down to twenty to twenty-five again.

It was during this time that I learned about South Haven's history: how it was founded in 1956 as a "strong, family-oriented" church; how it had grown during the '60s to have a worshiping attendance during the school year of 125 to 175. However, within twenty-five years the church went through what David Nore in his book *To Dream Again* describes as the "life cycle of a church."

According to Nore, the first fifteen to twenty years of a church's life are marked by growth as it engages in shared dreams, beliefs, goals, and structure. When the initial dream is realized and the goals are achieved, if a church does not have strong leadership with the ability to envision and articulate a new dream, it will begin to decline as it engages in nostalgia and questioning and then polarization and dropout. For South Haven this cycle was completed in twenty-five years.

Working in the association office, I read the profiles of many churches seeking pastoral leadership. For some reason I found myself drawn to South Haven; and after talking to the very discouraged chair of their search committee, I promised to pray that God would send them a pastor. I had no idea at the time that that pastor would be me! Six months after I began praying for this church, I preached my candidacy sermon there, and the small band of members voting that day unanimously accepted me to be their pastor. Exhilarated and feeling the power of the Holy Spirit moving among us, we began our ministry together on July 15, 1982, trusting that God had called us together and "God is not in the business of failing. God would not fail."

Though I honestly believed that God would not fail, I wasn't so sure about myself. I wondered if my own faith was strong enough to undertake such a project and carry it through. I questioned whether I had the necessary skills and leadership, and during the first few years especially I frequently found myself asking, "Lord, where will the people come from? What if they don't come?" It became immediately clear to me that leading the people of God in this time and place would require above all else an unshakable trust in God. I doubted my faith was that strong, and I knew it would be imperative to find ways to keep what faith I had alive and growing.

One of the first things I did after accepting the call to South Haven was to join a small group of four clergy who were committed to studying the scriptures and praying together weekly.

That was of course part of the good advice one received in seminary and from older, more seasoned clergy, but I never realized how important it would become in giving me the week-to-week under-girding of faith necessary to ministry. This little group became a place of challenge and nurture, providing a structure for my own ongoing study and spiritual growth. It also gave me even more impetus for disciplining my daily prayer life, as we tried to be accountable to one another each week for the time we spent daily with God.

A Midweek Quiet Time

At this same time I started a Wednesday service of quiet medita-tion and sharing of the eucharist at South Haven. This was as much to assure myself of some centering quiet time during the week as to offer such a time to others. It started small, with two or three gathered, and over the years it has grown to about twelve. I have tried different ways of structuring the half hour over the years, offering it sometimes at noon and sometimes in the evening, but it has always stayed rather unstructured, and it has been mostly quiet time, sometimes using music sometimes not, and a very simple sharing of prayers and the bread and the cup. We have found that different people come to the service at different times, according to their need.

The "demon of numbers" might cause one to question whether or not such a small, short service would have any impact on the life of a church, but it is my sense that this little gathering in the candlelit shadows of my study on a weekly basis was in some very significant ways "leaven for the loaf." If nothing else, it helped to keep the pastor more centered and focused in the midst of some very scattered and hectic days.

I have observed that many of us clergy believe that we can keep going strong on just one hour of worship a week, even though many clergy don't ever feel as though they've worshiped when they've led the service. As clergy we must find ways to worship that feed our souls, and I believe this must include figuring out how to lead worship and how to experience it at the same time. I think the myth of the pastor not being able to worship while he or she is leading worship has gone unchallenged long enough. The opposite may be the real truth. Maybe it is only possible for a pastor to lead the people in true worship when he or she is also experiencing true worship.

I continue to try all kinds of ways to keep my spiritual life vital. I often avail myself of retreats and quiet days offered by our association and conference and the local Catholic retreat house. I use writing a journal, meditation, dance, drawing, working with clay, reading, fasting, praying—anything at all that may put me in touch with myself and God. I have on occasion, when the ministry has seemed overwhelming or some particular need has emerged, declared a day of prayer for the church in which I did nothing but pray for the church and read scriptures, asking the congregation to join me throughout the day when and if they could. This has proven to be a powerful experience for me, and God has revealed some very specific direction and answers to prayer out of such intentionality. It is a continual adventure for me to discover new avenues of nourishing my spirit, and I rejoice at the vast variety of ways God gives us to revive our souls again! There is no point in thinking for a minute that we can lead others to faith if our own faith is dead, so the singularly most important thing we as clergy must do is to find ways to keep our faith alive.

Leading from Our Gifts

The second most important task for us as clergy, especially if called to a discouraged church, is to discover our own gifts and be willing to lead from them. If the most important thing I did when starting my ministry at South Haven was to figure out ways to nourish my own faith, the second most important was to refuse to sign my "call agreement" without discussing at length with the congregation what it was I felt called to. The call agreement in our association is the initial contract signed by the congregation and the minister stating the terms of employment. Everything was filled out (salary, housing, insurance, terms of notice) except that there was nothing listed under "duties." I assumed that that meant I was either to do everything or to do nothing, and I did not feel called to either.

I suggested that we hold a meeting with as many members of the congregation as possible and discuss my calling and their calling and together we might discover God's calling. This proved to be one of the most educational and enlightening evenings we would ever spend together in the church. The people, many for the first time, saw what was involved in the church's ministry and saw the impossibility of one person, the hired professional pastor, accomplishing that ministry. This may seem basic, but it is in fact an underlying unspoken assumption in many congregations that the pastor is hired to carry on the ministry of the congregation. When this assumption goes unexamined and unchallenged, the church is programmed to fail.

Whereas, in the overall design of leadership the clergy may in fact influence the total ministry of the church, the clergy cannot individually be responsible for it all. Each of us has been given a particular gift to contribute to the body of Christ. We as clergy must be clear about our own unique gifts; otherwise we will be expected to be gifted in all things, and desiring to conform to others' expectations of us, we will surely fail. If we can be clear about our own particular gifts, we can free others to be clear about theirs, and then we may have a chance (as Paul suggests in Ephesians 4) to have each part of the body of Christ working properly, growing, and upbuilding itself in love.

There is no question that the most helpful bit of advice that I received when I was in seminary was given to me by an adjunct professor who was first and foremost a local church pastor. "Lead from your strengths," he said. "Don't be afraid to lead from your gifts." These words of wisdom proved to be a key in unlocking the door for the Holy Spirit to begin to move in and through us at South Haven. They became not only a motto for my own leadership style but a theme that would begin to shape the direction of the church's ministry.

What were my strengths? I had a good singing voice, fifteen years of successful teaching and performing, a positive attitude, and a lot of creative energy. In discussing my strengths with the congregation, I indicated that I felt called to (1) encourage others in the discovery and use of their own gifts, (2) design and implement meaningful and creative worship, (3) preach and teach the word of God, and (4) set the tone for an atmosphere of grace and a ministry of welcome and hospitality.

What were my weaknesses? I am not good at almost anything routine or mechanical. I am not good at keeping track of details. I lose interest in an idea once a problem is solved, so it is sometimes difficult for me to stay with one task very long. I am terrible at saving money and anything that has to do with record keeping. As we began to talk, it became clearer and clearer what excited me about ministry and where I felt called to spend my time. (I was not, for example, interested in starting a youth group, even though I had just finished a successful job as a youth director—I simply was not feeling called to work with youth at this time. I would be supportive if the need was presented and someone else was called to respond, but I was not going to lead a youth group.) What started to emerge from our conversation was a vision of our ministry together, and all of us began to have a sense of the energizing power of the Holy Spirit calling forth our individual and unique gifts. What I was weak in someone else was strong in; what overwhelmed me energized someone else. The commitment to finding our individual calling within the body of Christ has been a theme of our life together at South Haven ever since.

Once it was clear that the minister was not going to do everything because the minister too had a special calling born of her own particular giftedness, the people began to recognize areas of ministry that required their own unique gifts. This gave rise to an air of expectation and anticipation as people began to believe that God actually called us as individuals for particular tasks.

One of the first acts of business that we did as a church was to rewrite our constitution so that it reflected who we felt called to be as a body and so that it would give us the greatest flexibility to grow and change. As a part of our life together we require that each person's church membership be recommitted every year in writing. This is done to emphasize the active decisional quality of our life in Christ. We take our membership and the use of our time and talent seriously. Each year, we fill out a time-and-talent sheet, assessing our gifts, interests, and areas where we desire to be active in the church. We try to have people do what they enjoy doing because we believe that our calling is where our greatest joy and the world's deepest needs intersect. We are trying to say no to guilt and no to "shoulds."

How do we help people find their gifts? We start with what a person likes to do—what he or she enjoys. Generally we like what we are good at. So we ask people what gives them energy, what excites them. We then try to match that up with some need in the church, and a sense of calling begins to emerge. For people having difficulty discovering their gifts we offer the Trenton Spiritual Gift Analysis, which some people have found helpful in identifying specific areas of accomplishment. Most often, however, people are led into the process of discovering their calling simply by talking about their interests and what excites them, and they are encouraged to pray about what they should be doing both inside the church and outside it.

The idea of calling is discussed during part of the six hours of inquirer's classes held for new members. New members and longer-term members are encouraged each year to assess their gifts and discover what God is calling them to do. They are also encouraged not to do what they do not feel called to do. Generally, doing what we feel we *ought* to do doesn't energize us; it only makes us resentful. That gets communicated to everyone around us, and the church can too quickly be turned into a place with a lot of disgruntled, guilt-ridden, unhappy members. There is a great freedom in being able to say no to things as well as yes, and it is amazing how God provides what is needed if we trust the process. It is also amazing to see the amount of positive energy generated by the Holy Spirit amongst a people discovering their own gifts and calling.

At South Haven we are trying to develop a sense of mission born out of our calling, and though it is a continual struggle to listen to where God is calling us and to respond faithfully, the process continues to bear fruit. We have engaged in a ministry of the arts, offering classes in recorder playing and drawing and painting; we have a clown ministry troupe, which performs throughout the area; we are ecumenically involved in running a hunger center and a Meals-on-Wheels program; we have been on a work camp to Back Bay Mission, Biloxi, Mississippi; and we are building a sixty-unit housing facility for low-income elderly and handicapped persons, in conjunction with United Church Homes. Members of the congregation are actively engaged in the ministry of music, and the lay people preach and prepare four out of the six services a year when the pastor is away. Our goal is to help everyone see his or her own unique calling and match it up with an existing ministry or to encourage people to start new projects to which they feel called. We are trying to develop an atmosphere of encouragement, where people feel free to fail or succeed without embarrassment; a place where grace abounds.

Once one has discovered one's gifts, the task is to step out on the word of God and trust one's calling. In my own case, one of my strongest gifts was my voice and performance skill, but it was difficult at first for me to trust that as a gift to be used in renewing God's church. I had some fear and apprehension about being a "singing pastor," and I wasn't sure it was appropriate for the pastor to lead the choir. I certainly did not want worship at South Haven to look like a three-ring circus with me playing the ringmaster or putting on a spinning-plate act with me keeping all the plates going! But there is no question that my eventual trusting of this gift and using it fully in my leadership has indeed been one of the keys in our church's renewal.

I mention this not because I think musical ability and perform-ance experience are in themselves particularly valuable skills for the pastor of a discouraged church to possess. I mention it as a matter of principle regarding gifts. We must have the courage to identify and use the gifts we've been given.

I have said thus far that the two most important things we as clergy must do in our ministry with discouraged churches is to keep our spiritual lives alive and lead from our strengths. We all have different gifts. The point isn't to wish you had mine or I had yours. The point is to know what we've been given and to trust that God has given our particular gifts to us for a particular reason. We need to dare to believe in our own uniqueness and our own calling. As we dare to move out on our strengths, others will be freed to discover their strengths, and the people of God will be em-powered.

In addition to the pastor leading from his or her own strengths, the congregation should likewise look at its own unique gifts and begin to build on them. Too often, our tendency is to feel our inadequacies so strongly and want so much to overcome them that we wind up trying to build on the point where we are the weakest. The issue of youth ministry at South Haven was a prime example of this kind of thinking. When I first arrived, I scheduled a weekend planning retreat for anyone in the church who was interested. We brainstormed many ideas for the church and tried to dream dreams and catch a vision for our ministry.

One of the strongest ideas to combat was that in order to grow, the church needed to have a strong youth group. At that time we had only two teenaged people in the church. Youth ministry was clearly not a strength, but the myth persisted that in order to grow we needed to be involved in building up the youth group. It took a great deal of persistent education over that retreat weekend, and even thereafter, to convince people of the logic of identifying the strongest areas of the church's potential ministry and beginning to build there. Because people remembered when the youth group was large and the Sunday school was full (which by now was twenty years ago!) it was hard for them to envision another kind of church that could be equally exciting, growing, and alive without the same kind of profile.

The task of identifying the church's strengths and beginning to build on them instead of trying to build up where we are the weakest is a difficult task but essential. Persistence is required, but if the task is accomplished it will bring many blessings.

Building on a Strong Worship Service

The *only* activity of its own that South Haven was engaged in when I became the pastor was worship, so that had to be the strength on which to build. As the Spirit would have it, leading worship was one of my own strengths, so the match was a good one. Also, since all of the literature on church growth stresses the importance of dynamic worship, concentrating on developing a worship service that was lively, engaging, and reflective of who we were as a people seemed natural.

When one is working with a discouraged church, the most important thing, it seemed to me, was to bring a sense of good news to the people. When people are disheartened and lack self-esteem, as individuals and as a church, they need more than ever to hear the good news of the grace of Jesus Christ.

In a time of despair and negativity the church needs to believe again that God hears their cries—that God knows their discouragement and will respond to their groaning. People need to hear again the great story of our salvation history—that once we were no people, but now we are God's people! They need to know that the church—the *ecclesia*—means the "called-out and-called-together ones" and that God has called them together for a special purpose. Perhaps the purpose is not yet clear, but in the risking it will be revealed, as we are a pilgrim people "on the way." A time of discouragement is a great time for preaching and prophesying—speaking forth the word of hope from the word of God!

Preaching

Though I believe in the practice of preaching from the lectionary on a regular basis, as I began my ministry at South Haven I felt that series preaching would meet the need of the congregation in a particular way. Stating a series of sermons and advertising their titles through the bulletin and newsletter seemed to give us a needed sense of focus and continuity, helping us to feel that we were on a journey together. This sense was important, as the church in the past had felt much discontinuity, fragmentation, and lack of direction.

I began preaching through Philippians, the letter of joy. How the people were hungry for some good news! I then preached through Ephesians, where one finds a balance of Christian doctrine and practice. This helped to give some grounding in basic Christian

99

beliefs and helped to shape the people's sense of being called to be the body of Christ, the church.

From there I moved to preaching through the Gospel of Mark, where one meets our Lord most starkly preaching, teaching, healing, and calling "follow me." I then preached from the great stories of God's call to Abraham and Sarah, Isaac, Jacob, Joseph, and Moses, all the while hoping to help people see and sense the call of God in their own lives and the life of the church.

What I sensed in the people was a hunger for a "word from the Lord." All of us need to hear the story again and know that it is true but especially a discouraged people! When people are disheartened, they need to know that God will deliver God's people, bring them up out of bondage, give them manna in the wilderness, and bring them to new life. We need to be reminded that the story of the Old Testament Hebrews is our story, and there is strength and power in the story for us because God is alive and real, and God's promise is sure.

Participation

I am convinced that in addition to hearing strong biblical preaching, the discouraged people of God need to have enough to do when they worship. Discouragement breeds passivity. Passivity feeds low self-esteem. Low self-esteem brings negativity. Worship can begin to lift people from this bondage if it is open to the Holy Spirit, deeply joyous, honest in intellect and emotion, and if it actively engages the people. We know that the word "liturgy" literally means the "work of the people," and yet so often a worship service doesn't give the people much to do. Sing a few hymns, read a call to worship, say a prayer, listen, listen, listen to the pastor, and go home. No wonder people have a hard time getting excited about Sunday morning worship!

One of the myths that I had been told before beginning my pastorate was that the pastor should not change anything in the worship service for the first year. I understood that it would be tactless and insensitive to come in and rip everything to shreds and start over, yet it seemed to me that not changing anything for a year was a good way to give away one's power to change anything ever. Especially in a discouraged church the people need leadership that is willing to offer something new. What they do not need is more of the same old way of doing things that has left them feeling joyless.

When a new pastor comes, the people are hoping that something will change. Not everything of course, but something. During the first year, which is often a "honeymoon" period, the pastor has a lot of freedom to make changes that he or she feels are important for the life of the church. We need to consider carefully what we think the most important changes should be and not waste our changes on what is trivial. Enlivening the worship service is crucial. Frankly, I can't imagine any church with a lively, meaningful, deep worship life being a discouraged, sad people. Worship is the heartbeat of the people of God, and if the heart is barely ticking, it's up to the pastor to perform some cardiopulmonary resuscitation quickly!

At South Haven the order of the worship service was relatively sound, but the execution had lacked energy and creativity. There was not enough for the people to do, and what they were given to do seemed to bore them. There was no theme to the service on a particular Sunday, and therefore the worship lacked a sense of focus and continuity. Week after week of lackluster calls to worship, prayers that have little or no relevance to the day, and psalms recited from the back of the hymnal is a sure way to deaden the soul of even the most faithful person in the congregation. I tried to keep the order of the service intact in order to give some sense of stability, but I began to add things and change things to liven up the pace and content.

First I counted up how many places in the service the people were doing something other than listening. There were eight such places, so I began to increase the number of opportunities for the people's participation. If there are not at least a dozen places where the congregation can actively participate in the service, then I believe the worship is too passive. We are up to an average of fifteen places for congregational participation, and during communion this increases to twenty-three. Actually, wherever the people can do the work rather than the pastor, then they ought to be doing it. They should be participating with the pastor all the way along—so that the only things the pastor is really doing by herself or himself is preaching and possibly the reading of scripture (although it is preferable to look for creative ways to involve the people here as well), and the benediction (although responsive benedictions can also be effective). The pastor's role in worship is to set the tone and direct the rhythm and flow of the whole service, and the goal is always to be engaging the community with the presence of God.

Singing

If it is true, as Pierre Teilhard de Chardin has said, that "joy is the one infallible sign of the presence of God," then we need to have the people singing. Not just three hymns and a doxology, but all through the service. There are many easy responses that can be used before and after the reading of scripture, before and after the prayers, calls to the table for communion, as introits and benediction responses. Anthems by the choir and other musical offerings of soloists have their place in the service as they minister to people by opening them up to the experience of beauty and grace and putting them in contact with the recesses of intuition and the unconscious. I suggest, however, that whenever possible let all the people sing, not just the choir. Why should just a select group of people be allowed to sing the responses to prayer or the benediction? Let's have the people singing! This may involve teaching the congregation new responses and hymns in the moments before worship. It might mean using the children's moment to engage the congregation in a song while the pastor and the children act it out or try the sign language for it. It could mean singing together more at potlucks and coffee hours, at church picnics and Bible studies, so that the people learn to feel comfortable when making a joyful noise.

At first it is hard for a discouraged people to sing. As the psalmist said, "How shall we sing the Lord's song in a foreign land?" But if we make an effort to sing through our discouragement, the singing itself can lead us out on the other side. We need to learn to do it. If the pastor is not skilled in this regard, then he or she must find someone who is gifted in this area to lead. It need not be the choir director or organist. There may be another person in the congregation who is gifted in getting people excited about singing together. What is really necessary is a love of singing and a love of people, a good sense of rhythm and pitch, and courage! I have seen people with hardly a voice at all get people involved and singing beautifully together if they are willing to step out with bold leadership and get it going.

Solid biblical preaching, a worship service with a unified theme and meaningful participation by the congregation (with lots of singing!), and finally an opportunity to pray together are the ingredients that we have found bring life to our worship. When I began as the pastor of South Haven, it seemed to me that if I and the congregation were to grow together in understanding and knowledge of what it meant to be a community of faith, then we needed to learn to pray together.

Prayer

Time needed to be given in the corporate worship for the prayers of the people, and I strongly believed they needed to give voice to those prayers themselves. This was something totally new for the congregation, who in their twenty-six-year history had never experienced praying aloud in their own words during worship. I had little experience with this myself, which I think was helpful—we were all in it together. I did not believe I could ask the congregation to so something I was not willing to do myself, and so we agreed that I would offer the pastoral prayer spontaneously and they would offer the prayers of the people spontaneously, and we would learn together what it meant to be able to express what was on our hearts before one another and before God.

For six Sundays there was complete quiet during the prayers of the people. But each Sunday I would gently encourage again, sharing with the people why I felt it was important that we learn to pray together: that it was one way in which the body of Christ was strengthened, for as we bring our hurts, our disappointments, our fears, our needs, our joys, our celebrations before God, we are witnessing to one another that we believe God is really alive and listening and responding to us. Our prayer life is a testimony to our belief that God is real and active in our lives.

Slowly the people began to respond. A sentence here, a sentence there. Each week before the time of prayer I would try to articulate what I perceived the fears of the people to be (which were of course my own fears as well). What if I don't know what to say? What if my words come out wrong? What if I start to speak and someone else starts at the same time? What if I start to cry? What if . . . The moments before prayer became a time of gentle teaching about the grace of God and the bond of our common humanness. Over the years there have been more and more people who have dared to utter their concerns and joys aloud before the Holy One, and I as the pastor still tremble every Sunday at prayer time. It is the part of the worship service that makes me feel the most apprehensive, because it is the one place where I have to let go. I might not know what to say; the words might come out wrong; they might be prosaic, mundane, boring; I might forget to say something I intended or say something I didn't intend; I might cry; I might fail. (But God will not fail!)

It has been our experience that people in the congregation now look forward to the prayer time as a very meaningful part of the worship experience. It is a time in our life together where people are touched and fed by the power of the living God. We continue to try different ways of structuring this time so that there is time for centering quiet and freedom for the Spirit to move, while we are still being conscious of the flow and rhythm of the whole service. The time of prayer continues to be a challenge Sunday after Sunday, but it is a key, I think, to our experiencing the Holy Spirit renewing us.

In some research done on church growth, "intercessory prayer" was one of the four top reasons people listed as to why they joined a particular church. In our church, opening up a time in worship for the people and the pastor to be vulnerable before God and one another has had a powerful influence on our life together. From the seeds planted in worship has grown a prayer chain of one quarter of the congregation involved in daily ongoing prayer for one another and the world. As we learn to pray together, we learn to listen more, to one another and to God, and we learn to walk more closely with Christ and trust the power of the Holy Spirit moving in, through, and amongst us.

A Teaching Ministry

Another area in which my own strength was matched with a strength and need of the church was in the area of adult education. I had a love of teaching and fifteen years of teaching experience, and the church had several adults who were eager to learn, so together we began a teaching ministry that has been the spiritual undergirding for much of our church's growth.

We started simply with a Wednesday evening Bible study for a small core group of adults who were hungry for some basic understanding of scripture and who had a desire to understand what it was they thought they believed. The first year we studied Ephesians and the Gospel of Mark, and I coordinated a lot of my preaching with the study. The second year we devoted the whole year to the study of the book of Acts, which empowered and deepened our understanding of what it meant to be the church and opened us anew to the workings of the Holy Spirit. The study group continued to grow in numbers and enthusiasm, and much of the leadership of the church began to emerge from its participants. Several new members joined the church by first coming to the Bible study, and there was a good deal of spiritual energy being generated from its ranks. The Bible study has remained as the mainstay of our adult education program with the numbers of participants growing each year and different people coming and going as different courses are taught.

We have added to the Bible study a "discovery group," which meets on a Sunday evening in someone's home, and rather than centering on scripture, concentrates on our personal growth as it relates to our faith. This group proved to be another avenue of invitation to nonmembers, and several people began coming first to the discovery group and then to church and eventually became active members. In addition, we began to offer the opportunity for a spiritual retreat in the spring of the year. It has met the needs of the people so well that we now offer two such retreats a year in addition to our annual planning retreat, to which all members and prospective members are invited. These educational opportunities have sparked so much growth in our church that it is hard to imagine our having grown at all without them. They have provided the spiritual undergirding for growth in faith. They have provided a chance to talk about what we believe, to begin to find ways to articulate our faith. They have provided fun and fellowship and have built friendships and made of us a family. They have challenged us to risk more and given us courage in the journey of following Jesus.

In addition to the structured groups for adult education, I have tried to see all encounters as opportunities for teaching. Whether it be in council meetings or choir rehearsals, in visits with prospective or existing members, in committee meetings or in informal conversations, we have continual opportunities to share with others the awareness of God's presence gently leading and guiding us in all things.

Our inquirer's classes for prospective members have also been an important part of our teaching ministry. We offer six hours of classes in which we discuss what it is we believe, who we are as the United Church of Christ, and what it means to be a member of South Haven United Church of Christ. As a part of these classes, each person will draw her or his spiritual journey, using crayons or clored markers, and we will talk together about our faith experience. Nearly everyone in the church has now had this experience, and drawing the spiritual journey has been a powerful tool in helping people begin to talk about their faith. As we share our faith with others, it becomes more real for us, and these opportunities have continued to strengthen us all. It is a powerful experience to hear how God has worked and is working in the lives of people, and each time we hear a new story it is another confirmation that God is indeed alive!

Hospitality

Another area in which a strength of mine was matched with a need and strength of the congregation's was in the area of creating a climate of welcome and hospitality. The one thing that a discouraged people need above all is to have a good time. They need to remember how to laugh, how to play, how to rejoice. It is so sad to see in so many of our churches how the chosen people of God become the frozen people of God. A good thaw can come in a lot of ways—through enlivening worship experiences, through dynamic learning experiences, through learning to celebrate.

At South Haven there were a lot of fun-loving people who had forgotten how to have a good time together. The years of decline in the church and the resulting despondency had left them in sad shape when it came to thinking about a party. At the potluck they had had for me when I was a candidate, hardly a word was spoken between anyone. Only a few people talked to me, and I was supposed to be the guest of honor. Luckily I had brought my guitar along with me, and so I got it out and with some effort got the people singing. Little by little the ice was broken and they began to show signs of life. It was then that I realized they had just forgotten how to be their fun-loving selves. They needed someone to encourage them to come back out of their shells and coax them to smile. It was then I noticed too that there were still some mighty good cooks left among them and enough hearty eaters to make for a good party. I decided to build on our combined strengths (mine being that I still knew how to smile and sing and I am good at finding reasons to celebrate).

I decided we would find every occasion we could to rejoice together and have a party and invite everybody we could (as Jesus said, especially those who don't get invited to parties very often). The church had gala events for my installation and ordination; they initiated a fall corn roast complete with a bonfire in the parking lot and a singalong into the wee hours of the moonlit night. They celebrated the church's anniversary and had a Christmas potluck, a

New Year's Eve open house, a Pentecost party, a clambake, a spaghetti dinner, a soup-and-salad luncheon after church—the people came alive! There was singing and dancing and game playing and deep conversation and laughing—the tombstone had been rolled away!

There is a good chance that the combination of discovering our gifts, renewed and deepened worship, biblical teaching and faith exploration, and opportunities for celebration helped bring about a resurrection at South Haven. But it was God who kept God's promise! Our task as Christians is ever and always to try to continue to envision and articulate where God is yet leading and to follow without fear, knowing that God is not in the business of failing. God will not fail!

Awaking a Sleeping Giant

First Plymouth Congregational Church, Lincoln, Nebraska

OTIS E. YOUNG

On Sunday morning, August 19, 1866, First Congregational Church was organized in what was then known as Lancaster, Nebraska. A representative of the American Home Missionary Society preached the sermon and celebrated the sacrament of the Lord's Supper. So was founded the first permanent church of any kind in what was to become the city of Lincoln. Lancaster then had six buildings—four dwellings, one store, and a blacksmith shop. The name of the city was changed to Lincoln in 1867, when it became the capital of the new state of Nebraska.

Early History

The church began its active life in the community as a mission church. The first pastor was to be paid $100 by the local congregation and the balance of his salary by the American Home Missionary Society. He requested that the AHMS provide at least $1,000 per year for support, noting that this sum was less than

Otis E. Young has been senior minister of First Plymouth Congregational Church (UCC) in Lincoln, Nebraska, since 1972. Before coming to Lincoln he was general secretary of the United Church Board for Homeland Ministries' Division of Church Extension and Evangelism. He has also served churches in Markham, Illinois, and Webster Groves, Missouri.

necessary. The society made it $500. In his plea, the minister wrote: "If we enter Lincoln at once and work efficiently we may be the first in the political and intellectual center of the state. If we delay for six months or a year at most, the opportunity will be lost. If we suffer the Congregationalists now in Lincoln to become discouraged, the Presbyterians will come in and take away a large part of the element which now we can secure."

His predictions were sound, as history has shown since then. First Plymouth Congregational Church, UCC, as it is now called, has gone on during these 120 plus years to become the preeminent church in the capital city of Nebraska.

In 1869 the congregation completed its first building, which was a 25-by-40-foot structure sheathed with boards and paper. Previously, the congregation had met in members' houses in the surrounding territory and outdoors in the bright summer weather. Public worship was the center of church life.

In 1886 Carrie Bell Raymond was received into membership, a noteworthy occasion because she was to serve as organist and director of music for the next forty years. She established a music tradition that has been a central part of the church's life and worship ever since.

First Congregational Church was instrumental in organizing Plymouth Congregational Church on October 25, 1887. These two congregations merged in 1923. In the meantime, however, First Congregational Church in 1890 sent out another colony of forty-five members to form Vine Congregational Church, which is still in existence in Lincoln.

Soon after the merger, the newly constituted congregation, having a membership of 1,073, divided almost equally between the two churches, decided to build a new building on the site that is now occupied by it, Twentieth and "D," about ten blocks from the state Capitol building. The plans were completed in 1929, and construction began in 1930. A total of $32,248 was paid for the site, and the estimated cost of the new building was $500,000, without a mortgage. The new building was dedicated on April 5, 1931. On dedication Sunday, 103 new members were received into the congregation.

First Plymouth Congregational Church continued to grow and prosper. Church membership reached 1,671 in 1946 and 2,076 by 1952. Thereafter, church membership remained static for a few years and then began a long slow decline so that in 1972, the congregation reported 1,233 resident members, a loss of 843 members in sixteen years. Average attendance at public worship each Sunday had declined to 250. Part of the decline in membership came about because of the congregation's long struggle with the proposed merger that formed the United Church of Christ. Before 1957, the church had voted 687 to 121 against the merger. Another vote taken a few years later was 443 to 314 against the merger. Finally on October 2, 1960, the congregation voted to join the merger 328 to 228. However, the years of struggle had taken its toll. More than a hundred members left the church. Some of these helped organize a new independent Congregational church six blocks away.

On the positive side, in 1962, the congregation began looking toward another major building program. A capital-improvements committee was set up to explore plans for improved educational facilities, a chapel, redecoration of the nave, a new pipe organ, and better parking facilities. In 1965 this committee presented plans to the congregation for improvements costing $538,000. A capital-funds drive was held, which obtained pledges for $422,708. There was already $126,000 available in other funds. The pledges and the funds on hand were not enough, however, to meet construction costs, which had risen to $775,000 by 1968. The congregation went ahead anyway, and the renovations and additions were dedicated on Sunday, September 22, 1968, with a debt of several hundred thousand dollars.

Strengths and Weaknesses

I arrived on the scene as the new senior minister in January 1972. The pastoral search committee was convinced that First Plymouth Church was, as the committee characterized it, "a sleeping giant." The congregation, according to the committee, was ready to awaken, ready to grow and expand. The church building, having been recently renovated and enlarged, was prepared for more use.

My first task, with the help of the various committees in the church, was to assess the strengths and weaknesses of the congregation. The strengths we found were these:

- A willingness and readiness to grow. Almost everyone I talked with believed that the congregation should be receiving many more new members.

- A tradition of leadership. Because the church was the oldest

111

congregation in Lincoln and had been a leader, this tradition was still in people's minds.

- A tradition of having a strong music program. Since 1886, when Carrie Bell Raymond became the organist and director of music, the congregation had had a vital music program. It was one of the first churches in Lincoln to have a full-time organist and music director. The church also possessed three fine musical instruments—a magnificent pipe organ in the main worship area, a fine smaller pipe organ in the chapel, and the only true carillon of forty-eight bells in the State of Nebraska.

- The church building, an architectural gem, in good shape and also very usable in a variety of ways besides worship.

- A tradition of its senior minister and other staff people being active in community affairs. In addition many of the church members had been, and were, leaders in the community as well as in the University of Nebraska.

- A congregation that had boldly used the media for its outreach. Since the 1940s the church had been doing a weekly broadcast live of its 9:30 A.M. worship service over a local radio station.

The church also had some significant weaknesses.

- Not very many young people in the congregation. Almost a whole generation was missing. As noted earlier, the church had been having net losses in membership since the late 1950s.

- An inadequate operating budget. There was a debt remaining on the building, and an operating deficit had been accumulating for the past five years. The congregation had been spending the advance pledge payments for the next year to pay the past year's bills.

- Not very many church members supporting the church budget with appropriate giving. Poor stewardship was evident.

- A lack of energy and excitement in the worship services. In spite of good music, worship had become a boring, routine exercise. Worship attendance was weak.

- A reputation of being an unfriendly, cold place. Visitors did not feel accepted.

- Lack of a sense of direction and purpose.

A Vision and a Plan

Gradually, we devised a vision and a plan that would utilize the strengths already present and overcome the weaknesses.

Improving Worship and Welcoming Visitors

At my first annual meeting of the congregation, after only three weeks on the job, I announced my personal goal of increasing attendance at public worship so that in a few years we would be averaging seven hundred per Sunday. At that time in 1972, average attendance was about 250. I told them I wanted to make worship exciting and interesting, so that when people left the services they would feel better than when they came in. In addition, I observed that as far as I knew, no one ever got angry for church ending early. We on the staff would plan the worship services very carefully, so that we would not ever run over one hour.

For more than forty years, ever since the church began broadcasting live its early service of worship, that service has been one-half hour long. I could also see possibilities there, keeping the service one-half hour long, yet making it more inspiring. We've accomplished that. In 1972, the average Sunday attendance at the 9:30 service was about eighty; now it's at least three hundred.

We receive more positive comments from visitors about the overall quality of our worship services than about any other aspect of our church program. They mention the way the service is put together, the movement, the music, the preaching, the use of inclusive language, the lack of "dead" time, the cohesiveness, and the sense of being in a spiritual atmosphere. Visitors and members alike appreciate especially the fact that due to careful planning, we never run overtime. The 9:30 service is one-half hour, and the 11:00 service never goes longer than one hour.

A few months later that first year at the board of deacons meeting, after much discussion, the deacons voted at my suggestion that we set a goal of receiving at least 100 new members in the next year and at least 150 in the year after that. The deacons further agreed to put into place a plan for greeting visitors and members as they entered the worship service and making sure to have all visitors to sign the guest book with name, address, and telephone number.

One of the deacons, a recently retired university professor with a friendly manner, agreed that in addition to being a regular greeter each Sunday, he would make it his personal responsibility to telephone each visitor who signed the guest book, that same Sunday afternoon and evening. He then went about setting up his system. When he called, he first thanked the visitor for being in our worship services and issued an invitation to return. He kept accurate records of each telephone call, and he also kept complete records of who returned Sunday after Sunday. In a short period of time, his system became one of our best sources of new members. This individual kept doing his telephoning each week for the next ten years, long after his term on the board of deacons ended. At one annual meeting, we bestowed upon him the lifetime title "Lay Associate for Evangelism."

We had now put together the central pieces of our action plan for waking the sleeping giant: a renewed emphasis on worship as the center of the church's life and creating a warm and caring attitude so that visitors at worship would feel welcomed and accepted. This attitude carried over to all the members who began attending worship with regularity again. And we set definite membership goals to be achieved over a period of time, and we made these goals widely known to all the members.

We also let it be known to the community at large that our church building was open for use. Soon more and more community groups began calling to request a room for a meeting.

Stewardship and Music

Our action plan included improving the stewardship of our members. We needed increased giving of money. In 1973 the congregation voted to have a special debt-reduction drive with the goal of wiping out the building debt completely within two years. That drive was successful. We also agreed in the board of trustees that we would never again have a deficit operating budget; and this aim meant not reducing the budget but increasing giving among the members. The year 1972 ended with a small surplus, and we have not had a deficit since then. In 1971 the operating budget, including benevolences, was $164,000. In 1987 our operating budget, including benevolences, was $605,000. In 1990 our total budget was $921,510.

In the fall of 1972, we employed a new minister of music and fine arts. The previous staff person had been there for seven years and had accepted a call to another church. The new minister has been ideal for our situation. He was a young man who had three years earlier graduated from the Union Theological Seminary School of Sacred Music in New York City and was filled with energy and ideas for worship. He has now been with us almost eighteen years, and we have a music program including the music in worship that is one of the best in the country.

Revised Bylaws

Next we realized that our outdated articles of incorporation and bylaws needed attention. The bylaws were too wordy and lines of responsibility were not clearly defined. A committee was appointed by the church council to make recommendations to the congregation for revision. This committee met regularly for many months and then presented its recommendations to a congregational meeting. Its proposed revisions were adopted.

Statement of Mission

The first parts of our action plan were in place and beginning to work. The giant was beginning slowly to awaken.

By 1975 the debt on the building had been eliminated, more parking had been provided, the church-membership decline had been reversed, and attendance at worship was continuing to increase, although not at the rate that I hoped for. I suggested that the church council appoint a special planning committee to take a look at the church and its future and make any recommendations it deemed necessary.

This committee decided that its most important task would be to draft a "Statement of Mission" for the congregation, so that together we would have a better sense of direction and purpose for the present and the future. After many meetings and long discussions, the following "Statement of Mission" was written and was officially adopted by the congregation at its annual meeting in January 1976. A list of "Imperatives" accompanied the statement of mission and it too was adopted by the congregation.

Statement of Mission

The church has been, is, and is to be a community of persons who acknowledge God as Creator and Sustainer, Jesus Christ as God's redeeming activity, and human beings as participating with God in the responsibility for the well-being of the created order. The church exists in history to increase among people the love of God and neighbor and to increase health and harmony in all the creation.

First Plymouth Congregational Church, a congregation of the United Church of Christ, in Lincoln, Nebraska, intends with the power of the Holy Spirit to continue to carry out the purpose of the church by being in its life a community of persons that, accepting Jesus Christ as Lord and Savior, is committed to following His example and teachings

a community of persons that, gathering regularly, participates in and experiences the presence of God in public worship through preaching, prayer, Bible study, the sacraments, and music and other arts

a community of persons that, seeking to nurture persons of all ages, provides opportunities for personal spiritual growth and learning the story of the Christian faith

a community of persons that, loving and caring for one another, supports one another in carrying out each individual's ministry at home, at work, and in leisure

a community of persons that, seeking to serve, is continually reaching out to minister to individuals who are lonely, oppressed, afraid, sick, poor, hungry

a community of persons that, recognizing our interdependence with all humanity, works for justice and harmony throughout the world

a community of persons that, recognizing our interrelationships with all creation, works responsibly for the care of the environment and natural resources

Adopted January 1976

First-Plymouth Church
Some Imperatives for the Present and Future

Part II of the Report of the Special Planning Committee
January 1976

The special planning committee believes that in order for First Plymouth Church to live up to the "Statement of Mission" and be a responsible and faithful Christian community, the following areas of our church life need special attention now!

We need
A system to improve the assimilation of new members into the life and work of our congregation. Presently we are receiving more than 150 new members each year. Therefore, we call upon the boards of deacons and deaconesses with the help of a staff person to work out a plan for the assimilation of new members and put it into operation as soon as possible.

We need
Four hundred families or individuals to face candidly the fact of their poor stewardship in connection with First Plymouth Church. One hundred-fifty families or individuals give no financial support to the congregation, and another 150 give less than $2.00 per week toward the support of First Plymouth. An analysis of our financial support also shows that at least another one hundred families or individuals give below their capability.

We need
Over the next four years an increase of 250 persons in regular attendance at public worship. We now offer one of the best worship experiences we know about. It waits on your participation. Our hope is that by 1990 we will have reached an average attendance of seven hundred each Sunday. Regularity in participation in worship needs to be a part of each member's commitment!

We need
To include the single persons of all ages who are members of our congregation in the total life of our church. One fourth of the members of our congregation are single adults. Furthermore, the largest population increase in our city is composed of young adults, many of them single. Many of our new members now and in the future will be single adults.

We need
A more comprehensive transportation plan. Many of our longer-living members no longer drive but still want to participate in the many programs and services of the church. We believe the gift or acquisition of a fifteen-passenger van that will belong to the church ought to be encouraged. Car pools and other methods of helping persons to be able to participate in church programs and services need better organization.

We need
A plan to encourage more of our members to include First Plymouth in their wills. We also need to promote the support of First Plymouth through "living trusts" and memorials. We have one of the most beautiful church buildings in the Midwest. It is an asset to the whole community. It needs to be well maintained and cared for now and in the future.

We need
More members to be engaged in the practice and study of prayer, biblical teaching, and Christian ethics and through these to exhibit the joy and power of the Christian faith.

We need
More members who understand that in their participation in the

117

life and work of First Plymouth Church, they are part of the
community of Christians all over the world and are thus related to
all humanity as brothers and sisters in Christ.

Members of the Special Planning Committee

These two documents provided a platform from which First-
Plymouth Church could continue to grow.

Reaching the Community

We have developed a number of ways to reach the community by
means of the media and through other programs.

Radio and Television Ministry

In the meantime, the church was continuing to use the media in
its outreach to the community. The radio broadcast live of the 9:30
service continued, and in December 1972, a local television station
asked if it could televise our 11:00 P.M. Christmas Eve worship
service. The estimated cost to the church would be about $1,500.
That money was not in the budget. After gaining the church council's approval, we raised money by asking members to contribute
toward the broadcast. Little did we know that we had started a
tradition. Our Christmas Eve worship service has been telecast
each year since then, and in 1980 the CBS network carried our
Christmas Eve service of lessons and carols live, nationwide.

In the spring of 1986, after much discussion and planning, we
had a capital-funds campaign that raised $1,000,200 for our
planned television outreach and building renovation. The television outreach ministry is now in full operation. In the fall of 1987,
we employed a full-time director of media, a woman who is a
trained television producer-editor-director. She trained a corps of
volunteers to assist her in operating cameras and sound equipment
and in other aspects of television production.

A television studio has been built in the church; we are using
four cameras of commercial-broadcast quality and we have a complete facility for postproduction. We videotape our Sunday morning 11:00 A.M. worship service and edit it to half an hour for use on
the local public-access cablevision channel. In addition, our edited
worship service "Reach Out and Live" is seen each Sunday morning on a commercial ABC affiliate from Omaha. This station
reaches eastern Nebraska, western Iowa, and northwest Missouri.
We are also seen and heard each Sunday morning on commercial

118

stations in Rapid City, South Dakota; Scottsbluff, Nebraska; Sheridan, Wyoming; and Lead, South Dakota.

We also use our television equipment for producing Christian education tapes, youth ministry, and videotaping of weddings and baptisms and other church programs.

We see the half-hour telecast of our worship service as a welcome alternative to present religious programming for these reasons:

1. The telecast comes from an active local congregation that is carrying on a vital ministry in its own community. We do not exist primarily to put on a television program.

2. Our telecast is a gift to the viewers from the members of our church. There is no fund raising in or on the program.

3. At the close of each telecast we invite the viewers to attend, participate actively in, and support the church of their choice in their own community.

We continue to carry on our Sunday morning radio broadcast. Thus we are using the technology of the past, which is still relevant, and at the same time are meeting the changes of the present and the future.

A Gay Men's Concert

An event in 1981 was significant in the outreach program of the church. The preceding fall we received a request for the use of the church building for a concert by the San Francisco Gay Men's Chorus. This chorus was planning a nationwide concert tour and wanted to sing in our church in Lincoln, Nebraska. I took the request to the board of trustees of the church and to the church council, both of which voted to let the chorus use the building. In March 1981 publicity for the concert began to appear in the local press, and the church office began receiving telephone calls and mail. People who were strongly opposed to the use of the building by the Gay Men's Chorus were letting us know about it.

There were numerous letters to the editor in the local newspaper from people who thought First Plymouth Church had sold out to the devil. There were also, however, some letters of support. Fortunately, most of the opposition came from individuals and groups who were not affiliated with our church. By and large, our church members were accepting of the concert, though there was some strong opposition.

119

The concert was held as scheduled on Tuesday, June 9, 1981. A standing-room-only crowd was in attendance. The chorus received a standing ovation as they processed. One newspaper reviewer said that it was the only concert he had ever attended where the choir received a standing ovation before it sang one note.

As I look back now, I believe the congregation's willingness to accommodate the chorus was a positive turning point in the church's life. Now the whole community knew for sure that we were an open and inclusive church. The publicity we gained could not have been purchased with money.

Preschool and Daywatch

Two other programs have played an important part in our outreach ministry. We greatly expanded and upgraded the weekday preschool, which is now recognized as the best in the city. It is open to all children of the community.

In December 1989 the congregation began renting a vacant storefront building on the main street of downtown Lincoln as another outreach of our ministry. The building is used as a daytime center, called Daywatch, for homeless and unemployed people. We are open seven days a week from 7:30 A.M. to 5:30 P.M. One of our associate ministers is in charge in addition to the volunteer staff. Free coffee and cookies are available throughout the day. Daywatch is a meeting place where people of all classes and races can feel welcome and safe. In this sanctuary people can tell their stories, enjoy one another, and learn to respect the sacredness of each individual.

Women's Ministry

While we were improving worship and stewardship and extending our outreach, I sensed increasing dissatisfaction with the women's association. Most of its members were older women, and it was increasingly difficult to find individuals to take leadership positions. As in most Protestant churches, the women's association, or women's fellowship, or ladies aid—or whatever term is used—was a parallel organization to the congregation, with its own officers, its own treasury, and its own constitution and bylaws. In our case the women's association board was made up of the leaders of each of the various circles; they were almost entirely older women, because the circles met in the daytime when most of the younger women in the church worked outside the home.

Thus, we devised a plan to replace the women's association. I suggested that the congregation elect at its annual meeting a board for women's ministries, which would be like all our other church boards. This board would then elect its own chair, as do our other boards. It would also be included in the church's budget instead of having its own treasury. After many months of discussion, a special congregational meeting amended the church bylaws to provide for a board for women's ministries and voted the women's association out of existance.

The women's circles continued to meet, and the monthly women's luncheon is still held, but all the planning for programs is now done by the board for women's ministries. As a result, many new programs have been added—for single women parents, for women who work outside the home, for women active in community affairs, and more.

In order to put the new board for women's ministries in operation, we were fortunate in being able to employ as a seminary intern a young woman from Yale Divinity School who had a particular interest in the project and the necessary skills to put it into effect. One of her major assignments during her year with us was to get the new system working smoothly.

She did the job well. When she returned to the seminary, the church was able to employ a woman from our congregation, part-time, to continue the staff work in women's ministries. After several years, she decided to enter seminary, and another woman from our congregation served in that capacity. She was also attending seminary in Kansas City at the same time. After becoming ordained, she joined our staff full-time as an associate minister. She continues to carry a major assignment in helping the board for women's ministries chart a new way for women's ministries in the local church.

A little over six years ago we were able to employ another lay woman from our congregation to be director of Christian education. Her willing spirit, flexibility, creativity, and experience in public school education have led our Sunday church school to more than double its size. She became a full-time commissioned minister in Christian education in May 1990.

A Plan for the Future

Our efforts in all these areas were bearing fruit. In 1981 we celebrated the fiftieth anniversary of our magnificent church building. It had been officially opened and dedicated on April 5, 1931. So we used April 5, 1981, which also came on a Sunday, to highlight the church's history. It also gave us the opportunity to launch a special building-fund drive to enable us to do some major renovation. In 1986, as noted, we had a capital-funds campaign for further renovation and for our television ministry. By that time we had reached our goal of an average Sunday worship attendance of seven hundred and had gone beyond it. Our church membership continued to increase. We were regularly receiving 150 or more new members a year, most of them younger people. Present membership is more than two thousand and continuing to grow. We have two complete church-school sessions each Sunday morning. In the past nine years, seven of our members have been ordained ministers in the United Church of Christ, and one, as noted, has become a commissioned minister. We are presently making plans for further building renovation and the addition of a large three-story wing. The estimated total cost is $2 million. We presented a proposal to the congregation, divided in three parts.

Part I

We propose to enlarge our church building by adding a new, three-level wing that would connect to our present parish hall on the northwest end and would match in design. This new addition would meet four strategic goals and needs.

1. A new wide entrance on ground level at Twentieth Street and an elevator would make our entire building accessible to the handicapped. We would also build completely accessible rest rooms.

2. We would have more space for our rapidly expanding weekday Preschool and Parents Day Out programs.

3. We would have additional space for our growing Sunday church-school programs for children, young people, and adults and for our expanding youth ministry.

4. A new, appropriately designed rehearsal room, robe-storage area, and offices for the minister of music and other music staff would provide space for our growing music ministry. This new music room would also be used for meetings and lectures.

Part II

We propose to redesign the chancel area of the main church auditorium. An integral part of this plan is the expansion and renovation of the main pipe organ. This proposal would meet three strategic goals and needs.

1. It would provide more space for the choirs and instrumentalists in leading worship and at the same time make the chancel area more flexible to accommodate concerts and other events. There would also be additional storage space in that area.

2. The present pipe organ would be expanded so that it has a wider variety of sounds available for playing a broader range of music. The plan includes a much needed new organ console.

3. A new organ case that is more in keeping with the architecture of the building would make the organ appear to be an integral part of the original building design.

Part III

According to our 1976 "Statement of Mission," we are a "community of persons which, seeking to serve, is continually reaching out to minister to individuals who are lonely, oppressed, afraid, sick, poor, hungry. . . ." One example is our radio and television ministry. We propose to expand our outreach ministry in two ways:

1. In 1988 the church council recommended that we pledge $200,000 to the Nebraska Conference UCC Development Fund, as part of any future capital-funds drive we might have. This amount would be paid over a period of three to five years.

2. A "First Plymouth Lincoln/Lancaster County Ministry Fund" would be established and set aside for future use. Once the fund is in place, a special committee would be appointed by the church council to recommend to the congregation how this money might be used for expanded ministry in the Lincoln/ Lancaster county area using the guidelines of our "Statement of Mission."

The Reasons for Our Growth

Looking back, I believe these are the key reasons for the growth of First Plymouth Congregational Church since 1972.

First, the congregation had a significant history of ministry in the city of Lincoln on which it was willing and ready to build and use as a base for reaching out.

Second, we were able to put together a committed and creative professional and support staff. There has been little turnover, and we have been able to add staff when needed.

Third, we have made Sunday morning worship the center of the church's life. The worship is carefully planned. The use of music with a variety of choirs, a resident brass group, and other instrumentation have all helped to make the worship exciting and inspiring.

Fourth, we renewed our program of Christian education for children and adults of all ages with special emphasis on the Sunday morning church school. The expanded weekday preschool has become a source of new members for the congregation.

Fifth, we took a new approach to women's ministries.

Sixth, we increased our outreach ministry in the community. Through the past eighteen years First Plymouth has become a vital center for community activities. The building is used day and night, not only for church activities but for community meetings and support groups. The main church auditorium with its excellent acoustics for music has become a concert hall for a variety of musical events and for our own separately incorporated concert series, Abendmusik: Lincoln, Inc.

We are known as the open and inclusive church in the community. Accessibility to older infirm persons and those with disabilities began more than twenty years ago with the installation of an elevator to the three main program floors and will be provided in our proposed building addition. We also have constructed an outdoor columbarium as part of a beautifully landscaped memorial garden, which is accessible for people with disabilities.

A few years back our congregation led the community in creating a playground for all people, parlaying a $5,000-dollar grant from the Neighbors in Need offering into a several-hundred-thousand-dollar, state-of-the-art playground—accessible to the disabled.

Seventh, the professional staff and lay leaders of the congregation have been able to put together a vision of what this church can be and do in this community, and we continue to find new ways of enlarging that vision.

The role of the senior minister has been particularly important. I am what Lyle Schaller calls an "intuitive leader." By understanding this congregation's past, discovering its weaknesses, and building on its strengths, I have been able to provide the overall vision and leadership for the staff and congregation. I have also been fortunate in being able to put together a staff of creative professional and support personnel who can work together. I trust each staff person to create and implement programs using his or her best abilities with support and consultation with me when needed but otherwise with little or no guidance or interference. I work out of the metaphor of the church as a community in which people may agree to disagree. The emphasis is on the positive and on reaching a workable consensus. Very few votes are taken on who or what is "in" or "out" of favor.

How an Old Historic Church Became New

First Church of Christ, Wethersfield, Connecticut

DONALD W. MORGAN

In the first year of my pastorate in Wethersfield, I overtook a young man in his twenties, apparently a tourist. He was walking along the sidewalk on the opposite side of the street from our handsome 1761 meetinghouse and eying our ancient structure quizzically. As I caught up with him, he sensed that I lived in town. "Tell me, sir," he asked, thrusting his head in the direction of the meetinghouse, "is that a church or is it a museum?" All but overcome by the implications of his question and at the time not quite sure myself, I gasped and responded fervently, "I hope to God it is a church!"

Is there life after the decline of an old, historic New England church? That was the question we faced over a decade ago as we undertook to revive a great New England church dating back to 1635. The answer to the question is today clear. There is!

The Situation in 1977

Picture the situation we confronted back then. Toward the close of the 1960s the First Church of Christ in Wethersfield, a suburb of

Donald W. Morgan is senior minister of the First Church of Christ in Wethersfield, Connecticut. First Church, which dates from 1635, is today the largest, fastest-growing, and best-attended United Church of Christ congregation in New England. Its membership, 1,660 in 1977, is expected to exceed 3,000 by 1995.

Hartford, Connecticut, had peaked at exactly two thousand members. From then on it began to lose members. Over a period of seven years it lost members at twice the national rate of decline for the denomination as a whole. First Church dropped to a membership of 1,660. Simultaneously, attendance at Sunday morning services was dramatically reduced.

Where was this old church headed? Would the decline continue? If so, how could the congregation maintain its facilities, which had been enlarged in the '50s and the '60s for a large-membership church? Would a declining, greatly reduced congregation be able to maintain its marvelous eighteenth-century meetinghouse, restored at the beginning of the '70s by a $1 million bequest? Were the golden years of First Church in the past?

When the search committee met with me in 1977, they made it clear their church was in serious trouble. They could see time running out. They knew fresh approaches were needed. They knew their church needed a new vision and a new spirit. They were hopeful God would do a new thing in their midst. They had no illusions as to what was at stake. Nor did I.

Shortly after beginning my pastorate in June 1978, I had occasion to drive into Hartford with one of our older members. As a retired businessman who had been highly successful in his field, he knew something about reading the bottom line. Further, he knew the city had plateaued in population at about 26,000, and that the Protestant population was declining. "Can a church in such a situation grow?" he asked me. "Absolutely," was my candid and convinced reply. Despite my optimism, my friend seemed uncertain. He really didn't think it was possible.

Some years later a high denominational official, aware of more recent developments at First Church, asked me: "How do you account for the phenomenal growth of the Wethersfield church? Is it demographics?" He had used the one word I have come to despise. It is the thinking of a deterministic mind-set. Not without reason, in my judgment, does the word bear a similarity to the word demonic. Within, I was thinking, "I wonder if they did a demographics study on the day of Pentecost?" But to him my answer was, "No, it has nothing to do with demographics. It may have more to do with the Holy Spirit."

The Advantages

Though in a critical state of decline, First Church had distinct and special advantages. To begin, the facilities were (and are) outstanding. The exquisitely restored Georgian meetinghouse provides an enviable setting and centerpiece. The additional buildings and grounds were (and are) superior. Good things had happened through the years to bring the church to a point of enjoying superior facilities.

Then, too, the location was strategic. The church stands at the corner of Marsh and Main in Old Wethersfield, a lovely New England setting suitable for a Christmas card. The village is an historic landmark, often compared with Williamsburg. But most of all, the church is near a convenient exit of Interstate I-91. This means people can come from a considerable distance and reach us without difficulty. More and more people have come to realize they can as easily reach First Church as a church in their own town. Yesteryear the church was situated on Main Street of the community as Main Street was then; today it is situated on Main Street of modern transportation and the current flow of life.

As well, First Church had a fine atmosphere. Unquestionably largely because of my predecessor, who served as senior pastor for thirty-five years, the congregation had a lot of love. Denominational figures have noted that the Wethersfield church people seem to have a special quality. They do, and to me this is a reflection of the warm and caring spirit of the previous pastor. My predecessor had overseen the expansion of exceptional facilities and had cultivated, by his own example, a loving spirit. We could build on that!

The Challenge

With all that going for it, First Church nonetheless was on the skids. The advantages were slipping away. In the course of time, given the direction of things, one could anticipate a church half or even a third its earlier, peak size. Eventually, deterioration would be evident to everyone.

Reductionistic thinking had already begun. Soon after my arrival the property committee began talking of closing down a building. Either rent it or sell it was the gist of the discussion. Right away, I saw the need to shift us out of that line of reasoning. Such a move as they were proposing would be a clear signal to everyone that First Church was taking the course of retrenchment and surrender. It would be one more step toward further decline. Far from solving our problems, it would compound them. I said to the committee, all men, "Gentlemen, before you close down part of the plant, may I suggest you check our shipping schedule." Knowing most of them were connected with manufacturing, I felt they would catch my meaning. They did. "You mean," they asked, "that we are going to have more people and more programs?" Softly but firmly, I responded, "Yes!" Then I added, "In a few years we may be asking how can we find more space for everything going on." The prophecy has proved to be correct.

We had to come to terms with the new day of church life. Gone were the heady days of the '50s and the early '60s when this church, like many a suburban church, enjoyed the benefit of massive population growth in the immediate community. Gone, too, was the post World War II church-going boom.

As mentioned before, the town's population had stabilized. No significant growth could thereafter be expected. Moreover, the population was becoming increasingly Roman Catholic. Once our church people "ran the town," holding many, if not most, of the major town positions. No more!

Given these developments, we could not afford to be complacent. Nor could we assume people would come to us just because we were here.

Additionally, there was more of a self-contained, turned-in-upon-itself attitude within the church than most people recognized. After all, we had been *the* church at the center of the town from its beginnings, going back three and a half centuries. The meetinghouse has an historic and architectural claim that one might think would assure its primacy and power. Symbolic of this inward-looking attitude was the door without an outside handle! Let me tell you about that.

Four or five months after arriving, I walked up to the main door of the meetinghouse. Actually it's not the main door, but the door visitors are most likely to approach, in light of its location. As I mounted the steps, I was dumbfounded to realize there was no handle on the door! No one could go in unless someone opened the door from the inside. This meant that Sunday after Sunday when visitors and newcomers came to First Church they had this inhospitable welcome: no handle! What frustration they must endure! What embarrassment did they experience running around from door to door trying to get in! How many had read the unintended message ("outsiders not wanted") and decided to leave, never to come back?

Absolutely beside myself, I set about to learn why there was no handle on the front door. Apparently at the time of the restoration five years before, it was at first believed no handle had been there originally. Since the committee wanted the project to be authentic, they would not install a handle. The project was more important than people, it seemed. At a later time, it was concluded there had been a handle, but with most of the work completed nobody bothered to make the correction.

Meanwhile, for five years people coming to First Church for the first time, if they approached the most likely door, ran into that incredible roadblock. How many gave up on us back then? To what extent could the decline of the church be attributed to that single thoughtless omission? Above all, this lack said something about the prevailing way of thinking—from the inside out, not from the outside in.

We had work to do!

The Approach

People today approach churches with a shopping-center mentality. Whether this is good or bad is beside the point. Incarnational Christianity moves into the real world where people live, and works from there. It doesn't stand around lamenting the situation or pontificating as to why it should be otherwise. Those are exercises of total futility. People seek churches that are prepared to meet their needs. We want to provide everything we can to meet those needs so that people will find it difficult to stay away.

People and Their Needs

The first thing we needed to do was relate to the people and gain a sense of their needs. My wife and I recognized that a thirty-five-year pastorate of a much loved man was a hard act to follow. How could we relate to the people quickly? How could we find out what they were thinking? Our solution was to hold three "Evenings in the Parsonage" every week for seven or eight months. Night after night, we welcomed groups of roughly thirty. Before the first anniversary of this new pastorate, we had had no less than fourteen hundred people in our home.

With each and every "Evening in the Parsonage," we asked questions that broke the ice, started people sharing, and also reflected their feelings about the church. One of the questions was "How do you see the church?" Then they had various selections, such as a lesson in history, a beacon in the storm, or a teacher. It was clear everyone thought of First Church in terms of history, but it was equally clear people did not want more of that. They wanted their church as a source of inspiration and encouragement and faith for everyday living. As a result of the responses of more than fourteen hundred people, I determined to ease up on the historical emphasis of the church and to stress the church as a center for faith. Happily, this shift was consistent with my own deepest convictions.

Our Image in the Community

The next thing we tackled was the image of the church out in the community. Of course, many were aware of its history and its historical place in Wethersfield. Many, too, admired its architectural beauty. But did it project an image of excitement, vitality, warmth, and outgoingness? My impression was that people did not see us that way. Perhaps once upon a time they did, but not now. What could we do to ensure that First Church be perceived as such an exciting and inviting place that people would want to make a point of coming?

We had to do something about how we saw ourselves. Why were we here? Just to be a church, whatever that means? Just to do our thing? Just to be the historic meetinghouse where George Washington once worshiped and John Adams once visited? Or are we a mission of Jesus Christ reaching out to people, caring dearly and desperately whether people are won to faith, whether people come among us and find a warm and caring congregation, and desire to join us in the walk of faith? Of course, the key to this happening was the style of the minister. I had to model this spirit of outreach and I had to do it again and again. I had to preach it and say it repeatedly. I had to convey the feeling that this was the most important thing we were doing, reaching out and welcoming people.

This approach meant shaking some people out of their complacency. It meant challenging assumptions that if people want us they'll find us. It meant giving real thought about how outsiders see us and why should they want to come to our church at all. It meant meeting head-on the widespread feeling that simply to be that old, historic church was enough. It meant everlasting vigilance against an "edifice complex" where the buildings were perceived as being the church or the most important thing.

Directly behind the meetinghouse and the adjoining buildings is the village cemetery. From what is called the connector, a spacious glassed-in walkway connecting the buildings, you can view tombstones within a few inches of our walls. On occasion I would remind people that we as a church are always only and literally just "one foot from the grave." We had better pay attention to the direction in which we were moving!

To put ourselves in the public eye we had, of course, to deal with publicity. This meant sending news releases to newspapers. We now do this well. By general agreement, we seem to have the best press of any church of greater Hartford. But it did not just happen. We have worked at it. The interesting thing is that when you do it and you are increasingly noticed, more and more attention and publicity flow in your direction. We have emerged as a very noticeable part of the church landscape of the area.

Equally, we had to start advertising. I discovered no funds were available for this in the budget. No one seemed to think it mattered. Through the years I have always put stock in getting your message out through advertising. Years ago an owner of Pacquin's hand cream told me of the disaster of America's number one hand soap, which during World War I stopped advertising for a year and went out of business! The church is in the communications business, and that means, in part, advertising, getting the word out!

Still, we had no money. Leadership apparently believed the counsel of some national advisers back then that church advertising does no good. Save your money! They were saving their money and losing people! So at my first church board meeting, I asked for $500 for a starter. I didn't make a case for it. I didn't spend a lot of time parading all the arguments and evidence for its importance. I simply said: "Friends, humor me! Give me $500 for advertising, just to get started and get us through the rest of the year!" They gave me the money.

The advertising had to be eye-catching. It had to communicate the spirit of the church. The name alone would never do it. "First Church of Christ," while meaningful to me and to us on the inside, does not grab people out there. So we began to use catchy and inviting phrases that helped create a bright and lively image of the church, such as "The Contagious Congregation" (not original, but my author friend George Hunter will forgive me), "Where the Spirit Is Catching," and "The Exciting Place on Sunday Mornings."

I must tell you some of my people didn't like these undignified slogans; not fitting, they felt. The issue was brought up in the board of deacons, as were a few other things in the course of time. My response was, taking a cue from Dwight L. Moody, that dignity is not listed among the fruits or the gifts of the Holy Spirit. I held firm to the importance of projecting a lively, up-to-date, attractive image. Eventually, not right away, the objections subsided, especially as we began to see results. Nothing succeeds like success, and I am a great believer in the saying, "the proof of the pudding is in the eating."

Of course, in all of this effort the preaching was important. You really must do your best in the pulpit Sunday after Sunday if you're going to turn a church around. You cannot skimp in this area and think to get away with it. If the church is in the business of communication, you must communicate effectively and enticingly in the pulpit. You must preach to inspire, encourage, build faith and vision, and help shape an image of what we as a church are about. Over a period of time, the message comes through and people increasingly understand. With this understanding comes a new self-understanding, a new self-image. People get turned on. The church sees itself in a new and exciting way.

Staff

With things launched, now we needed to look more carefully at critical areas. What are the things that a growing, dynamic church must deal with?

For example, what about staff? There is evidence that some ministers cannot lead a growing church. Their training, their assumptions, their temperament—all militate against this. Certainly if you don't think reaching people for the gospel is important, if you prefer to ignore all the book of Acts reports on the numerical growth of the early church, the chances are you won't cotton to leading a growing church. You may even feel threatened by it. Many ministers are. Then they sanctify their reluctance by resorting to a theology of "the faithful remnant" and "back to the catacombs." The true situation has to be faced. Soul-searching is in order. Those on the staff need to share the passion for growth. Moreover, do we have the kind of staff with expertise in the right areas to start the church really moving?

Lyle Schaller is on target. You staff to grow or you staff to stand still or you staff to decline. Take your pick. Whatever you decide you get. Ministers need to understand this. Churches and church leaders need to come to terms with it. We analyzed our church carefully and repeatedly in terms of our need to move off dead center. What are people looking for in a church? What are their needs? How can we serve them? And what kind of staff is required to make it all happen? Programs are important, but to have programs you need program staff that can make it happen. Steadily we have built our staff at First Church in the light of that perspective.

134

Program

Another critical area is program. What programs will meet the needs of people? What do people look for in the church? How can we help them? Having staffed for growth, we began programming for growth.

Bible Study

People want the Bible in their church. If they can't find Bible study in their church, where on earth will they find it? This became a major area of concentration of the associate minister whose sphere of responsibility became parish development. So we looked into the Bethel Bible program and decided to go with it. This meant launching a major Bible-study program with serious intentions that intensely involved great numbers of people. In the course of time, we adapted and expanded it to include even more people.

Youth

People want high-quality, effective youth programming in their church. We set out to provide the best youth leadership we could. We found a specialist who had both the conviction and the credentials to do youth ministry. It is my experience that generalists don't usually bring it off. Youth ministry is a specialty. As a consequence of getting the right person and then backing him with resources and coworkers, we have developed one of the finest youth ministries around. Where once we had a handful of young people, now we have seventy-five to a hundred out for a meeting and hundreds at special gatherings. As well, these young people evidence increasing enthusiasm and faith. We are very up-front about faith and Jesus, and the young respond. In today's world young people need faith that can really see them through. Some of the most moving statements I have ever heard in church have come from our young people speaking at a Sunday morning service.

Along with leadership, we set out to develop an attractive youth center. We wanted a meeting place that young people would feel represented the church's high investment in them. Having secured a sizable memorial gift, we developed one of the most attractive youth centers we could imagine. The young people enjoy it, and it lends itself to all sorts of activities and programs. In addition to the youth center, we secured a van for transporting young people and older people. It put our programs on wheels, and very attractive wheels at that. The van, too, was the result of a memorial gift.

135

When you set out to do important things in a big way, people want to help. They want to be part of a high-quality undertaking, especially when it affects young people and makes them a big part of the church.

Naturally people look to the church for the best in children's ministry. We decided to do the best we could for children as we nurtured them in Christian faith. We obtained a staff person, part-time to begin with but now full-time, whose focus and skills would be exclusively with children. We set out to fashion an atmosphere of love and faith, of brightness and joy, into which children could come. We have sought a creative curriculum that could do the kind of job parents and teachers want. We have considered every kind of curriculum available.

Singles

A few years ago we began to set our sights on singles ministry. At a conference for counselors, therapists, and other professionals on the growing singles population, I became aware that soon one half the adult population would be single—the yet unmarried, those "chronically" unmarried, those divorced, and those widowed. That meant most churches would be irrelevant to 50 percent of the people today. Here was a growing need, and we would fill it. We resolved to start developing a multifaceted singles ministry, one with a variety of programs to reach a variety of needs. It would not be a one-night-a-week affair but much more all-embracing.

My colleague explored various forms of singles ministry. He went to an extraordinary and highly sophisticated conference at the Crystal Cathedral and investigated other ways to approach this new challenge. Within a couple of years we really had something going. The singles ministry at First Church, "Single Challenge," has become one of the finest in New England. It enjoys an enviable reputation and draws people from considerable distances.

Again and again we have been told by these singles how churches had failed to meet their tremendous need in their singleness. They were often experiencing hell, particularly those going through divorce, and the churches had nothing to offer, nothing that would help. Often they found the churches unconsciously rejecting them as somehow out of place. Some singles even reported that their minister acknowledged the need but had no intention of doing much about it. Great numbers of these men and women had given up on the church, until they heard of us. They came to our "Talking It Over" sessions. They went on outings planned specifically for them, became involved in singles Bible study, and attended one of our excellent divorce recovery workshops.

We did not plan these as programs *of* the church but *at* the church. There was no effort to hustle people into the church itself. Nevertheless, singles would come to the programs and find help. Then they would look around, feel at home in the place, and decide to drop in for worship on a Sunday morning. There, too, they would discover that our congregation accepts them and loves them. They would keep coming, and then one day many would take the step of faith, make a commitment to Jesus, and join the family. The phenomenal success of the singles ministry at First Church has been a major element in our growth and vitality.

Caring Ministries

Yet another area of development has been our caring ministry. Seizing the concept of "the priesthood of all believers," we have sought to enlist many of our members in ministry to one another. This effort is headed by our director of caring ministries, another professional added to the staff. In this instance, she happens to be my brilliant and caring wife, who has a Master of Divinity degree from Union Theological Seminary. The church enthusiastically engaged her for this leadership role and just as enthusiastically continued to support and assist her. She has recruited well over a hundred members and trained them for the oversight of more than a hundred neighborhoods extending far and wide. She and the neighborhood lay ministers together provide the "net" through which no one can easily slip in this large, far-flung parish.

We also have a part-time minister of visitation. His main focus is our older members, and he helps with hospital and other calling. It is our desire that no one shall be neglected. We are trying, at least.

Another gain is a church administrator, a committed Christian businessman formerly with a major insurance company, who manages the financial and property affairs of the church. He relieves the senior minister and other program staff people so that more of their time can be spent in the areas for which they have specific calling and training.

Specials

One more thing I should mention: the "specials" at First Church. We deliberately began, early on, to bring national figures to the old meetinghouse. From time to time we have had speaking in our pulpit or leading a workshop or heading a retreat some outstanding people such as William Stringfellow, Elton Trueblood, Bruce Larson, and Robert Schuller. A few years ago we sponsored an all-New England event: "New Possibilities in Ministry," with Robert Schuller as principal lecturer. This conference drew hundreds, ministers and lay leaders, from all over New England. We met a need, and we added to the image of this historic church as an exciting place where things happen. In June 1986 Schuller brought his entire Robert Schuller Institute for Successful Church Leadership to First Church for a three-day conference, which attracted hundreds from as far away as Puerto Rico, Canada, and Australia. This was the first time the famed institute was scheduled away from Garden Grove, California. It was a stimulating time for the congregation and certainly enhanced their self-image. We have been thanked countless times. But again, it helped First Church to be perceived as something more than a sleepy church of ancient vintage located in a lovely, suburban New England town.

Service

We find that when a church is designed to relate to people's needs, people respond. They come running. Not only that, they respond in ever increasing numbers and with ever increasing quality. One of their needs is the need to serve others. We are able to support and participate in many mission programs to the inner city and other areas. According to the information we have, we contribute more to such outreach and mission efforts than any other United Church of Christ congregation in the state. These people flowing into First Church are so enthusiastic and committed, you can't hold them back! Turned on, they want to be busy. This is one of the exciting realities of church growth.

For example, we provide meals for the impoverished twice a month at an ecumenical agency in Hartford. We asked our congregation who among them would like to help—prepare food, make deliveries, serve meals, and wait on people. Within minutes we had over a hundred volunteers signed up! We are a major force in Habitat for Humanity in Hartford. We are providing key leadership in a whole range of service programs, so extensive another chapter would be required to describe it all.

The point of all this? Having staffed for growth, we program for growth. Where are people hurting? Where are people lacking? What can the church do which is not being done or others cannot do? "Find a need and fill it" is Robert Schuller's famous dictum, and we follow that dictum with a passion.

Atmosphere

Still another area to consider was the atmosphere of the church. How could we build fellowship and a sense of belonging? How could First Church be a place where everybody counts, "Where People Care About People" (a slogan we appropriated)? There are lots of things you can do to help achieve such a sense of belonging, and we have tried most of them.

For one thing, you simply bring the necessity to your congregation's attention. You remind them that people come to a church because they are looking for something. They have made the effort because of a felt need. Maybe they are lonely. Maybe their faith is slipping. Maybe they feel unworthy. Maybe they are going through a crisis. Maybe they want to end it all. What do they need? They need love. They need acceptance. They need to feel the love of God through other people. They need "a lift and not a load." They do not need judgment. How can we—each of us—communicate a spirit to meet such needs? Simply by making the congregation aware goes a long way toward reaching the common objective.

You also look at all the church's signs and signals in the hallways, outside the building, in the morning bulletin. What messages do they carry? Do they say, "Welcome!"? Do they say, "We're glad you're here!"? Do they say, "You are loved!"? The absence of a handle on the front door of the meetinghouse said all the wrong things. We changed that fast! The absence of helpful signs directing the stranger securely to his or her destination says we don't care and they're not important. So we installed signs. What about the morning bulletin? Is it easy to follow? Can you tell what's going on? Are there helpful indications that enable the newcomer or the person of another tradition to manage without feeling out of place or awkward? All sorts of things can be done to create the right atmosphere.

In our Sunday morning bulletin we say: "WELCOME! THANK YOU FOR WORSHIPING WITH US!" Then we add: "Welcome to First Church, dating from 1635, and worshiping in this meetinghouse erected in 1761. We welcome all who seek faith, hope, and joy, and for whom Christ is the Lord of Life. Find here an accepting, caring, non-judgmental spirit where lives are transformed, faith is renewed, and power for positive living is found. God loves you and so do we!" Such a statement, echoed in the word of welcome during the Moment of Fellowship, tells visitors what kind of church we are and how we feel about them.

Another feature contributing to the friendly atmosphere at First Church is name tags. It took a little doing to get the practice started. People can think up all sorts of reasons for not launching a name tag program in the church, but once they start, they love it. My advice to any minister or lay person considering name tags is: push it through whatever the initial resistance. Soon people find they can call one another by name. Gone are the awkward moments. Gone is all the uncertainty. Everybody is using them. We even invite our visitors and newcomers to let us know they want a name tag, assuring them if they fill out the form they'll have theirs the following week! Many respond to the invitation, and the next week they are already feel they are "in the family" and others are calling them by name!

One more feature that is very important is the friendship register. There is no substitute for it. During the moment of fellowship midway through the service, everyone signs the book in his or her pew and the book is passed along. That alerts everyone to the visitors. It also is a ready means for people letting us know, by an appropriate check mark or notation, that they want to know more about First Church—they want a call, they want to be on the mailing list, they want to learn about singles ministry, or they want to join First Church. We know who comes and when. We can make quick responses both to the newcomer and to the old timer. Our deacons are particularly alert to helping people feel at home. They watch for newcomers. They offer to show them around. They take their name and try to relate them to others. The whole church has become alive to what it means to be a loving, caring, welcoming church. It took some doing, but they have learned. And they are great!

Parking and Accessibility.

Parking and accessibility is an area needing special mention. We really had to tackle this one and we did. After we had seen growth coming along, we realized our parking facilities were no longer adequate. We needed to expand them. I saw the need, and I knew what it would cost—plenty! But I also saw that unless we dealt with the parking need, we would halt and perhaps reverse the development of the church. We would forever regret a neglected opportunity. We might see all our gains go down the drain! This was no time for timidity.

Our leadership more and more took the matter seriously. Finally we undertook a capital-funds campaign that would enable us to do several things, such as help the denomination start or renew churches (we have never backed off on the larger responsibilities, however pressing our local needs) through the New Initiatives program of the United Church for Homeland Ministries, install a computer for our increasing records, install an elevator or two to make it easier for people to get up and down in our buildings, and double our parking facilities.

Typically, some said, "Do we really need that?" Schuller points out that places for parking are as necessary as pews. Without the one, you will not need the other! People who cannot park will not need to sit. After going through the usual steps of obtaining congregational acceptance and developing plans while assuring the doubters, we had an attractive, beautifully landscaped, and greatly enlarged parking area with easy access in and out. Later we secured signs we could place at the entrances, clearly marking where to enter for "First Church Parking." Not long after the parking project was completed and we experienced a further surge of attendance and membership, people would say: "I wasn't wholly for it [the parking project] at first, but now I wonder what would we have done without it!" The doubters have gone. They are all believers now!

Worship That Lifts

At the center of the life of the church is worship. This is the pivotal act of the people of God. This is where we must be at our best. "I will not give unto the Lord that which costs me nothing." Worship must be exhilarating and exciting. How can we justify worship that is dull and boring? To me it is an insult to God. Equally, it is a disservice to people.

Worship is the first thing visitors and newcomers experience. How do they feel when they leave a worship service? Do they want to come back? Why should they come back? Is there anything about the experience that causes them to say, "Gee! I'm coming back next week!"? If not, why not?

Without getting into all the detail, let me say our meetinghouse is a choice setting for relevant worship. The arrangement of the box pews and slip pews creates an in-the-round situation. Intimacy is possible. People interact. They feel they are in this together. We make the most of this marvelous setting.

We must give the message of the morning our best shot. What an honor and privilege it is to speak for God and to proclaim the saving news of Jesus Christ! We take the opportunity seriously and try to give a message to which people can relate. The music is rich, alive, and thrilling. We intend it to be that way. We are blessed with extraordinary leadership in this regard, leadership that is creative, up-to-date, and committed.

All the elements of worship are carefully and dynamically brought together. The service is "tight"—there are no long delays while someone walks up or sits down. There is energy in the service. There is a flow and a building. Something happens. The presence of the Spirit is felt. The ecstasy and joy of worship in God's house are experienced. Again and again, people tell us of the lift they get from worship in the historic meetinghouse of First Church.

Of course, early on we moved from one to two services every Sunday morning. We did it before we needed to. Fighting all the temptations of reductionism, the prevailing sin of churches, we made this move to create a vacuum that had to be filled. It has been! Thus we maximized the opportunities for worship. Now we hold three services every Sunday morning. Christmas Eve we have four services, beginning with a late afternoon carol sing on the green and then three identical services by candlelight. In 1984 CBS came to televise our midnight service, live, nationwide, while 20 to 30 million watchers worshiped with us. That was a big moment, but we were up to do it. Easter, too, we hold multiple, identical services. People flow to where more is offered.

One further touch in our services these days is what I call the mystery guest. During the moment of fellowship—about three to five minutes—I interview someone—a guest, a member of the church, someone whose identity is not known until that moment. It is a stand-up interview at the microphone in front of the communion table. It is informal, relaxed, free flowing. It is often highly informational. It is often a real witness to the faith. It is a good opportunity for personal testimony, something frequently absent and lacking in many churches these days but surely part of New Testament worship. Now lay people can talk about faith, not just the minister. Some beautiful things are said, and the interview adds vitality and interest to the service.

Reaching Out!

"Can a church in such a situation grow?" Remember, that was the question of the parishioner. He had in mind the reality that our town's population was not growing, in fact had not grown in a decade, and that the Protestant population was declining.

But we had in mind a couple of other things. First, there are in every community across America 40 to 60 percent of the population who are unchurched. That includes Wethersfield. Lots of people out there were just waiting for a church that would grab them and win their devotion. Moreover, people today will go anywhere to find what they want. They no longer confine their living to their immediate community. We have had automobiles for a long time, and we have highways that carry people great distances. People will drive many miles just to buy a single item. So we began to rethink our market. It was far larger than the immediate town. With that assumption to work with, all things became possible!

Deliberately we began to think of ourselves as an area church, not as a town church. We are the First Church of Christ *in* Wethersfield, not *of* Wethersfield! If we are doing something exciting and fulfilling, people will come. They will drive the extra miles for that special, extra something. Increasingly our advertising was pitched to the larger area. During our services we consciously made fewer references to Wethersfield, which seemed to say to the out-of-towner worshiping with us, "You don't really belong here." Such thoughtlessness had to be avoided!

Consequently today, half our membership and half our Sunday morning congregation come from beyond the immediate town. New members joining at any particular time come from as many as fifteen to twenty communities. Additionally, one third to one half of our newer members are former Roman Catholics, and as many as 70 percent of our new members were previously unchurched. Obviously we are not "stealing" from other churches, as critics of church growth are quick to assume. We are reaching people that other churches had failed to reach.

Of course, outreach includes advertising. After our initial and modest start, we began to do more and try to do it better. We placed ads in expected places (the church page of the newspapers) and unexpected places (among "Best Bets" for weekend entertainment). We did direct mailings. We did thirty-second television ads. The TV ads have greatly enlarged our sphere of influence. One time more than half of a large class of new members first learned of First Church through our TV ad following Schuller's "Hour of Power." Now periodic television advertising is regularly a part of our outreach effort.

Setting Goals

At the start we had a goal to grow. In the course of time I began to see the need to have more specific goals. How large should we become? Realizing our 350th anniversary was coming up in 1985, in 1982 I presented to the church board a goal that we once again be a two-thousand-member church by our anniversary year.

I was uneasy about setting such a goal. I was uneasy about announcing it. What if we did not make it? Would our failure, my failure, be evident to everyone? If you can keep these things vague, nobody can hold you accountable. If you "spiritualize" it, nobody knows what's going on. If you are specific, you know and they know whether or not you made it.

But a goal is a challenge. It helps to give focus to what you are doing. It rallies support from others who want to share in the success. And it is an act of faith. The failure to set goals, to go out on a limb, to walk on water, is a sign of faithlessness. It is a sign of not trusting God to help us succeed in something good for the kingdom and totally consistent with the Great Commission. Why play it safe? Why not go for it?

The church board heard and accepted the goal. More and more, you could sense that our decisions were being affected by our clear and stated objective. We began to pick up momentum. We began to smell the lovely aroma of victory. The impossible was happening. First Church today is the largest, fastest-growing, best-attended UCC church in New England. Its membership has grown in the last dozen years from 1660 to more than 2,400.

Have we set new goals? You bet we have! Churches set goals for money for the church, how much they hope to raise through the stewardship drive. Why on earth don't churches set goals for people? We are in the people business, not the money business! People are what Jesus cares about, and if setting goals will help us do what we are expected to be doing, then, let us set goals. Our current goal is three thousand members within ten years following our anniversary year.

Moreover, we have developed a mission statement adopted by the church board. Like any such statement, it is not perfect. Others would do it differently and probably better, but it does express how we today see ourselves as a growing, stretching, faith-filled, and Spirit-driven church of Jesus Christ in the heart of New England: "We are called by the Lord Christ to be a model for our time of the finest and most creative in church life, worship, nurture, and out-

144

reach; proclaiming a positive, affirming, need-fulfilling faith-message; energizing and transforming human lives by the power of the Holy Spirit; and steadily enlarging the body of believers."

Fulfilling a Heritage

What we are interested in is dynamic fulfillment of a rich heritage, the faith heritage of New England. Everything about us speaks of that heritage—the meetinghouse, the setting, the length of the years of this ancient congregation. Everything about us speaks of vitality and commitment to the cause of Jesus Christ in our time. We delight in that heritage! We bask in it! We thank God for it!

It is remarkable that Jonathan Edwards attended Yale in Wethersfield before it was decided to locate Yale in New Haven. Three different locations were simultaneously tried, so that a student went to the town where his favorite professor lived. Indubitably Jonathan Edwards, leading figure of the Great Awakening, America's greatest revival, worshiped with this congregation.

Edwards' grandson, Timothy Dwight, president of Yale and key figure in the Second Great Awakening, also lived in Wethersfield, when during the American Revolution he was tutor of the evacuated senior class. Dwight, also, indubitably worshiped with this congregation and, as well, in the historic meetinghouse. Was he thinking of Wethersfield when he wrote, "I love thy Church, O God"? I like to think he was.

Thus, the two greatest figures of the greatest awakenings America has ever known were closely identified with the First Church of Christ in Wethersfield. We are thrilled to believe our current renewal and vitality are faithful reflections of the rich faith heritage of New England. We praise God for what God is doing among us and through us!

Anyone would tell you, First Church is an exciting place. We do not say that boastfully. We say it gratefully. If God is doing something beautiful here, it is not humility to make light of it. It is ingratitude. It is failing to let your light so shine that men and women will see these good works and glorify our Father in heaven. We celebrate what God has done, and we are confident and bold to believe God will keep doing it.

145

Witness to the Power of the Holy Spirit

Spanish Evangelical Church, Lawrence, Massachusetts

FELIX CARRION

The story of the Hispanic people in Lawrence, Massachusetts, gives rise to the story of the Spanish Evangelical Church (SEC). As a parishioner of the church once put it to me,

> Pastor Felix, I arrived here with my wife about twenty years ago when this was a desert for Hispanics. At one point we stood on the street with our meager belongings and had no where to live. What would become of us, we wondered? Then the founder and first pastor of the Spanish Evangelical Church came to our aid. He found a place to store our belongings, while we searched for an apartment. Through his deeds of love we became Christians and members of the church. Since then, we have worshiped God in the SEC.

This man and his wife came in search of a future and a hope, and the church was present to make this a possibility. At the same time, it can be said that their presence, their pilgrimage helped make possible the existence of the first Hispanic congregation in Lawrence. Along with the pastor, they met in the homes of church

---

Felix Carrion was pastor of the Spanish Evangelical Church in Lawrence, Massachusetts, from 1986 to 1990. He is now regional associate in the United Church Office for Church Life and Leadership. Carrion is a trustee of Andover Newton Theological School.

members. Today, numerically speaking, Lawrence is no longer a desert for Hispanics; and yet, a hope for a future still remains illusive—more than 45 percent of Hispanic families in Lawrence are below the poverty level.

Who would ever have thought that in this small New England city of immigrants—geographically and culturally far removed from Latin America—a sizable number of Hispanic people would settle to establish roots, secure a new home, and carve out a place for the generations to come. Stepping into Lawrence has been like having cold water thrown on my face; it has been an awakening experience, especially so for someone born and raised in New York City, a cosmopolitan center, a microcosm of the world. Of all the potential sites for a Hispanic ministry, God's providence led me to a small, obscure, but complex city enveloped in its own historical, political, socioeconomic, and spiritual contradictions, hostilities, and fatalities. I struggle with myself and God every day, hoping and seeking to make a little sense of what ministry is and can become here.

I know now, more than ever, that the apostle Paul, in the first century, comprehended the intricate dimensions and composition of reality we twentieth-century Christians too easily dispel as mythological, as primitive. To the Ephesian Christians he wisely stated: "For our struggle is not against enemies of flesh and blood, but against the rulers . . . authorities . . . cosmic powers of this present darkness, against the spiritual forces of evil in the heavenly places [Eph. 6:12]."

In his book *Naming the Powers* Walter Wink argues that much needs to be learned from the New Testament's language on power, for it yields insight into the inner and outer, invisible and visible, nature of power and how it can indeed become demonic and oppressive. In Lawrence, where children suffer from neglect, poor housing, and even hunger, power has absolutely been corrupted. Never will I forget the words of an anxious and perplexed mother, who said to me, "My children have not eaten any meat in months." (And this was so not because they were vegetarians.) A few weeks later she was evicted because she could not pay her rent. I felt powerless, terrified, wounded; even if I could help this one mother and her children, so many others would be neglected. In fact, of all Hispanic households in Lawrence 38 percent are headed by women, and in 1980 the average income of these households was only $4,326.

These encounters are the substance of the pastoral experience informing and shaping this chapter, this story in which my calling and vision and that of the SEC come together. This story is shared in the hopes that others will appropriate for themselves insights into the church's witness to the reign of God in the power of the Holy Spirit. At the Spanish Evangelical Church, we are endeavoring to *be* and *do* this one thing. Effective evangelization, the bold doing of justice, and holistic church growth result from the power of the Holy Spirit moving, energizing, leading, and empowering the faithful for their missional witness, involvement, and engagement in each local community. I intend now to share how this specifically happened in the SEC in the last two years or so.

Discovering Our Calling: Reclaiming Our Heritage

Entering Lawrence to pastor a small Hispanic congregation actually symbolized my reentry into an "oppressed ghetto." I remember clearly the day a friend tried carefully to prepare me for this reentry. Over dinner he shared his concerns with me, questioning me sensitively about my expectations, dreams, and perceptions of ministering in a place so unknown to me and so different from what I was used to. I was optimistic as I shared what I was hoping would be true once I was settled in Lawrence. In my excitement, he could perceive my naïveté; he knew, as I now do, that it would not be at all as I was painting it. Part of the problem was how unaware I was of the changes wrought on me while in college and seminary, away from the grass-roots reality in which I grew up with my people. I had gone from a tenement project, crowded with hundreds of people (below and above me, to my left and my right), to spacious campuses with plenty of room and with little sight of poverty. Reentry into miserable living conditions has shaken my being to the core.

I knew, however, that the oppressor within me had been defeated; I had been on the path toward liberation for some years now. I had known God in Jesus Christ to be my personal savior, my redeemer. And, yet, I did not know God as the liberator of the world, of society, of the historical reality of people and communities. In my life, God had been personalized, reduced to the invisible plane of my soul, my inner being. History was the domain of men and women, not of God.

A much closer reading of the scriptures had begun to reveal to me the God of history, of the world, the God who cares about the well-being of the whole human person. If God was love, then God could have no part of racism, discrimination, the institutional abuse of men and women. To reread scripture not through the eyes of those who painted God as an individualistic and privatistic possession but through eyes illumined by the Holy Spirit brought about the liberation I needed from the oppressor within me, the one who would say to me, "You are nobody, you belong to the lower class, and you deserve no better."

In 1984 what I was rereading in the scriptures came together for me at a deeper level, for in that year I visited Nicaragua and experienced what today I call a "conversion" to the God of the poor. After my experience with my brothers and sisters of that country, the song of Mary, the mother of Jesus, rang beautifully in my heart:

> [God] has shown strength with his arm; he has scattered the proud in the thoughts of their hearts. He has brought down the powerful from their thrones, and lifted up the lowly; he has filled the hungry with good things, and sent the rich away empty.
> —Luke 1:51–53

In Nicaragua, I saw the poor expressing their God-given right to be, to live, to shape their own histories; this experience gave me a sense of the fullness of liberation. Salvation was personal, but it most definitely included a transformation of society so that we should all live as equals, as sharers and inheritors of God's good earth. Decent, affordable housing should never be the luxury of the rich; it is a biblical mandate for all people.

The above mentioned statistics really have very little to do with numbers; they have everything to do with human life. Behind the percentage there is a face staring back at you, longing for peace, wholeness, love. In the case of the overwhelming majority of Hispanics in Lawrence, their struggle of faith is similar to that of the father in the New Testament, who had an epileptic boy.

> Jesus asked his father, "How long has this been happening to him?" And he said, "From childhood. It has often cast him into the fire and into the water, to destroy him; but if you are able to do anything, have pity on us and help us." And Jesus said to him, "If you are able! All things can be done for the one who believes." Immediately the father of the child cried out, "I believe; help my unbelief!"
> —Mark 9:21–24

As with this father and child, the situation of the people is destructive. It is a condition that has been around "from childhood"—that is, a long time. No one in society was able to transform his child's condition, and, strangely enough, not even Jesus' disciples were able to help. But, as with the father, the people do believe, and yet, there is present, in them and all around them, the unbelief, the doubt and pessimism, that arise out of the crises of their experience.

I have discovered that our calling is indeed the calling to be like Christ, to be agents of life where the forces of death are operating. The SEC is discovering also this calling; and this has stemmed from finding that in the scriptures God is the God of life, the One who promotes it, defends it, and creates it. Jesus Christ has been our life; we have been claimed by him; we have been resurrected with him. This experience is profoundly personal. Christ's life cannot shine through us unless his life has become one with our life, unless we ourselves have been transformed by him. But we have also grasped that this life of Christ in us is profoundly communicable; it is to be transmitted in our communities at all levels. This life is profoundly social; it is the life of the world and not just of individuals.

Two particular passages in scripture have been instrumental in understanding this truth, the one about the good Samaritan and the one about the widow of Nain. In both passages, destructive forces have operated against life. In both of them, agents of life reconstruct reality, bringing forth expressions of resurrection. On Wednesday nights and in our retreats we have reread these passages, allowing them to guide us in our calling. They have helped us to reinterpret our understanding of the church. We are not just the "gathered" community of Christians; we are also the "scattered" community of Christ present in our world. As a result, we adopted a new motto—a guiding principle—for the congregation: La Iglesia Evangelica, Iglesia con una Mision (The SEC, a Church with a Mission). Like the good Samaritan and like Christ in the story of the widow of Nain, our life and our calling are one and the same thing. As Christians and as a church, we have got to erupt wherever the stench of death rises, unmask its power, and summon forth life through word and deed. This is what witnessing to the reign of God is all about. Now, how has a small church, with limited resources, been able to do this in a city such as Lawrence?

It has been possible because we have intentionally begun to reclaim the power of the Holy Spirit for our mission. The Holy Spirit is not an appendage to the body of Christ; it is its power, its energy, its dynamism. Traditionally, in most Hispanic churches,

151

one usually hears much about the Holy Spirit being present, moving in the midst of the people, speaking to them, leading them. Charisma is not usually lacking in many of our Christian communities. I grew up in a church where the Spirit's gifts for the church were claimed and put to good use. People who were not formally educated or who were not ordained could and would preach regularly. In a real sense, laity Sunday was every Sunday, for in each worship gathering, the laity ran the show. I come from a tradition where women lay preachers were invited regularly to preach at our church. Seminars, conferences, sermons, and teachings quite often focused on the Spirit's role in the church.

This is the heritage we are reclaiming at the SEC. We have been careful not to create an unhealthy fixation on the Spirit. Nevertheless, we are taking seriously the Spirit's presence and power in our midst. For example, this has become evident in worship services where the order of worship has been changed to meet the needs of people who are sick or struggling or in crisis. We have spent most of the worship service singing and praying and ministering to one another. This is no small thing; it is real, it is powerful, and it brings new life. The beauty of such an event is that everyone is involved, from the elderly to the children.

This same experience we take to our community when we "invade" with love our tenement housing projects and share God's life. We do this in our street meetings. We bring chairs from the church, an amplifier, and a microphone, and we give the laity the opportunity to share their journeys in Christ. Then, together we pray for people, speak with them, and connect them to the life of the church. I guess what I am saying is that when a church lives its life in the power of the Holy Spirit, then all sense of shame or embarrassment or fear begins to dissipate; and a new boldness emerges. With the Holy Spirit, religiosity begins to disappear, and mission emerges as the new nature of the church.

Discovering Our History:
Reclaiming Our Double Identity

I can vividly remember the night of December 31, 1986. The church was gathered for its traditional New Year's worship service; together we prayed awaiting the New Year to arrive. The sermon was based on Jeremiah 29:7, 11: "But seek the welfare of the city where I have sent you into exile, and pray to the LORD on its behalf, for in its welfare you will find your welfare. . . . For . . . I know the plans I have for you, says the LORD, plans for your welfare and not for harm, to give you a future with hope." Obviously, for me, we were going to seize 1987, settle down, and seek the welfare of the city. No time to waste; we had an urgent mission to carry out. By the end of the sermon I was mentally and physically exhausted. I think the people were tired, also, for I gave them my whole theology and vision in one sermon.

Today I look back upon this event, and I see how insensitive I was about the people's history and pilgrimage as immigrants. These were a people in exile, strangers who had been uprooted from their homelands. I failed to grasp their double identity. On the one hand, they were Christians, and on the other hand, they were the Hispanic people of that particular city. Unconsciously, I was separating their existence from their historical reality. As a result, I failed to raise some very critical contextual questions. They were Christians and at the same time victims of their larger community. In his book *Savior, Savior Hold My Hand*, Piri Thomas captures brilliantly this struggle when saying,

> I'm not putting God down. I'm just wondering why . . . we've allowed certain people to put us down. I can't carry no cross and be nailed to it at the same . . . time. . . . To us people of the Barrio the ghetto is our church, and the only way we're gonna make a heaven out of this hell is by getting together.

How could they settle down in a place where they were rejected? To settle down is not simply a matter of ideology; it is about life and death. For some of the Central Americans in the congregation, settling down could lead to being apprehended for being illegal immigrants.

Did God bring them here? Surely, God did not lead them into poverty and oppression. Their plight cannot be falsely legitimized or spiritualized. What I knew at an intellectual level needed to be transferred to a gut level. Ministry—mission—begins not with an idea of the people but with the people themselves. Although I meant well, I ended up confirming the way the church people had already been thinking of themselves and the rest of the people. It is a "we" versus "them" perception upon which they interpreted their own identities. If this view was going to change, then the SEC needed to understand both their double identity and their calling to reenter history—their communities—from the perspective of God's dealings with their own people.

One concrete way in which I began to share this need with the church was by leading the church to own a vision not just for the local church but for the city of Lawrence. The vision could not afford to be narrow or provincial; it had to include the wider family already experiencing God's dealings with them. I became a member of the board of directors of a multi-social-service agency for the Hispanic community, and eventually I was elected president. I became intentional about making the presence of the church felt in the community and also about making te presence of the community felt in the church. The SEC now talks about drug-addiction programs, day-care centers, and housing for the needy. Those members of the church who work in human-service agencies are encouraged to share their concerns and vision with the church. Through one of our parishioners, the Women's Resource Center of Lawrence will be offering seminars on Acquired Immune Deficiency Syndrom (AIDS), domestic violence and abuse of women, and other related subjects. Another sister working with a hospice program brings the church in touch with those in crisis.

The fact that the church was not accustomed to a pastor so involved in the social arena raised questions. I capitalized on this situation, however, in order to raise consciousness among our people. Many of our discussions were wonderfully intense. One sister of the church said to me, "I just don't think the church should be about politics; that is not our arena." We engaged in dialogue, and the more we talked the clearer it became that her way of thinking would be changed not through the rhetoric of a biblical and theological rationale but through example. She was more impressed by my public witness than by my words. We have embraced each other; she respects me and I respect her. We continue to grow together, even though there exist some differences.

The biblical stories of Esther and Nehemiah have inspired greatly our sense of peoplehood, not just as church but as a pueblo (the people) with a culture and a historical pilgrimage. Esther's life and future depended on the survival of her people. When her people, as Jews, were being threatened with extinction, she remembered her roots, her history, and interceded bodily in their behalf. She risked her life for the welfare of her people. And so it was with Nehemiah as well, who heard of the ruins of the walls of Jerusalem and was compelled to leave his comfort and return to his homeland to inspire the people to rebuild the walls—indeed, their security. Nehemiah's words have become inspirational to us:

"You see the trouble we are in, how Jerusalem lies in ruins with its gates burned. Come, let us rebuild the wall of Jerusalem, so that we may no longer suffer disgrace. . . . Remember the LORD, who is great and awesome, and fight for your kin, your sons, your daughters, your wives, and your homes. . . . Our God will fight for us.
—Nehemiah 2:17; 4:14, 20

The reclaiming of our double identity is leading us into a struggle for the life of our people. Moreover, a social consciousness is emerging. Now, in our Bible studies, such topics as housing, drug addiction, and immigration and naturalization are addressed. These subjects are not foreign to the church people, for they represent the needs of their families and friends.

Discovering the Wholeness of Education: Biblical and Theological Expansion

The scriptures have always played a key role in the Hispanic church tradition; they are the authoritative written word of God. Recognizing the central place of the scriptures, I began to articulate a vision of a church well grounded in them. Our people usually embrace the scriptures wholeheartedly without critically questioning their content. This is not to say that they don't study scriptures. Quite the contrary, many of the members of the SEC can quote the Bible by memory and apply its meaning to their lives. In fact, they keep me very honest about my knowledge and interpretation of scripture. You can always feel the energy and excitement of the people when they know that for several weeks we will be studying a certain book of the Bible or some doctrinal teaching.

In our first month in the SEC, we incorporated into our prayer service, held every Wednesday, a time to go through the epistle to the Colossians. Attendance immediately jumped from fifteen people to about thirty-five. This was very exciting; it created new energy for the church. In addition, we began using our weekly house services, held in the homes of parishioners, to wrestle with biblical and theological themes that were practical—that is, that had to do with matters affecting the local church and community. At these services, together we taught ourselves; we affirmed the contribution that everyone had to make. This was a new approach for many of our members, considering that they were used to having people tell them how they should think and how they should interpret scripture. Each person's interpretation was considered in

155

the light of the interpretations of others. This sparked a new process of questioning, which was, indeed, liberating.

In one of our all-day educational retreats, away from Lawrence,
more than sixty church members dealt with the theme of the
integration of evangelism and mission and the bridging of what we
had previously analyzed as being material needs, on the one hand,
and spiritual needs, on the other hand. It was one of our most
productive educational endeavors. I did not sell the people short.
The speaker who was invited truly challenged them; he pulled no
punches. As a result, people questioned their ideas about what was
material and what was spiritual, what was secular and what was
sacred. The new insights gained led them in that same year to bring
food on Thanksgiving week to the many needy families in the
community. I remember vividly how we all prayed together and
affirmed that with this food God's love in Jesus Christ would be
concretely embodied through our ministry. On that day we left the
church as a scattered community, spreading the good news of Jesus
Christ. As a pastor, this was a very high point for me. I cried and
rejoiced, knowing that we were all growing together.

I do need to mention, nevertheless, that not everyone has embraced this new vision of the reign of God and of our public witness
to that reign. On that same Thanksgiving Day, one sister of the
church said to me, "Instead of giving food to the people, we ought
to be giving them Christian literature, the word of God. That is
what they need." Her concern was genuine; she did not want us to
become simply social activists, doing good deeds. We had a message to proclaim, one of forgiveness and healing in Christ. She
knew that the needs of the people were also profoundly spiritual.
What she failed to grasp was the connection between material
needs and spiritual needs. When Christ fed the multitudes, he was
attending to their whole well-being. In the epistle of James, we read
this same message:

> What good is it, my brothers and sisters, if you say you have faith
> but do not have works? Can faith save you? If a brother or sister is
> naked and lacks daily food, and one of you says to them, "Go in
> peace; keep warm and eat your fill," yet you do not supply their
> bodily needs, what is the good of that?
>
> —James 2:14–16

This has been my vision for the SEC. A church that incarnates—
embodies—God's word through works; that sees liberation taking
place in the deliverance of food to those who are hungry. The sister
mentioned above eventually left for another church, although I

continued to talk with her. Even though her leaving was painful for me, it has created new space within the church for others to embrace a more holistic gospel. There can be no resurrection without death; her leaving represented the new transition the church was undergoing. Biblical and theological expansion does not come without some struggle and pain.

The youth and the children of the church needed to be included also in this educational program; and this I did. On Sunday mornings we have at least six classes in session: four for the children and two for the young people. These classes are bilingual and bicultural. We have even encouraged our young people to teach the classes of the children.

It has been through our educational emphasis that we have integrated the children and youth into the life of the church. A few weeks into my pastoral ministry a young man came up to me and said, "We are tired of not being important in this church. We want to play an important role here. I hope you will help us with this." His speech indicated that the SEC was about to undergo a period of transition. No longer was the focus going to be strictly placed on the adults; for now the new generation was demanding its rightful place in the church. This change came about immediately after the young were given high priority in the educational life of the church. If young people are treated as second-class citizens, they will feel it; they will lose faith in the church.

Since then, the young have taken over the musical ministry of the church. The music is now livelier; it reflects how the young people want to worship God. Monthly bilingual services have been created. The youth now are participants in the liturgy of the church. Some of their dramas have been used for sermons on Sunday morning. A recent high school graduate, Eliezer Reyes, has become a true leader in the life of the church. He was given the attention he needed and he has blossomed, serving as a liturgist, the musical director, and the president of the youth group. He sits in at our important meetings where decisions affecting the SEC are made. His contributions are highly respected by the adults of the church. In essence, what has happened is that the church now belongs not only to the adults but to the young people as well.

I am perceived by many of the adults as a young person with not much experience. They want me to see and deal with youth as they do. Thus, when I speak on youth's behalf, at times, my words do not reach the adults. My vision includes them—that is, the adults. However, I know that there is no future for the Hispanic church unless we bring in the younger generation, unless we give high priority to youth ministries, youth evangelization, and the education of our young people.

Again, I must mention that Jesus' raising of the son of the widow of Nain is a paradigm for my vision. Christ ministered to her, gave her a future and a hope by raising up her child. The death of her child meant the death of her livelihood and her hope. Today, so many young people, especially in the Hispanic community, are withering away, are dropping out not only of high school but of society. I cannot help but feel that the future of our church and community is at stake; and we can't just stand there and keep things going as they have been for the sake of tradition. I am compelled by who I am, a young Hispanic minister, to make a difference for the young Hispanic people of today, of Lawrence. I think this is true not only for the Hispanic church but for all churches. If we neglect our young people and children, we neglect our future.

One of the greatest compliments I have received from the SEC has come from the young people: "Pastor, you do not sell us short; you give us the best of what you have. Thank you!" Every time I hear these words, I rejoice and continue dreaming of a church filled with the new life of young people.

Affirming the Fullness of Spirituality

In an all-church meeting, in which we evaluated ourselves, one sister of the church came to the conclusion that "we need to pray more, to fast more, to battle Satan through our devotion to God." She was right!

In the process of being zealous for mission, it is easy at times to think that many of the victories we experience are the result of our efforts, our work. We forget that we do battle, as the apostle Paul said, with "principalities and powers." These powers need to be confronted in prayer, in fasting, in meditation, and in silence.

Evil is very real; this I witness every day in Lawrence. And we cannot overcome it without a spirituality that is holistic, that includes the disciplines mentioned above. I often grow tired of waging war against oppressive forces. Where I renew my strength and courage is in those moments when I go to God and place all my concerns upon God's loving care.

The people of the SEC take this side of spirituality very seriously. They know it emerges from the fact that they endure so much pain, which could not be overcome unless prayer and fasting (a spiritual discipline) were a part of their lives. They don't earn God's favor through these disciplines; but, rather, through them they express the truth that without God's love and power we are utterly hopeless. It is God, in Christ, who has ultimately triumphed over evil. With us, the way of triumph can be no different; it utterly depends upon God's presence in us, working for the well-being of humanity.

As a church we pray together every Wednesday night. On Friday nights, a small group of the church gathers in different homes to spend two hours in prayer. During these times, local and global concerns are lifted up to God. The SEC also makes it a point to spend at least four to six Saturdays of the year in all-day retreats praying, fasting, and studying together. I know from experience this is not mere escapism; neither is it pure fanaticism. Churches that pray together can engage in mission together.

When this side of spirituality is linked to a spirituality of compassion, then what one has becomes explosive, powerful. Mission is not reduced to mere social activism nor does it become pietism. Indeed, the spirituality of Christ has been our pattern here. On the mountain of the transfiguration (Matthew 17) the disciples were in the wonderful presence of God. But when it came time to descend into the valley of human need, Christ was not swayed by Peter's request that they be secluded, on a mountaintop.

In this chapter, I have highlighted key areas in my pastoral experience up this point at the Spanish Evangelical Church. Instead of being a story about what has happened with our church from day one to now, it has been a story that focused on those events and learning experiences that were instrumental in bringing together my vision and the reality of the SEC and the Hispanic community of Lawrence.

At this point in my pastoral ministry, I don't pretend to have the wisdom of those who have been in ministry many more years than I. Indeed, I have much to learn from those ministers. Nevertheless, in the coming years, my vision will continue to grow, along with the vision of the SEC, as we continue to engage in being witnesses to the reign of God in the power of the Holy Spirit. I seek above all things now to be faithful to my calling; I pray that I will never sell out on the vision that God has placed upon my heart. As new experiences come my way, I pray that my vision will take concrete form in the lives of all my brothers and sisters in Lawrence, Massachusetts.

Miracle at the Asylum

Asylum Hill Congregational Church, Hartford, Connecticut

JAMES L. KIDD

What are the chances for an old, downtown city church? What are the chances for a church that has been around for well over one hundred years, with a great history but a consistently declining membership? In the past ten years it has received, on average, eighteen new, adult members a year. From its 1950s height of more than fourteen hundred members, it's down about seven hundred and is heading in the wrong direction. The church is in Hartford, Connecticut, which has the third-highest crime rate in the nation per capita, and it is located in the section of the city that has the second-highest crime rate. It's on a main drag—there are big corporate headquarters all around it—right next door to the Hartford Insurance Group, just a block away from Aetna, across the street from the Roman Catholic cathedral. But right behind the facade of these big institutions is one of the biggest ghettos around, inhabited primarily by blacks, Hispanics, and the elderly; yet the constituency of the congregation is primarily suburban, upper and upper-middle-class, affluent people—a blue stocking congregation in a church in the middle of the city, surrounded

James L. Kidd has been the senior minister of Asylum Hill Congregational Church in Hartford, Connecticut, since 1970. During these years the church's long decline has been arrested, average weekly attendance has risen from under two hundred to well over six hundred, and the budget has more than tripled. In 1989 the church gave more than $600,000 in benevolences.

primarily by poor people. What kind of chance does that church have?

When I was invited to be the pastor of this church in 1979, I was leaving a church in the upper-middle-class suburban community of Wilmette, Illinois, which had done well; but that church and my previous church had both been characterized primarily by social-action concerns. We were involved and engaged in ministry to the world. All through the 1960s, in Wellington Avenue Church in Chicago in the heart of the North Side, we worked for racial justice, and in the 1970s, in Wilmette, we continued with that, built a several-million-dollar, racially integrated housing project for the elderly, and worked to get the United States out of Vietnam. We had a peace center with staff, supported by the church. We were involved in all kinds of things like that. Finally I decided I wanted to make the church grow, but it was hard to change roles in a church where I'd been for ten years. So I began to look around, and the Asylum Hill Congregational (UCC) Church in Hartford was looking for a minister to reverse their membership decline. They invited me to come in September 1979.

That year, the average attendance was 184. The pledging was $179,000. The membership was 770.

In the last eight years, the Asylum Hill Church has received 817 new members. We average more than five hundred people in worship on Sunday morning, at two services. If you count the older children who are in attendance for part of the service, average attendance is more than six hundred each Sunday. Total membership is 1,248. Our annual canvass had a pledge goal of $581,000 for 1988 toward our total budget of just over $800,000. In every way the church is growing, alive, and vibrant, and is making an exciting witness in the city. Our formal outreach budget is almost $150,000 a year.

Why We Are Not Especially Different

Now, you can look at that story and those statistics and interpret them in a number of ways. First, you can say, "Well, of course you've grown because you're a rich church, and we're poor." And it's true; this church has a big endowment, with an income of more than $100,000 a year. But this church was just as rich in the past, and it was dying. Other churches in Hartford have bigger endowments—some of them have endowments of $7 million or $8 million—and they continue to decline. The fact that we are rich is not the reason we have made these dramatic increases in membership.

Second, you may say, "Well, you are a pietistic church and we are a prophetic church." But that's not the answer either, because if you ask people to name the reasons they go to church or don't go to church, they never say it's because it is or isn't a prophetic church. Anyway, we've been involved in all kinds of prophetic things—we started a Hispanic church in our chapel; we helped start a local community organization, the Asylum Hill Organizing Project; we've spearheaded low-income housing; we've hosted meetings on abortion rights; we started Interval House, a shelter for battered women. We've been threatened with bombs. We have an increasingly racially integrated congregation. So you can't say that our growth is because we're not prophetic. There have been very few churches that have been more engaged, more prophetic.

Third, you might say, "Well, look at you. You are a charismatic, exciting leader, and you're the reason that church has grown." Well, I surely appreciate it if somebody thinks that, but the fact of the matter is that I've been in the ministry a long time—thirty years—and never before have I had a church grow like this one. My other churches did all right, but none of them ever had dramatic growth like this one. The reason this church is growing is *not* because I'm a charismatic leader, because I've been the same kind of minister all my ministry, and none of my other churches grew like this.

Finally, people might say, "You're growing because of the demographics. It's the demographics that make you grow." Well, as I indicated in the beginning, it would be difficult to find a church where the demographics were more difficult than they are in this situation. We are a city church; we are in a dangerous area; we have people come to church only to have their purses snatched, their cars broken into, their cars stolen. People come here and they know they're in the midst of a jungle. Most of the people who come to this church don't live around here. The demographics are the last reason this church is growing.

I think we are growing because, first of all, I have become convinced personally that Christ calls us to make disciples for him. I believe literally in Matthew 28:19 in the Great Commission, where Jesus sends the disciples out to "make disciples . . . baptizing them in the name of the Father and of the Son and of the Holy Spirit, and teaching them to obey everything that I have commanded you." I believe that is our assignment. So I have decided in this church to try to achieve that goal and be obedient to that calling.

I was aware of the fact that churches were dying all over the

163

place—especially in our denomination and especially city churches—and I felt called to see if it was possible to make a center-city UCC church grow. So I collected all the books I could find about it; I visited ministers who were making their churches grow; and I came up with a program to *plan for growth*. I worked at persuading the lay leadership to make growth a high priority. We did it together. It would have been impossible without them. Some didn't like it and left the church. Together, I and the lay leaders decided that was OK! If you don't plan for growth, then you plan for no growth. You have to make a decision. So we first chose a goal of eighty new members in 1980: "80 in '80."

The Five Elements for Church Growth

But what could we actually do differently to bring many more people to this church? As a consequence of all my reading I found a simple structure that we call "the 5 Cs." If you're going to make a church grow, you have to have "the 5 Cs" in some form. If you're going to have new members, you have to make *contact* with them. Once you've made contact, you *cultivate* them. Once you culti-vate them, you have to persuade them to make a *commitment*, a decision. Once they've made a commitment, you have to take care of them, teach them the things Jesus has commanded us—you have to teach them how to be a *churchperson*, how to be a disciple, an apostle, and how to grow and mature in the faith. And then finally, once they're in, you have to keep them in; you have to have *conservation*; you have to conserve the members you have.

Contact

So first of all, contact. Now, I believe it's clear—at least to me—that if you're going to have any of these things, then you're going to have to build enabling structures. Nothing's going to happen unless you have a structure that will help discipline and force you to do what needs to be done. Of course, you also have to persuade the leaders of your church, your governing board, that this is something that needs to be done, that making the church grow—making disciples—is a high priority. And the leadership for that is to be taken by a persistent senior minister. That's a way of making it clear that growth is a high priority. This church had come to realize it was "grow or die," and they wanted to live.

A Contact Committee

So if you're going to have contact, then you have to build a contact committee. Select them with care; they should be people who have some expertise in how you reach people, if at all possible, but the most important characteristic is that they care about their task. In our church we called this group the communications committee, or the public-relations committee. This committee has now become so important that it has become a board with representation on the board of deacons, which governs the church.

So the first thing is contact. How do you make contact with people? You have to sit down with this communications group and figure it out. So we went about doing all the things we could think of and that we could talk the board of deacons into letting us do. We did several mass mailings telling people how wonderful we were and inviting them to come to our church. We placed newspaper ads, and we didn't advertise just on the religion pages but in other sections—entertainment, business, and so forth. We put ads on the radio, ads on television. We put regular mailings out to newcomers in the community, people who purchased homes in the suburban area around the city and also in the city itself.

But we were also very clear that if you're going to make a church grow, it's going to grow because the present church members, the worshipers, are people sufficiently enthusiastic about their church that they go out and tell their friends that this is a wonderful church and invite them to come. Roughly 80 to 85 percent of our new members have come because our present members have been enthusiastic and invited them to come and participate in the life of the church.

One of the things that I did when I first came was to tell this congregation from the pulpit that it was their obligation to decide that I was the best minister in Hartford. Now, obviously, I have a lot of shortcomings, and they wouldn't have to wait long to find out what they were; but it was important for them to decide that their minister was OK. And maybe if they believed that, and if they supported me from that conviction, then maybe I would become the best minister around. It was important for them to be convinced of that so they would invite their friends to come and hear the sermons I would be delivering, because whether we like it or not, the fact of the matter is that the first reason most people are committed to a church is because of the minister, the personal relationship they have with him or with her.

Potluck Dinners

What else do you do, then, to convince members to invite their friends, something a lot of people are reluctant to do? We organized a large number of potluck dinners in members' homes with twenty members or so at each one, and then we tried to make them acquainted. We had a fellowship period before the dinner to loosen them up a little bit, and we had grace together—we believe in prayer—and then we had a conversation. I'd say, "What brought you to this church for the first time? What brought you back? And have you invited other people to come? What's happened when you invited them? And what was the message from all of that discussion?"

Then we showed them a movie. The movie was one from the Fuller Institute for Church Growth, called *I'm Only a Layman*. It talks in evangelical language unfamiliar to our people—in fact, sort of off-putting to many of them—but it was the only thing we could find like that, so we showed it. It talked about the necessity for present church members to invite their friends if new people are going to come to church. After the movie, we had a discussion, asking what scenes they remembered, what they laughed at, and whether any imperative came out of this movie, anything they felt they had to do as a consequence of its message.

Then we gave them a piece of paper and a pencil, and we asked them to list their unchurched friends and family and acquaintances. We asked them to prioritize, to decide which ones were most likely to respond to an invitation to come to worship. We said, "OK, that's your assignment, to call on the first three names on your list and invite them to come to worship with you." Then we broke them up into groups of two each, and we had them role play the task of inviting one another. Then we reassembled and discussed how it went and how they felt and the things that were most helpful. People talked and jotted down notes and went out and invited their friends.

Friends' Sunday

Another way of making contact is to have a "Friends' Sunday" in church, with special music, a special program, and a special sermon. We urged people to bring their friends for this special Sunday, which we continue to celebrate, and gave them something, such as a button or flowers. Or we had a brunch after the service, or suggested that people go out with their guests after our coffee hour. We made a special effort to welcome them.

In addition, we had a lot of special days (as we still do), and I'm always telling my people how terrific they are, because they go out and do these things, and they are the kinds of people that other people will respond to. That has worked very well. Not everybody does it, of course—not everybody comes to these meetings, and not everybody who comes to the meetings invites friends; but enough do so that we're receiving a lot of new people. Last year we received 136 new members, and that's a long way from 18 only eight years ago.

Witnessing Retreats

Still another means of contact is witnessing retreats where we talk about different ways you can witness to your faith, ways you can talk about what the Christian faith means to you. We have "journey" workshops to help people identify the points in their own lives where their religious experience has been defining, enabling them to become the kinds of persons who call themselves Christians.

And then we talk about things like the old "Roman Road," an old evangelical tool that's been used for a very long time. We take them through particular passages in Romans and talk about them existentially. We start off with Romans 3:23—"For all have sinned and fall short of the glory of God"—and talk about that; what does that mean, that "all have sinned"? And everyone has a chance to talk about what sin means to him or her; what is the human condition of sin? Then we turn to Romans 5:12 and have that read aloud—"Therefore just as sin came into the world through one man, and death came through sin, and so death spread to all because all men have sinned." We talk about death and the human experience of dying, and how we feel about that, and whether there is any hope for us. Then someone reads Romans 6:23 aloud—"For the wages of sin is death." We discuss what that means and what it means in terms of life, in an existential context—or any context that's comfortable for them. We read the whole thing over: "For the wages of sin is death, but the free gift of God is eternal life in Christ Jesus our Lord." We talk about that and about Romans 5:8, which we read out loud together: "But God proves his love for us in that while we were yet sinners Christ died for us." We compare that to John 3:16 and what that says in terms of our faith. Then we read Romans

10:9–10 aloud: "If you confess with your lips that Jesus is Lord and believe in your heart that God raised him from the dead, you will be saved." Then we move to Philippians 3:12–14—"Not that I have already obtained this or have already reached my goal; but I press on. . . . forgetting what lies behind and straining forward to what lies ahead in Christ Jesus."

That's an outline of the kind of training that we sometimes do in our witness retreats so that people can become clear about their faith in order to be able to talk about it. On witness retreats we also have people write down the names of those they know who are not part of any Christian church and reflect on who might be open to an invitation to the church.

Signs and Ties

You can look around your building and ask what could be changed about it to make it more receptive. Our communications board decided our signs were terrible! They were parallel to the street so that people driving by had to stop to read them. People who were driving by wouldn't do that, so we put up new signs at right angles to the street. We looked at the appearance of the church. We repainted our doors and installed glass exterior doors in some places to look less forbidding.

We did everything we knew how to do to improve our visual communications. We redid our church stationery. We designed a church logo. We came up with church neckties for the men—a tie with tiny pictures of the church on it—and buttons with the current theme ("Visions" in 1986, "Thanks" in 1987). We even have church watches that say on the face, "Asylum Hill Congregational Church!" I went to a party one day wearing my church tie, my church button, and my church watch, and one man there said, "You're a walking billboard!" It was true. I talk about my church everywhere I go, and the members do, too. Otherwise we wouldn't have had the kind of growth we've had. People are really reaching out. They wear their ties to work, and when people say, "Hey, what's that tie?" they tell them about their church and invite them to come.

Our communications board is also responsible for overseeing our church newsletter and for the public-relations pieces we mail to new people who move into the city or into the metropolitan area.

Well, that's the first thing. If you don't have contact, you're not going to grow, so that's the first thing to concentrate on.

Cultivation

Once you've made contact, you have to build a cultivation file, a list of all the new people and who they are. Get their names!

Ushers and Greeters

We also started a hospitality committee. We begin by having ushers out in the parking lot to welcome people when they come, to help them with parking, and to hold open the doors and tell them where to go for worship. And if they have children, ushers direct them to the Sunday school area.

Inside the church, we have greeters at the doors every Sunday. We have ushers trained to touch people, of course discreetly on the shoulder or arm, and welcome them; they lead people forward in the sanctuary and touch them and give them their bulletin only when they reach the pew. The ushers smile at the new people and touch them. The reason for touching is that studies show that when people are touched they think the people touching them are friendly; otherwise they think them neutral. In one study a hotel clerk touched every other person who came to the desk, and then someone asked the hotel guests their impression of the hotel. Those who weren't touched had no impression of the clerk, but a very high percentage, 90 percent of those who were touched, said, "Oh, he seemed like a friendly, nice person." Well, that's the kind of thing we try to be aware of so we touch our people and welcome them.

Coffee Hour

Hospitality is an important part of our ministry. We have coffee hour after both services, and we really go out of our way to make it nice. For people who feel that formality makes things special we have a table set up with formal service, and for people who want something more casual we have coffee pots and disposable cups where they can help themselves. For people who don't want coffee we have tea, and for people who don't want either we have juice, and we have doughnuts every Sunday. Every week ten or so of our people receive a letter inviting them to be hosts and hostesses at one of the coffee hours after both services. They have a little badge, and their task is to go around and look for people who are standing alone and greet them, make them feel welcome.

Worship Service

We especially try to have excellence in our worship service—attractive space, the best music possible, the bulletins neat and with no mistakes—we have them printed so they're very attractive. The laity participate in worship every Sunday. They write the words and lead the congregation in the confession and the assurance of forgiveness. We have the older children in the service, and at the second hymn they march out following a banner one of the classes has made. Finally, I work very, very hard on my sermons to make them the best that I can.

Fellowship Pads

In the service, we have folders containing fellowship pads. I know a lot of churches have them now, but some don't; and I make a big issue of that every single Sunday. I say,

> We invite you to participate in an act of fellowship. Those on the center aisles and on the outside aisles will find that there is a fellowship pad at the end of the pew. We invite you to write your name and pass the folder down to the other people sitting next to you, and then pass it back so that you can notice the names of those who are sitting with you and greet one another by name after the service. There are also name tags there, and we invite you to put down your name in large block letters and place the tag high on your shoulder so we can read it. If you are a visitor, we especially welcome you to our service today. We thank you for coming to worship with us. It's important to us that you come and be with us and we're so happy to have you here. We want to encourage you, if you will, to give us your address and telephone number so we can send you some information about our church. We're so pleased and honored to have you here. Please take a blue name tag and put your name on it so that we can identify you as a guest and can seek you out and especially welcome you to our service today.

We go through that every single Sunday at both services.

Then, that week, we take the names from the fellowship pads, and every visitor receives a short note from me with a welcoming statement, hoping the person will come back again. Then we put the names on the mailing list to receive *The Hill Church News*, the newsletter that goes out every week. A lay person from the membership committee telephones them and makes a report back to the church office, where the information is put on their card in the cultivation file.

Follow-up

After a visitor has been to the church two or three times, I receive the card. I try to go see the person, if that's possible, or telephone to make an appointment to see the person at home or invite him or her to come and see me here at the church. That way I'm able to make as many as eight or ten telephone calls or face-to-face visits every week, about four hundred a year. Then we try to assign a lay sponsor, a church member who works with that person or who lives nearby to take special responsibility for making the newcomer acquainted in our church.

After a person has been coming for a while, we invite him or her to a membership class—we send a letter and also telephone—we work on commitment.

So that's cultivation. Once you have made contact you can't just say, "Well, it's nice to have you here," and ignore the person; you have to work on a relationship. You have to be like a suitor, a lover; you have to track the person down and work on your quarry. If you don't do that, the person is not going to join—at least, not this church. Our church has to make all the effort because we have the world's worst demographics; it's a long way to travel, and it's dangerous to come down here. So why should anyone come unless it is to experience the very best in this church—the very best preaching, worship, music, fellowship, and really caring people? When people do experience the best, they come, and as I said, they've been coming in large numbers.

Commitment

What about commitment, the third C? Well, we invite people to have three contacts with us in the process of becoming members of the church.

In the Minister's Home

The first contact is a meeting in my home; we're very nice to them; we have refreshments and really welcome them. They like to came into my home; it's important to them.

Because in this church we try to begin every meeting with prayer, we begin this home meeting with prayer. Then we make introductions all around, and we talk about the church. We ask people why they're there and what they think about the church, and we go around the group and they sell one another on being in

171

this church, because they testify to how wonderful it is and how they love everything about it—the fellowship, the preaching, the music, the building—they just talk about all the things they like. When it's my turn, I say, "Gee, that sounds like a wonderful church. I think I'm going to join!"

Then I tell them a little about the history of our denomination and about our local church, and we go through our bylaws and talk about the expectations of our covenant and our statement of purpose and statement of faith, and I ask them about *their* expectations of the church. We talk about our faith as a Trinitarian Christian community. But mostly we talk about the covenant, our expectations. Our covenant says, "I promise to live a Christian life, to attend the services of this church regularly, and I pledge the stewardship of my time, talent, and money both within the ministry of this church and in the world."

Then we talk about that. And I'm hard. I point out that it says a member is going to live a Christian life, and if a candidate is doing things he or she knows are un-Christian, then I don't want that person to join this church, because we take our covenant very seriously. So first of all, I say,

> You're going to make a commitment to try to live a different kind of life, a Christian life; that's important. Second, you're going to be at worship regularly. Worship is not a sometime thing for Christians; worship is essential. And if you're not prepared to make a commitment to come to church regularly, then I don't think you should join the church.
>
> The third thing is that you're prepared to make a commitment to be involved in the church, in the ministry of the church, in some way.

People come some distance, so commitment can be in a big variety of ways. We have one person in the church who volunteers sixty hours a week. We have other people who can only be here on Sunday, and they will serve sometimes as a greeter, or a liturgist, or an usher, or they teach Sunday school. But everyone is asked to do something. We're in the process of building a gifts ministry, and we've just employed a part-time staff person to help bring that about. Then we tell candidates that we also expect them to make a financial pledge and that the amount of the pledge is up to them. We don't have any law that says you have to tithe, although many of us in the church do tithe our income, but the average adult pledge in our church is almost $1,000. The largest pledge is $18,000 a year, and I tell them that if anyone here would like to become the largest pledger in the church, the person who holds that position now is not a person of pride and would be glad to relinquish that position.

Each candidate receives a packet very carefully put together with all kinds of information. It has our annual report, our program guide, our church directory, the bylaws, a UCC pamphlet, an information sheet, a covenant sheet, information about our annual Boar's Head Festival at Epiphany, and a pledge card.

At a Mini-Retreat

The second commitment meeting is a mini-retreat, which is held at the church on a Saturday. There the candidates go through the statement of purpose of the church. Our statement of purpose is one we try to have everyone memorize; it's on the front of the Sunday bulletin and it's repeated frequently. It says, "The purpose of the Asylum Hill Congregational Church is to work for the increase in love of God and neighbor in Jesus Christ through caring, sharing, outreach, and worship." Then we talk about the whole program of our church in terms of those four categories—caring, sharing, worship, and outreach. That mini-retreat is led by other members of the church staff, and it has become a very exciting, important part of the preparation for membership, in which candidates and staff come to know one another better.

On Joining the Church

The third occasion for contact is the Sunday the new members join the church. We meet with them before the 10:00 service for prayer and to explain what's going to happen. Every new member has a sponsor, a person who has special responsibilities for the new member. Then we have the ceremony in the worship service where the new members own the convent and the statement of faith, and the congregation make their vows. We give the new members a white carnation as a symbol of being washed clean in the love of God in Jesus Christ and forgiven, and a handsome certificate of church membership. A whole lot of us shake hands with them—myself, one of the associate ministers, the moderator, the chair of the membership committee—and we welcome them. While we are doing that the whole congregation sings a welcoming hymn. Then the new members turn around to face the congregation. Their sponsors put a big, fancy name tag on them and give them a hug, and they go back to their seats.

After the service, at the coffee hour, the new members are greeted by everybody, and then there's a brunch, with food provided by the sponsors and the membership committee. It's a celebration, and it lasts one hour. We have wonderful food and fellowship together at small, round tables, where everyone has a chance to visit. The children are included. Earlier, we have given them a special card to invite friends or family they would like to have come and be with them in church on the Sunday they join, and they are invited to the brunch as well. We sing a couple of songs we've written to familiar tunes. One of them goes, "Asylum Hill's the church for me"—and we point to ourselves—"the church for you, the church for us." We hug one another and point to one another, and it's just terrific, and we laugh and have a great time.

Then people who have been members for a long time stand up and look at the new members, especially those they've sponsored, and sing, "Consider yourself at home, consider yourself part of the family." The lay leadership stand up and say a word about what they do in their groups or on their boards and invite the participation of everyone. Then I always have a couple of long-time members stand up and say how the church has become increasingly important to them through the years, and they're so happy they joined and they know these new people are going to be just as happy. Then we close with prayer. A lay person always leads us in prayer. Some of those prayers are the most wonderful things, really whiz bang; people really listen when lay people do the praying.

That following week, we send a letter to the sponsors reminding them of their obligations—to invite the new members to church, make them welcome, and invite them to meet people for dinner or some kind of social occasion. That same week, a letter goes out to all of the new members from me, personally welcoming them again and telling them how happy we are to have them in the church. Then we refer all their interests to the various interest groups in the church, and we ask our new members to be greeters at worship in the following weeks. After three months they have a reunion brunch with the ministers to see how they're doing.

We have a friendship committee responsible for working with these new members and enabling them to assimilate into the life of the church. Their task is to call on them and make sure they're participating to the level of their interest.

174

Churchpersonship

The fourth C is churchpersonship.

Courses and Fellowship

Each year we publish a little booklet called "Hill Lights," filled with descriptions of all kinds of courses and groups. I teach courses; my outstanding colleague Peter Grandy, who has been here twelve years, teaches courses—on theology, history of twentieth-century thought, basic twentieth-century theology, essentials of Christian belief. Some of our members teach courses. There are all kinds of courses on the Bible. We have hundreds of people who study the Bethel Bible program, taught by lay members in our church, and other Bible programs as well. We have prayer groups, home groups, a book discussion group, and Christian witness breakfasts during Advent and Lent; we have special things all the time. We have a part-time lay staff person working on spirituality, teaching, and group leadership. At the latest count we had 110 different educational opportunities in which people can participate.

We have fellowship opportunities, too. We have a couples group, a young adult group, an over-thirty-five singles group, a Dine with Nine program, youth groups, the very important ministry of our women's association, and the church school. Every Sunday before and after services we have forums and courses, discussion groups, and that kind of thing.

Going Out in the World

In addition, we try to have our lay people go into the world. Churchpersonship and growing in faith and being a disciple mean that you love the world, and loving your neighbor means not only your next-door neighbor and your fellow Christian but people in need out in the world. A lot of our people are engaged in tutoring adults and children. We have a Saturday morning program of basic Christian education and recreation for neighborhood children. We have a West Middle School committee that works with the local elementary school in all kinds of things; in fact, the principal said we were essentially the Parent-Teachers Association in that school. We participate in a cooperative, ecumenical human-needs center and soup kitchen; and we're involved with all kinds of agencies in the community. We help to fund the Asylum Hill Organizing Project—a local community organization—and we have a housing task force building low-income housing for people in Asylum Hill who are having a serious problem finding a place to live.

Our building is open to the community at no cost. In the course of a week we have several thousand people using our building, and sometimes a lot more than that—as I say, Epiphany weekend, when we give our Boar's Head Festival, we probably have seven thousand people using the building. So it's used a lot. In fact, right now we're in the process of proposing to raise $1 million to enlarge and renovate our building, because it's not adequate to handle all our programs. Our building is receiving such a tremendous amount of use that now we need to redo a whole lot of things that we did just six years ago. Rugs are worn out and so forth because of all the people coming in and out.

We're thinking about a very specific proposal to raise an additional $500,000 for outreach. Four hundred thousand dollars would be for "I Have a Dream," in which we as a church, will adopt an urban school's sixth grade and guarantee those children that if they stay in school we will pay for their college education; these are all children from poor families. The other $100,000 would be for seminary education. These fund drives have already been approved by the diaconate, our governing board.

Once every year or so I preach a sermon in which I affirm the ministry in the world that members are about; what an inspiration that is for me and for all of us to see the ways in which Asylum Hill Church cares. And our people really do care. They head up the United Fund and fund drives for the Red Cross and the Salvation Army and everything else; they serve Meals-on-Wheels and do lots of little unpublicized acts of kindness—they are really terrific people. So we pass out blank paper with the bulletin, and I ask them to write down their names, if they will, and what they're doing in the world. We put it all together in a booklet and make it available for people, sort of an annual report of mission, the nuts-and-bolts mission of our people to the world in addition to the many thousands of dollars they give away. If you add up *all* the money that goes out of this church for missions, it's about $200,000 a year, much more than our formal outreach budget. That's churchpersonship, discipleship, and the kind of care we try to have for the world in which Christ has placed us.

Conservation

Those are the first four Cs—contact, cultivation, commitment, and churchpersonship. And the last one is conservation. Conservation has to do with conserving our members, especially people who are like the outer skin of the onion—they're falling away; we want to minimize that. We've had people in our church go through the "Leads" program, the John "Tim" Savage program (he wrote a book called *The Bored and Apathetic Church Member*), where we identify the people who are no longer interested and who have reinvested themselves elsewhere. We try to identify and reengage them.

Every Sunday we take attendance with the fellowship pad—we know who's in church and who's not. We have a group called the calling and caring ministry. These people have received training in listening skills, and they go out and call on people who have stopped coming to church, people whose patterns of involvement and participation have been changing. A part-time lay person is in charge of that ministry. She's our director of parish caring, and she's involved in doing all kinds of things to help us prevent people from falling away. We also keep track of new members, because that's often where you lose them, about six months after they've been members and they're not fitting in. So we try to have somebody call on them and find out what we can do to help incorporate them into the life and ministry of our church.

Then the director of parish caring has another group of lay people that go calling on the elderly. I hardly ever call on shut-ins or the elderly any more; I just don't have the time to do it; I do a little, but not very much. This group of about twenty people goes out to call, and they reach our shut-ins and our elderly at least once a month, either by telephone or by personal visit.

The third group working with the director of parish caring is called the pastoral-care team. These are people who are trained to do the more serious tasks, such as calling on people who have lost a loved one. They do grief counseling—again, it's mostly listening—or they visit a person who is going through a divorce or something like that. Incidentally, we also have a divorce-therapy workshop from time to time; it's going on as I write this essay. In addition, my associates and I are out calling on people in the hospitals and caring for them all the time.

So those are the 5 Cs.

The Three Ps

We also talk about the 3 Ps: *participation, permission,* and *positivism*. We try to give people permission to grow and become the full persons that God created them to be: "Not that I have already . . . reached the goal, but I press on to make it my own [Phil. 3:12]." Positivism. We try to take an attitude of positivism, to be positive—as somebody said, "a Home on the Range church, 'where seldom is heard a discouraging word.'" It's not that we don't have a prophetic ministry or witness, that we don't complain about things, because we do; but primarily we try to be affirmative, because people are motivated by positive reinforcement. And we believe in miracles, doing something that can't be done. That's wonderful, to have something that can't be done and to go ahead and do it with God's help.

One of the things I think is essential is to establish goals. It's very hard to persuade a church to do that, to have goals, because first of all you might fail, and if you make your dreams public and fail, you'll be embarrassed and discouraged. Then, people think it's wrong to compete with other churches. But we are in competition with other churches, and we have to do the best we can to draw as many people to this church as we can. We want to help other churches do the best they can and grow, too; in an annual workshop we tell them what we're doing and encourage them to do the things appropriate for their situation.

Some people only hear and see the limits and the problems, so they won't ever accept goals, dreams, and possibilities. But we must have specific goals because they motivate us to assess the way things are, to brainstorm, to move and to act; and I believe that God never leaves the people without possibilities. In every problem, in every limit, there's a possibility. Jesus says, "When you have faith, you can say to this mountain, 'Move,' and it will move." And I think that's very, very important, to have those goals.

Those, then, are the things we're doing. And the basis for it all is our belief in the Lordship of Jesus Christ. We believe that in the life, death, and resurrection of our Lord, he has called us to be with him in his ministry to the world.

We have a lot of shortcomings, I know, and we often fail, but we've done a lot of very exciting things. I think right now our church is poised for a major leap. We're going to have a big period of major growth, with new members and attendance and more missional participation. Putting up our new building and bringing about this dream of dramatic outreach will make our members very enthusiastic. We're excited about the future here at Asylum Hill Church.

Somebody said, "Well, that's a funny name, 'Asylum Hill!' " and I tell them it's called "Asylum" because we have a lot of "committed" members; but it's true, we do have a lot of committed members and an outstanding staff. They are a loving people, and together we have been trying to witness effectively to the love of God in Jesus Christ.

A New Church in a New Land

First Filipino-American United Church of Christ, San Bruno, California

ERASTO L. ARENAS

n February 1979, the Northern California Conference of the United Church of Christ in partnership with the UCC Board for Homeland Ministries approved a proposal submitted by the Reverend Angel B. Taglucop of Hawaii and duly endorsed by the Pacific Asian American Ministries calling for the organization of a Filipino United Church of Christ in the San Francisco Bay Area. A committee headed by the Reverend Mineo Katagiri, then conference minister of the Northern California Conference, called me, an associate of Taglucop, to be the organizing pastor and invited me to come to San Francisco to look over the situation and to determine the viability of the project. For five straight days in April, I made an on-the-spot survey of the area and pinpointed locations where there are heavy concentrations of Filipinos. I visited social-service agencies and Filipino organizations. I paid a courtesy call on the officers at the local Philippine Consulate. I visited the homes of families I knew back in the Philippines or people who were

Erasto L. Arenas is the founding pastor of the First Filipino-American United Church of Christ, San Bruno, California. He initiated the organization of several other Filipino congregations in the greater San Francisco Bay Area and in other parts of the country. Previously he was a minister in Hawaii.

referred to me by friends. I identified families who would want to join this new venture in faith and compose the core group of the church-in-the-making. To cap the week-long survey, I gathered twenty-one of these people for an exploratory meeting with the Reverend John Deckenback, associate conference minister. Convinced that a church could be organized and stood a very good chance of growing, I reported back to the conference minister, who expressed deep satisfaction at the result of the survey. On August 1, 1979, I moved from Hawaii to San Francisco and officially began the organizational work.

Why a Filipino Church?

The question why there should be a Filipino church has been asked so frequently that I feel I must address it. The organization of Filipino churches to minister to the spiritual needs of Filipinos is imperative if we are to demonstrate our genuine concern for their souls. Approximately 90 percent of the Filipino immigrants are Roman Catholics. Of the remainder just a small percentage is evangelical. Many of them put off church commitment until they are properly adjusted financially, culturally, and socially. Their main concern when they arrive in the United States is economic self-sufficiency. The intense problems of becoming secure economically, socially, and culturally absorb most of their energies and attention so that making a vital church commitment is often relegated to a secondary concern. It has to wait until a convenient time. For many, that convenient time never comes at all. Many, many more have fallen along the way, spiritually that is, in their hot pursuit of the American Dream.

There are several reasons why, for the moment, the United Church has to shy away from integration and assimilation of Filipinos into existing "American" congregations and instead opt for all-Filipino congregations.

First, Filipino church-leadership potentials usually are not used or not fully developed when Filipinos join Anglo churches. That is because Filipinos have preconceived notions that white people are the natural, excellent leaders and whatever Filipinos have to offer in terms of leadership skill is "inferior." But placed in a situation where they are with their own people, their leadership ability finds full expression and shines forth.

A second reason for having Filipino congregations is that in Anglo churches the Filipino evangelicals' sense of stewardship and giving potential is not tapped to the fullest. Again, because of the preconceived notion that the white Americans are the richest people in the world and their churches are almost always affluent, Filipinos tend to think, "They do not need my dollar." In that context, they lose any discipline they may have learned about giving. When they are placed in a situation where they are with their own people, they give because they see the need for money, and they feel they themselves are needed.

Third, let's face it, many Filipinos, especially newly arrived immigrants, are not comfortable in a church other than one that is composed of their own people. Somehow, it is difficult for them to feel a sense of belonging and the kind of welcome they want in a non-Filipino church.

Fourth, for others, the problem is communication. They are searching for a type of worship experience with Filipino flavoring, that is, where they can hear their own language used in the entirety of the service. For many immigrants, communication is still a very serious problem. Some of them do not speak English at all. That is why, from the beginning, I have always dreamed of starting a language-service department in the church to cater to this particular group. Last month, we finally realized that dream. San Bruno First Filipino-American United Church of Christ started a purely Tagalog worship service on Sunday afternoon. This is the first of its kind among the Filipino churches of whatever denomination in the San Francisco Bay Area, and we are proud of this achievement. Interestingly, the excitement of having a service conducted in the native tongue was such that even those who are very proficient in English attend. Indeed, it is a beautiful experience to be able to sing the song of Jerusalem in your own tongue in a foreign land.

The Need for a Local Sponsor

Daly City, which has a total population of 67,000, 60 percent of them Filipinos, was originally the target area. But unlike the Presbyterians and the Methodists, the UCC has no facilities in the area. The nearest city with UCC presence is San Bruno, where the San Francisco International Airport is. Together with Mineo Katagiri, I visited the pastor of Saint John's UCC in San Bruno and convinced him to sponsor the proposed Filipino congregation. Sponsorship meant that Saint John's would

1. allow the use of available church facilities for group meeting and for corporate worship free or for a minimal fee

2. provide office space for the organizing pastor

3. recognize the Filipino pastor as an affiliate staff member for the purposes of establishing relationship with the Golden Gate Association

The Reverend Champ Taylor, the pastor of Saint John's, was only too happy to agree, and he convinced his congregation to accept the challenge.

A Pioneering Venture

On August 16, 1979, forty-seven people met in the sanctuary of Saint John's UCC, and during this historic service the First Filipino-American United Church of Christ was born. For many Bay Area Filipinos its emergence was the realization of a long cherished dream. For others it was a tangible and unmistakable response to their fervent prayer.

This ministry being the first of its kind in the mainland United States under the umbrella of the UCC, we were aware that we were blazing a new trail. It was basically a pioneering venture. The presence of a core group somehow made it a little easier for me to launch a movement that I was convinced was viable and would grow. But in order to succeed I knew I must work very hard. Under the terms of local church sponsorship, the sponsoring church must at least provide a small office space for the organizing minister, as I have said. St. John's did not have any space to spare. Rather than be dismayed, I used that limitation to my advantage. I was on the road everyday. I was everywhere where there were Filipinos, visiting and witnessing not only in the San Francisco-Daly City area but all over the Bay Area within a radius of 60 miles. I asked for referrals to Filipinos who might be interested in our venture. I dispatched press releases to the local Filipino paper. I sent personalized letters and invitations. I organized home Bible study groups in key cities in the area and in the homes of people who were attending the San Bruno services. I admonished and encouraged people to advertise the church by word of mouth, to go and tell, spread the word, that the Filipino United Church of Christ had come. Indeed it had. These efforts bore fruit. In three months' time the membership rose to one hundred strong.

A Wider Vision

When we reached that point in so short a period of time we knew we had to think a little bigger. Sitting down with the interim council, I shared my dream and my vision with them. Equally enthusiastic and on fire, together we came up with the following major goals—to be achieved within a period of five years:

1. San Bruno First must have a minimum membership of three hundred.
2. San Bruno First must have its own house of worship.
3. San Bruno First must be financially independent.
4. San Bruno First must have organized another five congregations in the Bay Area.

How We Fared

Today, after seven years, how has San Bruno First Filipino-American Church met its goals?

Membership

Because of the strong presence of several other Filipino churches in the Bay Area, I saw recruitment of members as the area in which I had to hustle the hardest. The membership of San Bruno was coming from all over the place—as far away as Stockton, Vallejo, San Jose, Fremont, Hayward, and Marin County—and, of course, San Francisco and Daly City. In a little more than three years, we had three hundred members on the roll and were maintaining an average weekly attendance of 65 percent. Not that impressive, perhaps, but it must be noted at this point that San Bruno First was already implementing goal 4—forming new congregations. So we were a feeder church, a tributary, sending away many of our members to form the new satellite congregations, as will be discussed below.

Our House of Worship

It was noted wryly in a conversation among realtors in the Bay Area that the Filipinos are to a certain degree responsible for the spiraling of real estate prices in the area—why?—because of their penchant to own their home. To them owning a home is the most

185

tangible sign that they have climbed up one step higher on the socioeconomic ladder. It is one concrete expression of the fact that they have arrived, that they have it made. Somehow, the fledgling congregation felt exactly the same way.

We wanted a house of worship we could call our own. Moreover, afternoon worship was not for us. Morning worship is "the" worship. After nineteen months of renting the facilities of Saint John's, San Bruno First moved into its newly acquired sanctuary at 461 Linden Avenue, San Bruno. We borrowed $170,000 from the UCBHM, payable within ten years, and bought a building worth $202,000.

Self-support

Our church was a recipient of an $80,000 leadership subsidy, which started August 1979. In four years' time, the subsidy was exhausted. But from the beginning, the congregation showed considerable strength in giving, as evidenced by its ability to pay the building's monthly mortgage of $1,830, plus other expenses after only nineteen months of existence. It bought a brand new van that picked up people from their home to take them to church. (It now owns two vans.) It did a major renovation of the sanctuary, spending a considerable amount of money on it. It has consistently contributed to Our Church's World Mission and this year gave $3,000 to three seminaries in the Philippines. The congregation has been most generous, by Filipino standards, in its support of the pastor. The budget in 1988 was $110,000—good enough for a congregation our size.

Outreach Program

When we started San Bruno First and sensed the kind of enthusiastic response we were getting, I knew this congregation would look far beyond its walls, its immediate environs, and spread far across its own Jerusalem into "Judea and Samaria." The vision was there. The dream was there. But more important, the will was there just as well.

Earlier in the game, I thought something should be done for the scores of people who drive miles and miles just to be able to come and attend the worship service in San Bruno. I thought it would be unrealistic, wishful thinking to expect them to keep on traveling such a long distance forever. Before they got tired, fell away, and were lost to our membership, I thought it would be wise to anticipate that danger and minimize it by bringing the church right where they were and thus keep them in the fold.

Through constant home visitation and Bible study, we managed to organize five satellite churches; four of them are remarkably strong for new congregations. One already has its own building. Another, in Fremont, is in the process of borrowing a loan for its projected building; it shows considerable promise in terms of membership growth. We even managed to move across a conference boundary line to organize a church in Southern California. The church in Eagle Rock is doing extremely well even as it survived a crisis due to a split in the membership.

Problems

Today, after seven years, San Bruno First has far outgrown its facilities. There are Sundays when attendance is so high that space becomes a real problem. But what vexes us most is our Christian education program. We thought that we had solved it as soon as we bought the building, only to find out that the fellowship hall just was not big enough to hold five classes simultaneously. We have no classrooms that would make it conducive for children to learn. Three classes go on simultaneously in the sanctuary with each teacher drowning out the others' voices. There are no spaces where the children can go out and play. So after their own junior worship service, they go every which way, with most of them playing along the street and endangering their lives in the process. Also, there is no place where the thirty-odd members of our young people's group can hang around and be on their own. The condition is simply chaotic.

The number one problem, which defies solution, is parking. Traffic along Linden Avenue is terrible on a Sunday because of parked cars on both sides of the road. We have lost several people because of their inability to find parking spaces when they came to worship, and we have antagonized a number of our neighbors because of the presence of so many cars.

Attempted Solutions

During the last four years, the church council has consistently wrestled with these problems, which, admittedly, have slowed down our growth. There were a couple of options open to us. The first was relocation. There is no question that what we needed was more space—a bigger sanctuary, more Sunday school classrooms, a playground for our children, and a much bigger parking space. We engaged the services of several realtors to find us a place that would meet there needs—a ready-made building with all these amenities, but somehow, there was no such place available. Through these realtors we offered to buy a couple of church buildings from churches with smaller memberships than ours, but neither wanted to sell. We considered simply purchasing a choice piece of real estate and putting up our own building and facilities, but the price of real estate was so high that there was no way we could afford it. It was not that we did not have faith, it was simply that we were being cautious and realistic.

Renovation of our present facilities was our second option. We hired an architect to draw a plan for a building that would maximize the use of the available space we have. He came up with a plan for a three-tiered structure that would use the entire ground floor area for parking, put the fellowship hall and the Sunday school classrooms on the second floor, and put offices and a conference room on the third floor. A number of our neighbors fought the planned expansion. The city planning commission, bowing to pressure from our not-so-friendly neighbors, balked and would allow us only two floors; they also imposed a great many restrictions. The church council dropped the idea, arguing that it was not worth the struggle. Meantime, we continue to wrestle with the problem.

Projections for the Future

It is estimated that there are now more than a million Filipinos in the United States, and due to the liberalization of United States immigration laws, thousands upon thousands more are expected to arrive during the coming years. It is said that at this point the Filipinos are among the fastest-growing ethnic minority groups in California, second only to the Mexicans. It is imperative therefore that the United Church address this social issue. Toward this end, the Filipino Ministry of Northern California, spearheaded by San Bruno First, submitted a project proposal that calls for the organization and development of twenty new Filipino churches all over the continental United States during the next ten years. Demographic data are now being collected. Strategies and methods of approach are being designed according to specific needs. Cities where there are sizable numbers of Filipinos and where the project is deemed viable have already been identified. We are eyeing qualified pastors who can be called upon to be the organizing ministers in these different target localities, The need is great. The challenge is before us. The harvest truly is plenteous—indeed it is, for the Filipino ministry. And time is of the essence. We must be ready to respond and move as fast as people and facilities can be made available. We do not have the luxury of time. The time is now or it will be too late.

Where in Heaven Is Angels Camp?

Union Congregational Church, Angels Camp, California

ARDIE KENDIG-HIGGINS

Where in Heaven is Angels Camp? I remember reading about it in my high school English class in Doylestown, Ohio. That's where Mark Twain lived and wrote *The Celebrated Frog of Calaveras County*. I've taken several hops. I was born, raised and ordained a Methodist—as a child I believed that John and Charles Wesley, whose portraits hung in my preacher dad's office, were my grandfathers—and served in a Methodist church in Mount Gilead, Ohio (no balm there!). But I married a wonderful man and United Church of Christ minister, Daryl Higgins, and took a long jump to Southern California. I was minister of Christian education at a UCC church in Lacanada Flintridge (if you can't beat 'em, join the UCC yourself) and associate minister at another UCC church in California before landing on the lily pad of Angels Camp, a touch of heaven.

I must admit I really didn't want to come here. I was serving a wonderful black church with fabulous people, a good youth program, and a tremendous music ministry. Why go to a small church with fifty-six members and a part-time salary? Because "darn it I

Ardie Kendig-Higgins has been pastor of Union Congregational Church, Angels Camp, California, since 1982. Previously she was associate minister of the Church of Christian Fellowship (UCC) in Los Angeles and minister of Christian education at the Church of the Lighted Window in La Canada-Flintridge, California.

love those people!" That's how I explained it to my husband after my interview. Besides, the Lord kept bringing up Angels Camp at every turn in the road. So with a U-Haul behind my car, my feet dragging, and tears running down my cheeks, I headed north into the foothills and the Gold Country.

Why did I love them almost immediately? They were different—they loved their church and it showed; they were talented and interesting people; they wanted leadership (something I felt I could provide); and they wanted to work toward having a full-time ministry. I felt God in their midst and a challenge to me.

Divinely Called

Union Congregational Church was formed in the 1860s during the gold rush in California. The town was a mining town named after a fellow called Angel—it was his mining camp. The people who moved there felt the need for a church. So the Protestants built their church at the edge of the business district on the top of the hill. It was a Congregational church served by circuit riders, who rode from one gold-mining community to another in the Sierra foothills. In the early 1900s the church was yoked with the Murphy church nine miles away. The two churches were served by the same pastor until the late 1950s, when the Murphy church became a full-time enterprise. Angels Camp could not afford a full-time minister, so they hired men with other careers or retired clergy to serve a few days a week. From 1869 to 1982, church records show thirty-nine ministers (with no record of any ministers from 1884 to 1899). In April 1982 I became number forty.

God called me into the Christian ministry many years ago (well, sixteen years ago seems like many years). God gave me gifts and appointed me to work in the local church, building up the body of Christ. Union Congregational Church was also divinely called by God to be part of God's body and minister in Angels Camp and across the world. Now God was calling us to work together! We felt this call. And within this call we both heard a challenge for growth—both spiritual and numerical. After all, how can a church go from a part-time to a full-time pastor without growth?

So here we were together; now what? Average Sunday school attendance was eight, and worship attendance ranged from fifteen in summer to thirty-nine in winter. Certainly divine guidance was needed. At least on my part! For our church to grow I believed, and still believe, that there are three spiritual disciplines essential—

prayer, seeking God's will, and being led by the Holy Spirit. In our covenant with each other we pledged, "We look forward to a significant and fruitful ministry to our church, and promise our whole-hearted cooperation, love, prayers to this end."

A Prayer-and-Praise Chain

Prayer being the key to communication with God, thus knowing God's will and the line through which the Holy Spirit can flow to and through us, we started there. A struggling prayer circle was meeting each week. And a prayer chain was in existence, but it needed to be revised. We began by organizing a seven-week study of prayer—its meaning, types of prayer, the history of prayer (including Jesus's teachings), and different ways to pray. Based on our study, we reorganized the prayer chain into a prayer-and-praise chain. You see, we realized that we are called to pray for things for which we are thankful as well as for our needs. So we added praise to our chain. Also we came to believe that it is important to let others know that we are praying with and for them.

We started sending a card to each person in our prayer-and-praise chain whom we have in our prayers. We leave each person on our prayer list for two weeks. If a person needs to remain on our list at the end of that time, we put the name back through the chain. When a prayer is answered or when something good happens to a person, we send that news through the chain also. We also list the prayer-and-praise chain telephone number in our bulletin along with the church number. Periodically (every six to nine months) we change the order of the chain to insure that the flow continues to go well. This allows us to delete and/or add members to the chain. (The telephone number, however, remains constant.)

Studying prayer helped us gain fresh insights into what the prayer circle should be doing. Upon gathering, the circle (not to be confused with women's fellowship circles) begins by reading some scripture and having a short devotional period. It then prays for our church, our pastor, our church officers, our shut-ins, and our Sunday school and its teachers. After that it prays for each person on the prayer-and-praise chain list. (Some people who are in the prayer circle are on the prayer-and-praise chain, but this is by no means a prerequisite to being in the prayer circle.) After praying for any other needs or noting answered prayers mentioned by circle members, the circle closes its meeting with the Lord's Prayer. We also put up a prayer board in our friendship hall listing prayer needs and answered prayers. The board, along with letting the church and Sunday school know we were praying for them, added a dimension of importance and confidence in ourselves.

There are several other areas that have helped our church grow. I guess you could say that each of them compliments prayer, seeking God's will, and being led by the Holy Spirit, making them become more of a reality in our work together for the Lord. I'd like to share them with you. They are in no particular order of importance; each is simply a piece that makes our picture whole.

Long-Term Commitment

There is a mentality, almost an expectancy among many churches, that the church is merely a stepping stone for the minister—he or she will be here today and gone tomorrow. This certainly held true at Angels Camp. My first day there as my husband and I were unpacking my books in my new office, the moderator (who also chaired the search committee) stopped by to welcome me. I asked if everyone was as excited as I was. A hesitant "Sort of" was the response. A chill ran through me, at the same time giving me cause to think. "Some people are wondering if you'll be here long—you are so highly qualified," continued the moderator. This remark was a disturbing affirmation of my ministerial gifts. She left, and after recovering from a mild case of shock I realized that the congregation's initial excitement and anticipation had given way to some typical fears of a church that has had short pastorates (especially, since it was only able to afford a part-time salary). The people begin to expect each minister to have a short pastorate . . . and so it happens! With these underlying attitudes, no firm commitments are made. No "leaps of faith" are taken. No close relationships develop. No five-year plans are formed.

With this type of a barrier set in place everyone, the pastor and the people enter into a holding pattern. The entire ministry of the church in the community is thereby undermined. I didn't want this to happen to us. Besides, hadn't I always said I enjoyed challenges? Well, here was another one!

From what I've seen and read, great churches—large or small— aren't built overnight. There are years of sweat, toil, and tears along with the laughter and joy before God gives the increase. So that was what we had to look forward to. Also I believe that a long-term commitment on the part of the church and the pastor, to each other, is essential for significant growth. We had already established the fact that we both wanted church growth.

So, I began from our first Sunday together to talk about our covenantal relationship as a commitment, like a marriage in which parties vow "till death do us part." I admitted that there would be problems, but if we worked together they could be resolved. There would be difficulties, as there are in any relationship, but they could be stepping stones instead of stumbling blocks. I continually lifted up our covenantal relationship. This has had a growing, positive influence on our ministry together. It has been exciting and fun to count our anniversaries.

Our church, like most growing churches, is a rather homogeneous group. This does not mean we have a church full of clones—not by a long shot! We are about as diverse as they come. However, all the members feel that they "belong," that they are a part of the fellowship; they like one another. They want their pastor to fit into their homogeneous group, too.

I've never thought that pastors, or anyone else for that matter, ought to be put on a pedestal. I definitely don't want to be put on one (besides, I'm scared of heights, and as my people have learned I sometimes fall off high stools). Anyway, most people want their pastor to be "like" them—not too far below or above, not too far ahead or behind. They want a person who will struggle with them in living a Christ-like life, minister to them, and allow them to minister to him or her. In other words, church people want their pastor to be a "real" person, who hurts, and feels, and loves.

I've tried to be a "real" person (of course, I don't know how to be anyone else but me). This means I have shared my interests, faith, joys, disappointments, needs, and dreams. I've been vulnerable, and that has freed others to be vulnerable also.

A Dating Church

During a courtship, people date. After the marriage, dating often falls by the wayside. But if the relationship is to remain alive, exciting, and fresh, the dating must continue. We at the Union Congregational Church consciously date one another. The third Sunday of each month we have a potluck after church and celebrate all the birthdays for that month. Often after church, members go to brunch together, and during the school year we get together at different places and eat dinner (it is dutch treat, and we change from homes to restaurants, from sit-down meals to buffets). We go to sporting events together to watch our young members play or just to be spectators. Once a year we go to a nearby state park for an outdoor church service, an all-church picnic, and an afternoon

195

of fun and games. We have formed a group of people who enjoy going to plays. Our social committee not only organizes our fellowship hour after church but sponsors special fellowship dinners every few months. We like being together. Besides it's fun.

I can see the wheels clicking and hear you saying, "Sounds like a clique to me." We consciously try not to be. We encourage everyone to invite others to all of our functions. We think that if people have fun with us they will want to worship with us also. This doesn't mean we don't think that people need to enter the church through the front door also. Four times a year we have Bring-a-Friend Sunday. We ask everyone to bring someone who is not involved in the life of a church. We emphasize *bringing* them, not just inviting them. We also encourage everyone to bring people to the many special services such as communion, renewal of wedding vows, baptisms, and services celebrating the Christian year.

Community Service

We have also made a conscious effort to be of service to the community. We have opened our building during the week (when we are not using it for Bible study, women's fellowship, youth meetings, or other gatherings) to other organizations. We sponsor the distribution of government-surplus commodities, and we let groups such as Alcoholics Anonymous, Alanon, Alateen, Hospice of the Sierra, 4-H, and Head Start use our facilities. We see this as part of our "mission" to our community.

Mission emphasis has also helped us grow. We realized we need to look outward to be able to grow inward. We collect food each week for the county food bank. We try to help others who have emergency needs, and we are becoming more involved in corresponding with some of our UCC missionaries. We are studying together what is happening in UCC mission fields. Once a month we have mission moments during our worship. Our vacation Bible school and Sunday school are also involved in mission projects now. It has been exciting watching our children become personally involved by collecting pencils, writing letters, saving dimes, and visiting the elderly. Their enthusiasm spreads to all of us.

Leadership Style

By now you are probably wondering about my leadership style (if you can call this style). First let me define several styles for you. A *permissive* style is trying to keep everyone satisfied (a tough job). The object here is pleasing all the members and steering clear of anything that "rocks the boat" (no one likes to be seasick). An *autocratic* style is being the one who calls the shots (you can't be afraid of needles), the decision maker, the pilot. A *participative* style is spreading the decision making among many. This creates "ownership" and obligations rather than dictation; decisions are self-imposed. A *bureaucratic* style is marked heavily by reference to rules. The church is run by majority rule according to parliamentary procedure. The pastor is a diplomat. In a *laissez-faire* style people and things are allowed to take their own course.

I have learned to use all of these various styles (of course, being an action person I find some are easier for me than others). It is important that the church style and the pastor's style match. In our church most of the time I use the participative style because it best meets our needs. But by listening to the Lord we have found that when a situation calls for a different leadership style, both the church and I have been given the grace to accept and use it.

I'd like to say a bit about the role of the pastor here, because it goes hand in hand with style. Pastors can be pompous, remote, and preachy. But if we are to be true to our calling we must follow Christ's example and be a friend. A friend shares or, in other words, communicates. It is a pastor's job to communicate the Bible. If a pastor does not want to do this, he or she had better not be in ministry. A large part of our task as Christians is to evangelize. The best way to evangelize and communicate the Bible is through preaching and teaching. Pastors need to state Bible truths in simple, understandable terms interspersed with stories and personal experiences. Here again, Christ is a good example! Once this is honestly done, lives will change. Then—celebration will happen!

This isn't to say the Bible isn't communicated by counseling, social action, and administration. It is. But as pastors, we must put first things first. We are called by God and by our people to preach and teach. The other three aspects of our job are a reflection of the first. This doesn't mean that the reflection is not seen. Indeed, it must be seen or the job is not complete. All it means is that the reflection is not the original. Without the original there is no reflection. Without the word of God told and understood, there can be no Christ-like life lived, mirrored, in response.

An Involved Laity

I have already said that I mainly use the participative style of leadership. This can only work if the laity are involved. There are basically two types of members in every church; ours is no exception. There are those whose energies primarily turn outward toward the community in an effort to bring others into the body of Christ. There are also those whose energies mainly turn inward toward maintaining the organizational structure of the church. It takes both types of church members to maintain a balance. And it's important to enable all of the members to use their gifts. When this happens, a turning point occurs, and growth results.

Common sense tells us that people like doing what they do best. It makes them feel comfortable, good, and worthy. So in our church we let them do it! Early on in our "marriage" we took an inventory of each of our talents. Each person has a list of talents on a sheet, and as new talents are acquired they are added. We also have been working with one another to teach others how to do what we do best. This training has been very rewarding individually, as well as for the church as a whole. In the process of sharing our talents there are the joys of laughter and the tears of frustration. But we love one another just for trying. Besides, we don't need everyone to be able to quilt or teach or cook. And now that we have tried doing some other things, we either have gained a new skill or have an appreciation for the person who already has that skill. We have learned to celebrate one another as well as God.

Probably the most honest expression of the involvement of our laity is found in our Sunday bulletin. It reads, "Ministers: All the Members. We want everyone to know that this is a partnership. We are all ministers—to and for and because we love Christ!"

Visitation

The involvement of the laity is very important in all aspects of the church, especially in visitation. People expect the pastor to make calls when they are in the hospital, shut-in, or ill. After all, that is what he or she is paid to do! But what makes a lasting impression is when lay people visit them. We realize that some people are very uncomfortable making such visits, but those that enjoy it we use. This doesn't mean that as pastor, I get out of calling. I still do it. But I'm just one of the team. We also have members who are ready and willing to make telephone calls to these people. So telephone contact from the laity adds another dimension to our visitation team. The diaconate board keeps up with the needs for visitation and sets the ball rolling for us. They also choose a sunshine person for the year. This person sends the appropriate greeting card. "Visits" come in many forms for the members of Union Congregational Church.

We have many people who are unable to drive, so the diaconate board set up a transportation service to help out. Those who are in need of rides always have someone to bring them to church on Sunday. But our caring doesn't last just for an hour or so on Sunday. Many times these people need to go to the doctor, post office, or grocery store. So rides are provided for these occasions also. It has been a blessing for everyone involved, because new and deeper friendships have emerged. We have learned that involvement and service are fun, as well as beneficial to those in need.

We have several shut-ins who can no longer take part in the life of our church. We were concerned about how to keep them involved. The diaconate board through visitation found out that most of them missed coming to worship. So we have tried taking worship to them. We established a tape ministry. A tape and a recorder are taken by a visitor, who spends some time with the shut-in and leaves the tape. A day or two later that visitor or another returns for the tape and spends some time with the shut-in. Not only is a worship experience provided from the person's "own" church, but he or she has an opportunity to visit with other members. We also take the person communion several times during the year, and Sunday school children visit and send cards.

The tape ministry has been used in another way that we never really expected. When people realized we were taping the service, they began asking for it when they were ill or out of town. This came as a pleasant surprise to us. It's nice to know that people don't want to miss out on this important part of our life together. You're probably thinking, "That's a great way to get a Sunday off." But you are wrong! We don't let anyone off the hook that easily. We ask all of our members to attend church when they are out of town. Now we don't require them to bring a note from the pastor of the visited church that says they were there, but we do ask for a bulletin. The bulletins are posted on the wall in our friendship hall. Everyone enjoys looking at them. And we have been able to try new ideas from some of our sister churches because of this way of sharing. This custom has also encouraged us in our commitment to try to be in worship every week.

Involving Young People

I've shared a great deal about how our adults are involved. But we feel that our teenagers and children need to be involved also. We have them participate whenever possible in leading the worship service (a few times they have even done the entire service).

We have developed a program for training our fourth to sixth graders to be acolytes. It is good to have them involved in the worship service in an active way. We have the second to third graders ring our church bell every Sunday morning. I'm not sure whether they have more fun ringing the bell or the adults have more fun watching them swinging up and down the rope! They ring it about fifteen minutes before church and right as the service starts. Letting the children ring the bell has increased their interest in church and has added excitement to the pealing of our bell.

The Good Use of Time

Good stewardship of time is also important to the life and growth of our church. This begins with the pastor's use of time. It takes quite an abundance of effort and time to prepare a sermon that will educate, stimulate, motivate, comfort, and provide spiritual nourishment in a fresh way every seven days, especially when leading Bible study, calling on members, and community involvement are also high priorities the people have for their pastor. Our people believe that time for reading, prayer, and study are important for the pastor and for the life of the church. They not only encourage it, they constantly bring me things to read and study.

Calling by the minister is needed in every church. Usually this is done only at times of need. But it needs to be done also when there isn't a crisis situation. Too often it doesn't happen because the pastor has too many other duties. I find myself in this bind all too often. But with the help of the laity in other areas of leadership, I am finding myself freed from some administrative duties so that I can have more time to visit in homes and businesses. I am constantly amazed when people tell me I am the first pastor to visit them. People appreciate the pastor meeting them where they live— it lets them share an important part of who they are. It also frees them to call for support in times of need. Making calls also has made it easier for me to share in significant and important family occasions. In addition, my home is open to the members of the church (that is, when my husband and I can be caught at home). We have had an annual open house for all the church members, which has been a fun evening for everyone.

The members of the church also view my activities in the community and the UCC association and conference as part of their outreach. They willingly have freed me to be involved in other activities. This has also provided new ways for our church to be involved beyond our walls. The good news is information that needs to be communicated to those outside the church as well as to those inside. Along with the activities of our members in the community, my activities in the community help us grow in awareness of the needs that are present to individuals as well as the community as a whole. Once these needs are identified, we can pool our resources and respond in a caring, loving, Christ-like way. Being part of the world's brokenness is an unmistakable reminder for us of what God wants us to do. Involvement outside the church often presents opportunities for evangelism because barriers are broken down. Some of these barriers exist because of lack of knowledge—people don't know what the Christian life or the church is all about. Loving, caring words and deeds through interaction with people on their ground can break down these barriers of ignorance and negative experience that result from past inappropriate actions of Christians and churches in the community.

Personal experiences such as sickness, accidents, births, divorce, business failures, marriages, anniversaries, and promotions are common to persons outside the church as well as inside. Friendship, words of comfort, and invitation at those times can open the doors of the church, the gospel, and eternal life. In order to use this tool for church growth, I have to spend time with people outside our membership. Few people seek out the gospel. It has to be taken to them, for they seldom recognize that they even need it. As I have already mentioned, John Wesley has had a great impact on my life. He once said, "The world is my parish." I see the community, as well as the church, as part of my parish. It is my commitment to win for the Lord everyone I can in our community. Some people are resistant to the Lord today; tomorrow they may be receptive. Therefore, even those who are resistant I consider part of "my parish." I love them and try to keep contact with them until they are ready, even though the majority of my time is spent with those within the church. One cannot witness the good news to someone with whom there is no contact.

Well-planned and efficient meetings are also a way of being good stewards of time and achieving church growth. Praying and hoping that our church will grow are not enough! Commitment to planning and hard work produces results. None of us really like to be in long meetings; we'd rather be "doing" ministry. But we found that if we are going to be able to "do" ministry, it always takes a plan. God has never done anything without a definite plan. Moses was given clear plans to build the tabernacle. God had a plan for creation and for the growth of the early church. If planning is good enough for God, it certainly is good enough for us! So we set goals, establish ways to carry out the necessary work, do the work, and evaluate the process and the finished product.

We struggle hard to stick to this plan of action so that things run as smoothly as possible. It saves us time, and we aren't worn out from spinning our wheels or bored from too many diversions. Thus we have an important ingredient left—energy! We have learned to let committees do the work and report back to the main body. This keeps our meeting times to a minimum. We also try to limit debate on whether to do something and how. Our meetings usually last about an hour. Since this time frame has been established, we have found people more willing to serve.

Repeatedly in scripture there is emphasis on the need to learn God's will. If we believe in God, we are expected to commit time to learn God's will. We believe that education happens in almost everything we do in the life of the church. But it takes place principally in worship and in Bible study.

Worship and Celebration

In our church the responsibility for worship belongs to the pastor and the diaconate board. While preparation for baptism, communion, ushers, greeters, acolytes, and flowers are all important, they aren't the main emphasis of our service. The word of God must be proclaimed in a vibrant way! Our services are often centered around a theme from the scriptures. The word is reinforced by related prayers, hymns, anthems, the sacraments, and banners. We try to make all of our services opportunities for those who participate to feel the presence of God.

There are many elements in our worship services that involve people (this isn't a spectator sport). The children are involved in sharing things they learn in Sunday school, in the children's message, in baptism, and in singing. We have lay persons involved in reading the scripture, giving the opportunities for the week, and bringing us the morning message. Our altar guild has organized the decorating of the church for various seasons, and the altar decorations are the handiwork of our members or the product of their gardens. Banners, butterflies, balloons, birds' nests, and even cats have provided the theme for our worship celebration. One member designed and made two stained-glass windows for new doors for the church.

We feel that we are growing because we are celebrating. We celebrate our baby steps as well as our leaps of faith. We renew our church covenant together every year. We rejoice in the birth of a baby into the families of our church by placing a rosebud on the altar and sharing the vital statistics with the congregation as we thank God for this new life. We do this all the way from child to great-nieces to grandchildren and great-grandchildren. We have a roll of honor for those who have been members of the church for twenty-five years. It is called the Silver Cross, and a silver cross is given to the person being placed on the roll. Often we have special services of communion, reaffirmation of wedding vows, and wedding anniversaries. We have even had a baby show for our nursery (plans are available on request). Job promotions, graduations, house blessings, and retirements are causes for joy within our worship services and special programs. We enjoy celebrating any event that is important in the life of one of our "family" members.

As one of our men said recently, "You know you're involved when worship is fun, it takes you two hours to get out of church after the service is over, and you go home feeling good and glad you came." It's great to lift up our loved ones as we share the Word of God, and it makes them and us feel loved and warm inside. This doesn't mean it's all party—we challenge one another all along the way! We continually remind one another of God's call as well as God's promises. We lift up our need to heed the Great Commission "to go and tell" and the great commandment "to love."

Bible Study

We believe that our main job as a church is to open the Bible for one another. More than anything else, reading the Bible is what makes our church (or any church for that matter) a church. We challenge one another to study the word of God individually and in groups. We offer Sunday school for adults and children. We went to a two-hour program, scheduling Sunday school an hour and ten minutes before church. This gives us time to get to church without being out of breath or cheating our lessons. Not only did our attendance in Sunday school increase, but so did the ease with which we gained teachers. To our teachers we offer training sessions, substitutes for each class, and a star in their crown! People volunteer to teach, now that we give them the summer off and tell them it is no longer a lifetime commitment!

Besides our adult Sunday school class, which ranges from ten to fifteen members, we offer mini-courses of Bible study and topics of special interest throughout the year. Sometimes the topics are chosen by me, other times by requests. Depending on the subject we have ten to twenty-five in attendance. In both Sunday school and the mini-courses everyone has become very good about studying between sessions. It has made it easier on the leader and more interesting for the participants. And hardly anyone asks, "What page is that on?" when we look up scripture now.

During the summer we have vacation Bible school for a week. We are now averaging fifty-five students. Once again we offer teacher training, since it is a whole different staff from the Sunday school staff. Each day the children add a new piece of clothing to their wardrobe so that by the end of the week they are dressed to fit our theme for the week. They have bible study, crafts, snacks, and games. They also work on a musical play and program, which they put on Friday evening following a potluck supper. Parents, the congregation, and many townspeople come to join in the fun, and we usually have an audience of more than one hundred. It has become such a popular week that people even plan their vacation around it now.

Vision for Growth

Last, but by no means least, we have a vision for growth. We know that there are many possibilities for our church and we are determined to achieve them! We needed not only plans for each of our meetings but an overall plan for the life we share together. So we began by sharing our dreams of what we wanted to see happen. Talk about wisdom—we needed to put on our glasses and open our eyes. Once they were open and we could see some dreams, we needed to focus. So we put our dreams into a five-year plan and arranged them in the categories of administration, worship, evangelism, education, care, and service. After we affirmed them as a congregation, we posted them in our friendship hall. As a goal is completed we marked it with a colored dot. We also celebrated these accomplishments during worship or at some appropriate church function.

We didn't want to concentrate on numerical growth alone, but we did feel that we needed consciously to work on increasing our numbers. After all, we are committed to carrying out the Great Commission—the winning of new disciples and the growth of Christ's church. But we knew that merely showing a net gain is not necessarily a sign of faithfulness. So we aimed at a 10 percent increase in membership and participation. We also knew that if we were faithful in planting the seeds of the gospel, cultivating new disciples, and letting the "Son" shine on them, we and they would grow, and God would give the increase!

This has been a significant time in the life of Union Congregational Church. Daily in our ministry I see signs of genuine Christian commitment among individuals and families for whom the gospel has become not a toy but a tool. I can see persons who are truly taking to heart Christ's commandment to join in the service of God and the human family. I can see decisions being made by loving concern rather than by selfish desires. I can see occasions where sadness has been faced courageously, crisis met constructively, disappointment overcome by hope—all because faith is real and commitment is deep. What I see convinces me that God continues to work in, and through, our lives.

Part of the mystery of our growth is that we have stopped struggling to survive and to preserve the past. We are looking ahead with anticipation, rather than back with longing. God is making something new and meaningful out of our church that is allowing our past to become seeds for our future.

A particularly happy dividend that comes from being the pastor of Union Congregational Church, Angels Camp, California, at this point in its history is to be able to share in the growth and expectation that continue to mark its life. We have ninety-three active members (and we are expecting)! Our average attendance in worship is seventy-five and we're hopping right on up toward one hundred. We're on our second five-year plan—more leaps of faith.

Someone—I think it was T. S. Eliot—once wrote that the church must be forever building, for it is subject to attack from without and decay from within. We can be forever grateful that, in terms of personal commitment, in our common concerns as a fellowship of believers, and in the resources needed for our local and wider mission, our foundations are strong for building a bright future!

You see, ours is a love story—me for my "special" people, "special" people for me, and us for God.

Where in Heaven is Angels Camp? Just this side of the "Pearly Gates."

Journey Toward Interdependence

First Spanish United Church of Christ, Chicago

SAMUEL ACOSTA

The purpose of this essay is to share the struggle of the journey of First Spanish United Church of Christ, Chicago, toward interdependence seen through the eyes of its pastor. Of course, it could be said that this approach will lose objectivity and face the temptation of bias, but I think it is necessary to run that risk in order to assert myself. After all, it is time for me to see the church with my Hispanic eyes in order to understand its role. I have been seeing the church through other people's eyes long enough.[1]

The Story of First Spanish Church

To understand First Spanish United Church of Christ, I have to describe the type of community where it is located and the phases of its development toward self-determination.

The church is in northwestern Chicago in Logan Square. Logan Square is an area where the Hispanic population has risen sharply over a twenty year period—from 0.6 percent in 1960 to 50 percent in 1980—[2] and it has increased considerably since then.

Samuel Acosta has spent the last ten years ministering to the Hispanic community at First Spanish United Church of Christ, Chicago. Born in Colombia and coming from a Presbyterian background, he arrived in the United States in 1969. He regards his Hispanic ministry through the UCC as the "best thing that ever happened to me."

SAMUEL ACOSTA

The first Hispanic group that appeared in Logan Square was the Cubans between 1960 and 1970. They began to move into the area of Kedzie Avenue and Fullerton Avenue and around Logan Boulevard. Some of the small stores along Milwaukee Avenue began to change to Cuban hands. The newcomers were mostly young and with limited education, but they had a great desire to move up on the economic ladder.[3] Later, Puerto Ricans and other Hispanic groups arrived. Unemployment among Hispanics was 6.5 percent in the male labor force and 8.2 percent in the female labor force.[4]

Because of the increase in the Hispanic population in Logan Square, the white population, mostly of northern European descent, began to move out to the suburbs farther north, where they could be safe from the newcomers. The churches in the community, in 1970, were still predominantly white. First Spanish UCC was, in some ways, a pioneer enterprise.

Nomadic Period (1962–1970)

In January 1962, the Reverend Vicente Milian was called by the Community Renewal Society (the mission arm of the UCC Illinois Conference in Chicago) to work with six Puerto Ricans who used to meet at Warren Congregational Church, in the near North Side of Chicago. He arrived in the area at the time that it was changing from a Hispanic to a black population. The Hispanic community was moving farther into the North Side. Milian began his work with the Puerto Rican community but also worked with the Cubans. The group began to grow out of the Cuban immigrants, whom Milian had great skill in reaching. At this point, the group was 50 percent Puerto Rican and 50 percent Cuban.

Because of the migration of the Hispanics out of the area, the group decided to move north, where most of the Hispanic population was going. In 1965 they began to worship at Wellington Avenue Congregational Church on the North Side, where they continued to grow. It is curious that at this point the group was not organized formally as a church. The members were part of the Wellington Avenue Congregational Church roster. The composition of the group still was 50 percent Cuban and 50 percent Puerto Rican. In 1967 the members of this group began to settle in Logan Square, and by 1970 almost 70 percent of the congregation was living there.

In 1969 the group began to think of the possibility of having their

208

own building where they could operate as a separate congregation. Some conflicts developed at this point in terms of style of worship and use of the Wellington Avenue facilities. By January 1970, the group decided to rent an old Methodist church in the heart of Logan Square. They found the right location, but in the move they lost some of the families that were not in the area of Logan Square. Only eighty families were in the new location, but the composition of the congregation changed: about two thirds were Cuban and the rest were Puerto Rican.

At the end of 1969, Milian decided to retire, and the group began to search for a new pastor. In July 1, 1970, I arrived from Colombia, where I was working for the Presbyterian Church, to take responsibility for the congregation.

Covenantal Period (1971–1976)

My arrival marked the beginning of the group's covenantal period. It began with the initiation of conversations between the congregation and the Community Renewal Society in order to participate in the Churches in Transition project, designed by the society to help churches in an area of change.[5]

This is the period when the congregation planned to recruit twenty-five members a year in order to come up with a membership that could support the work after the resources from the Community Renewal Society came to an end. The covenant was designed for five years—1971 to 1976. With the economic support and technical assistance of the Community Renewal Society, the congregation was able to jump from 80 members and a parish of 150 persons in 1972 to 250 members and a parish of 400 persons by 1976.[6] The budget rose steadily: $400 in 1962, $9,000 in 1972, $45,000 in 1976, and $200,000 in 1987.

We celebrated the culmination of the Churches in Transition project in June 1976, when the congregation accepted the task of becoming the first self-supported church resulting from this project. At this particular time, I did not realize and the church did not realize the impact that inflation and the energy crisis would have on our budget. I now consider that this celebration was too grandiose because it did not visualize the problems that the church would have to face in the future.

In 1976 we began the period of independence in a state of great fragility.

Period of Independence (1977–1987)

In my annual report for the congregational meeting of the church in December 1976, I said:

> We have come to a point where a big change has happened in the life of this church. We were before [by] reason of the mission of the United Church of Christ. Now we are participants in the mission of the church. We can no longer wait for help; we have to help ourselves.

This experience of independence and self-determination was very important as a means of gaining self-esteem, but we forgot, or we were not reminded, that we were part of the family of the total church. A great sense of isolation and despair came after the celebration. I felt that the Metropolitan Association, the Community Renewal Society, the Illinois Conference, and the denomination were telling us, "Good bye, you are on your own." The situation was more difficult for me, the pastor, because there was no other brown face in the structure of the denomination where I could go for counsel and support. To put it in biblical terms, it was like the experience of the disciples at the Transfiguration. They were with Jesus on a mountaintop having a good time, but they had to come down to the valley to face the world of conflict and problems.

Pretty soon we began to see some realities that had not been so evident. One reality was inflation. Another was the cost of heat. It began to affect the fragile budget of the congregation. After the cruel winter of 1976, the upwardly mobile Cuban community began to move to Florida. The congregation that we spent five years building began to crumble, as we transferred member after member to Miami. During 1978–1979 we lost a hundred members and with them, pledges for $12,000 from our budget. You can imagine what that meant in economic loss. The board of trustees, the pastor, and the congregation were aware that we were in trouble and we had to do something about it.

In order to face the problem, we began to open our doors to the new Hispanic population that was coming to Logan. We could not afford the luxury of being just a Cuban or Puerto Rican congregation; we had to appeal to all the Hispanic groups in that area.

In economic terms, between 1979 and 1981 I had to negotiate with the congregation a freeze on my salary to give the congregation the opportunity to recover. I was not doing anything special because the congregation itself was suffering unemployment and other ailments. By the beginning of 1981, the church was able to replace the hundred families that we lost from 1978 to 1979 with a hundred new families, and we also picked up twenty-five additional members.

During the journey toward independence I did not feel alone in relation to the local church because this congregation had a big heart and a great desire for survival, but sometimes I felt very lonely and lost in the middle of my denomination.

Since 1976 the board of trustees and I have been involved in planning long-range programs that would bring in the revenues to maintain the work of the church in the middle of this population mobility. Two of these programs were the day-care center and the college program. The day-care center was organized as a private enterprise where the parents pay on a weekly basis for services. Since January 1980 it has been operating at full capacity. It provides the church with more than $10,000 a year in exchange for the use of its facilities and also helps the church with repairs and insurance.

The Elmhurst North Park College Program (described below) also pays for the use of the facilities—more than $9,600—and for secretarial service, janitorial services, insurance, and repairs. The money coming from these programs gave the church the break during the period when we lost most of our members. In addition, the programs gave us the opportunity to serve, and bring the church into the lives of, many people in the area.

At the same time that the board of trustees and I were working together to gain the proper financial support at this critical period, we realized that we had to make our Hispanic constituency more pluralistic. In other words, our church had to be able to attract Hispanics from all the Latin American countries. With that idea in mind, we designed our Hispanic Festival to open the doors of communication, identification, and celebration with all Hispanics in Chicago.

As a result of our annual Hispanic Festival, we have been able to build a more pluralistic church. The Cuban-Puerto Rican combination began to change to a Cuban-Puerto Rican-Mexican-Guatemalan-Salvadorean, and South American mixture. Actually we have fourteen countries represented in our fellowship. The festival has become a moment of celebration that tends to unite all the different traditions from the Hispanic community. We maintained our relationship with and commitment to Logan Square, but we began to draw a good number of members from different areas of the city. The community church became a metropolitan church in this process.[7]

How We Accomplished Our Goal

In order to accomplish our goal of independence, after careful study, we chose four areas to develop: (1) membership, (2) economic growth, (3) Christian education, and (4) community. Rubem Alves's *Theology of Hope* gave us the frame of reference for our work. Alves explains why Latin America lives between the necessity of a revolution and the impossibility of having one. The main reason, he says, is that Latin America has not had the opportunity to create its future; the future has always been brought to it. It seems to me that the tragedy of the Hispanic churches in the United States is precisely the fact that we have not been able to create our own future. We have a mission for the larger church, but we have not had the opportunity to create our own future. First Spanish United Church of Christ decided to create its own future.

Membership

There is no way we can talk about church growth without including membership growth. The mainline denominations are losing members and are therefore afraid of talking about membership growth. First Spanish UCC decided to grow in order to become a self-supporting church. The idea was to enroll twenty-five new members every year. In order to do that, every program and activity of the church had to be directed toward evangelism. The women's circle, the youth groups, the choir, the deacons' board, the day-care center, and the college program were oriented toward the idea of bringing twenty-five new members into the life of the church each year.

We had to remember that this church started twenty-five years ago with four members from Puerto Rico and a budget of $400 a year. The big change came when we decided to be a church that could attract all the Hispanics in the city of Chicago. From being a church of four Puerto Ricans we developed into a church of four hundred people from fourteen Latin American countries

We created a series of festivals in which we celebrated the life of all the Latin American countries and the things that in some way could unite us. The folklore, food, and music were elements that we emphasized strongly. Every Sunday we celebrated the new families incorporated in the life of the church. We also celebrated the older families in the church. This practice created a sense of church family. As a result, membership began to grow, and every member of the Latin American community began to identify with this church. Finally we began to explore the possibility of being a metropolitan church instead of a local church. We now have families that drive from the suburbs to the city every Sunday.

All these elements contributing to membership growth were related to our desire to assert our identity. We were very intentional when we invited Hispanic people to our church: "You are worshiping in a Hispanic church, and we do not make any apologies for it." It is important for our people to accept that Hispanic is beautiful and that there is nothing wrong with us because we want to worship in Spanish. After all, God is multilingual.

Economic Growth

Membership growth brings with it economic growth. It is a misconception to believe that only rich churches can have economic growth. The truth is that the poor usually give more money to the church than the rich do. One of our goals was to teach *all the members* to be happy givers. This was not an easy task because we had to create a rather sophisticated stewardship campaign that would teach every member why we give. We had to remember that 90 percent of our membership comes from a Roman Catholic background where the concept of making a financial pledge is not yet developed.

The starting point was the development of a good stewardship committee that could translate giving into Hispanic terms. Various church committees had some innovative ideas. One was to add to the pledge card the things that the church had done for its people during the year and the cost in dollars. For example, in 1988 the church gave an average of five hundred hours of counseling to the community. This service, if paid for, would have cost $35,000. Through examples such as this, people could visualize what the stewardship committee was talking about. We also told the congregation that we wanted to be free of any aid from the denomination so that we could survive on our own.

We had specific goals that we wanted to accomplish every year. At the beginning we wanted to increase our income by $5,000 every year. We had some setbacks to our plans, notably the mobility of the Hispanic community, especially after the cold winter of 1976. We cannot deny that Hispanics want to be in the Snowbelt for ten years, more or less, and then go south to Florida, Texas, Arizona, California, and Puerto Rico. There is nothing we can do about this phenomenon. We have to accommodate ourselves to it, and we have to increase membership by 10 percent a year to break even.

We discovered that one of the ways to improve our economic growth was to concentrate on education. Education is a top priority among Hispanics because it gives us the key to open doors in this country. Therefore, First Spanish UCC decided to concentrate on the education of the Hispanic community of Chicago. We created what is now the Elmhurst North Park College Program, the first bilingual college education program for Hispanics in Chicago and probably one of the first of its kind in the country. The idea was to develop a college that Hispanics could enter without any proficiency in English, with the understanding that they would build proficiency and later be able to function entirely in that language. We have already graduated sixty Hispanics.

What did this program gain for the church and the community? For the church we were able to graduate ten new members in different disciplines, who brought new knowledge and economic resources to the membership. When I came to the church in 1970, I was the only college graduate the church had; today 90 percent of the board of trustees have a college degree.

For the benefit to the community, let me tell you about Dulce Susana, a young woman who came from the Dominican Republic more than six years ago. She had a little girl and a failed marriage, so she was on public assistance. One day she came to our church and heard about the college program. She enrolled and in 1987 she graduated with honors. One week after graduation she started her first job, making $20,000. Two weeks later, she had her first increase, $1,500. Of course, she happily left public assistance. We have more than ten stories like this one resulting from this program. I do not have to tell you what that means for the economic growth of the church and the community.

When I sat at one of the tables at our conference on AIDS (discussed later), I found that the other people at the table were graduates of our college program who had responsible jobs in Chicago. Thus the entire community was affected by our growth.

Christian Education

We decided from the beginning that First Spanish UCC would a family church. The reason was that Hispanics tend to be family oriented. When a Hispanic is looking for a church, he or she wants to know what kind of activities for the family it offers. With that in mind, we decided to create a solid department of Christian education. We trained Sunday school teachers and developed our own Sunday school material. It is bilingual and bicultural with a solid biblical emphasis.

Over the years we have developed a Sunday school for all ages. We have incorporated into it membership classes for adults and confirmation classes for youngsters. We recently discovered that our emphasis on the family was not doing justice to divorced people, single people, and widows, so in 1987 we created some programs for these groups. Now we are maintaining a center where more than sixty people come every Sunday to learn about the church, the community, and the world.

Community

We believe that if the church grows, the community should grow too. We made up our mind from the beginning that we wanted to have roots in Logan. We cannot afford to be moving from one place to another, so we decided to "buy Logan." That sounds arrogant, but it is not. When I came to this church, only one member owned a home in Logan. Today more than sixty own property there. That did not come about by itself. We planned for it. We discovered which banks were making loans to residents in the area, and we asked our members to move their accounts to these banks. We also made contact with people who were selling homes in the area because of the arrival of the Hispanics and secured direct contracts with them in order to save the new buyers money. Homes that were bought eighteen years ago for $24,000 today are worth $100,000.

In addition, we have created a coalition with other Hispanic groups in the area to bring new parks and new housing to Logan. As described above, we built a day-care center for working parents and started a college program for Hispanic adults.

We are in the process of creating another program for the community concerned with Acquired Immune Deficiency Syndrome (AIDS) education. Statistics tell us that Hispanics are a group that is in increasing danger of infection, and we also know that Hispanics are very afraid of dealing with this epidemic. For theological reasons, some do not want to address the problem at all. Our church is probably the only one that has started a program of AIDS prevention and education. We are also counseling families of persons with

AIDS. We are looking forward to the day when we can create a center for AIDS prevention and education that could become a resource for schools and colleges in the Chicago area.

When you put our efforts in these four areas together, you can understand why First Spanish UCC has become one of the strongest Hispanic churches in the country. We have created our own future and that of our children and have contributed to the future of the community at large.

Interdependence

This journey toward independence has made us aware of a critical issue in the life of this church—the tension between dependence and independence.

From Dependence to Independence

On the one hand, is the desire of a young congregation to be fully responsible for its future and, on the other hand, the need of the congregation to have a community on which it can depend.

During its nomadic period, this congregation functioned under the umbrella of Warren Congregational Church and Wellington Avenue Congregational Church. Its dependence was almost total. We had to adapt ourselves to the time and conditions of the Anglo churches and the resources we received from the denomination.

During the covenant period, there was another kind of dependence, the kind that deals with progress, meeting deadlines, and accomplishing goals. In order to participate in a particular project the congregation had to do certain things.

From 1976 to 1980 the church went to the other extreme. As a result of its new status as an independent church and probably because of some anger that developed in that process, the church acted so independently that in some instances it became very isolated from the body of the denomination. There were times when the board of trustees was aware of some pressing needs for the congregation and the pastor, but the independent status created a false pride that prevented openness on the part of the leaders toward the organizational levels of the denomination. Admitting such needs seemed like falling again into a condition that was considered bad and embarrassing.

Sometimes I think that the struggle of First Spanish UCC between dependence and independence has been in some way my own journey, and I have seen in the church the tension I that I have

216

felt for many years in my own life. I lost my father when I was seven years old, and I was taught by my mother: "You have to study and learn to be independent. You cannot expect anything from anybody. You have to be in control of your life." The reality is that I studied, but most of my studies were accomplished through scholarship from the church and help from friends whom I still do not know. I have felt that tension between independence and dependence. My experience was the classic struggle of a person who goes from the dependence of childhood to the rebellion and independence of adolescence. But from there I went on to the interdependence of adulthood.

This cycle that was real in me was also real at First Spanish UCC. The church went through a period of dependency in its formative stage and from there went to the independent stage. To have remained in the first stage would mean to be a child forever. To remain in the second stage would mean to continue a life of constant rebellion.[8] We are beginning to reach a period of maturity when our congregation is searching for fellowship with the broader church. The congregation, too, must move from dependence to independence to interdependence

The Importance of Interdependence

I believe that this struggle is a serious theological issue. Therefore, I would like to consider it in the light of some passages that have been illuminating us in the last seventeen years of my ministry in this church.

The apostle Paul, in his first letter to the church in Corinth, has a beautiful image:

> For just as the body is one and has many members, and all the members of the body, though many, are one body, so it is with Christ. For in the one Spirit we were all baptized into one body . . . and we were all made to drink of one Spirit.
> —1 Corinthians 12:12–13

This passage suggests several things to me in the light of the experience of First Spanish Church. The Hispanic church and Hispanics in general are an important ingredient in the body of Christ. They make a unique contribution to its total life. Using Paul's analogy: in the body we have many members and every member has a specific function. The Hispanic church has to maintain its identity as a Hispanic church because this is important to

217

every member of the body. The best contribution of the Hispanic church to the total body of Christ is to remain faithful to its uniqueness. To assimilate or to be fearful because of the small number of our members will not be of any help to the total body. In the human body the organs that are less visible are as important as the ones that are more visible. By the same token, in the body of Christ every part is important, the ones that are visible and the ones that are not so visible. That means that the body of Christ will not be itself without the presence of the Hispanic church.

It is equally true that no part of the body of Christ can exist without a deep connection and relationship with the body. Paul in his first letter to the Corinthians expands this idea when he says:

> Indeed, the body does not consist of one member but of many. If the foot would say, "Because I am not a hand, I do not belong to the body," that would not make it any less a part of the body. . . . If the whole body were an eye, where would the hearing be? If the whole body were hearing, where would the sense of smell be?
> —1 Corinthians 12:14–17

That means that the Hispanic church cannot exist and makes little sense unless it is closely related with the other members of the body. Paul M. Harrison dramatized this point in his book *Authority and Power in the Free Church Tradition,* when he quotes from Harry H. Kreuner's book, *A Baptist Theology of Church Order.* Kruener noted that American churches, in the name of freedom, carried the autonomy of the local congregation to an extreme. He held that local congregation is an organic part of a greater whole. If it insists on maintaining its independence, it will be deprived of life and nourishment like a branch torn from the parent vine.

We can say again that the Hispanic church, a branch of the whole church, cannot survive separated from the vine. This sense of interdependence with the total body of Christ gives wholeness to the Hispanic church. I think we miss the point when we emphasize our self-determination and independence too much and forget that we need our connection with the other members of the body of Christ.

If the whole body were Hispanic, where would the blacks and whites and native Americans and Asian Americans be? If the whole were blacks or whites or native Americans or Asian Americans, where would the Hispanics be? If we are all part of the body, the church, then interest in every part of the body will come as a natural thing that does not have to be forced. Paul expresses that feeling in his second letter to the Corinthians, where he mentions the churches in Macedonia:

> We want you to know, brothers and sisters, about the grace of God that has been granted to the churches of Macedonia; for during a severe ordeal of affliction, their abundant joy and their extreme poverty have overflowed in a wealth of generosity on their part. For, as I can testify, they voluntarily gave according to their means, and even beyond their means.
>
> —2 Corinthians 8:1–3

The relationship between the members of the body of Christ has to be a natural one. When the church, the body of Christ, does not operate in that way, then any work that is related to one of the parts will be considered as a project and not something that is done in the name of the body of Christ as a whole. Paul adds that thinking when he says in reference to the churches in Macedonia: "With much entreaty begging of us the grace and communication of the ministry that is done toward the saints [2 Cor. 8:4]."

Yes, the church serves one part of the body in the name of Jesus Christ in the effort of ministering to the people of God. The sad thing is that sometimes in our effort as a particular church to emphasize our congregationalism we forget that we are part of a greater body and that we have the opportunity to serve one another as part of that body. Walter E. Ziegenhals says the same thing in his book *Urban Churches in Transition*, when he addresses the responsibility of religious institutions in relation to transitional communities.

> Investments in transitional communities by religious institutions, while never sufficient in themselves to alter the overall economic picture, do represent a plus in the balance of payment of that community. Equally important, they are a symbol of that institution's concern for racial and economic justice. Investments are not only the denomination's responsibility, but its privilege.[9]

We have to realize that the church has sociological and theological responsibility to the parts of the body, and it is a privilege to serve in the name of Christ, any part of this body.

Finally I want to say that every part of the body is important and should have equal attention. When the church gives more attention to one part than to another, then the neglected part suffers and, in the long run, all the body will suffer, because when one part of the body is ill, the whole body will feel the illness. Because Hispanics are a part of the body of Christ, the church has to take this part seriously and allow it to express its uniqueness in union with the total body.

Lessons for the Future

I have learned a number of lessons from my experience with First Spanish Church. They affect both the local church and the denomination.

For the Local Church

First, I have learned that independence is not an end in itself but an opportunity to exercise the capabilities of a community, an opportunity to discover the unique ways a community deals with its problems. Second, I have learned that independence has to become interdependence and has to be exercised in the context of the whole church; otherwise a congregation can become an isolated community centered on itself. Humility has to be a very important ingredient for a community; otherwise the Hispanic community will be in danger of making the same mistake that has kept the white community in the United States isolated from other groups.

Interdependence gives us freedom to reach other communities, other parts of the body of Christ, in order to learn from them, to share with them the good news, not with false pride but with the humility of the children of God. Interdependence gives us the opportunity to celebrate our accomplishments but also to recognize our failures, because we have failed in good faith. Interdependence gives us the opportunity to celebrate the fact that Hispanic is beautiful, but at the same time it gives us the opportunity to celebrate the fact that black is beautiful, white is beautiful, and Asian is beautiful. There is no independence for Hispanics unless there is independence for the rest of the body, and by the same token, there is no independence for blacks, white, Asians, and Native Americans, unless Hispanics have it too.

I have learned that interdependence is also the opportunity I have to share with the body my needs and the needs of our church. To hold in the pain would be the equivalent of denying the fact that we are part of the body.

Further, interdependence implies the freedom to be dependent on the body when one chooses and to be independent when one chooses. Interdependence is also the freedom of one of the parts of the body to take control of its future as regards its responsibility to the total body. Nobody can plan the future for us, but it has to be designed in the context of the whole church.

The severing of the Hispanic church from the whole church has been damaging for both. First Spanish UCC has to take a road of more intensive participation in the life of the United Church of Christ, at the local level, at the denominational level, and at the national level in order to begin a new era of growth and interdependence.

For the Community Renewal Society

When First Spanish UCC finished its covenant with the Community Renewal Society in 1976, the church felt that all relationship with the CRS was ended. We are sure that this was not the intention of the CRS, but that was the way we perceived the termination, and it created a feeling of isolation and anger against the CRS. To avoid a situation like this in the future, I would like to see the CRS help churches that are going through this process to make the transition from one stage to the other less painful.

The involvement of the CRS with the local church should not end with the conclusion of a program. If the CRS does not mean to continue a project that deals with a part of the body, then it should encourage this part of the body to find new options; otherwise it is not taking this part of the body seriously.

Hispanics have something to offer to the total body and should have the opportunity to do so. It is a waste of talent and energy not to use the potential that is present in the Hispanic church; depriving the CRS of the input of a part of the body of Christ will be a disfavor to the body of Christ as a whole.

At the same time, the CRS has a lot of resources to offer to the Hispanic community and the local church. The amount of information and technical assistance that it can give is great. First Spanish UCC is lucky to be in Chicago, where such an organization exists. I believe that our experience with the Churches in Transition project has given us maturity and knowledge that can be shared with the CRS. This essay is an attempt to do so.

For Other Denominational Levels

If Hispanics are an important part of the body of Christ, then something is wrong when the regional and national levels of our denomination do not reflect that reality. Somebody is not taking seriously theological reality. Our denomination is still not an inclusive one. It is a denomination that has great difficulty incorporating into one life the talents coming from Hispanics, Asian Americans, and Native Americans. To overlook talent is a disservice to the total body of Christ. I came to this denomination seventeen years ago from the Presbyterian Church in Colombia, where I worked only with Hispanics. In the United Church of Christ in the United States I was exposed to a ministry to whites, blacks, Asian Americans, Native Americans, women, and homosexuals. This exposure forced me to change some of the patterns I brought with me. My ministry has never been the same since, in a good sense. If that has been true for me, can not the Hispanics and the Hispanic church be an instrument of change for other parts of our denomination? I believe that the salvation of the denomination rests on the shoulders of the minority groups. It is there where the growth in our denomination is particularly striking. But this salvation will be possible only if the local and national offices allow us minorities to make our contribution to the body of Christ.

It is time for the Chicago Metropolitan Association, the Illinois Conference, and the national instrumentalities of the United Church to structure an urban agenda where Hispanics and other minority groups will sit to plan for the future. There is no such agenda at this point. The First Spanish United Church of Christ experience of the last seventeen years can provide some sociological and theological ingredients for it. The denomination at city, regional, and national levels should encourage discussion among minority groups so that we can plan together, not as enemies but as organically related parts of the body of Christ. I am looking forward to the day when this dream becomes reality.

NOTES

1. Plutarco Bonilla, *Theology and Culture* (Chicago: UCC, Council for Hispanic Ministries, 1979).

2. *Chicago Tribune*, 21 April 1981.

3. Water E. Ziegenhals, *Urban Churches in Transition* (Philadelphia: Pilgrim Press, 1978), p. 47.

4. Ibid.

5. Edward W. Bergstraesser, *The Third Year Evaluation of the Churches in Transition Project* (Chicago: Center for Scientific Study of Religion, 1974), pp. 1, 2.

6. Community Renewal Society, *Churches in Transition in 1978* (Chicago: CRR, 1979).

7. Gaylord B. Noyce, *Survival and Mission for the City Church* (Philadelphia: Westminster Press, 1975), pp. 100–56.

8. Erik H. Erickson, *Childhood and Society* (New York: W. W. Norton & Co., 1963), pp. 247–69.

9. Ziegenhals, *Urban Churches*, p. 107.

Creative Caring
in a Growing Church

Immanuel United Church of Christ, Shillington, Pennsylvania

ROBERT I. RHOADS

There's an old story about a traveling salesman who found himself in a strange town on Sunday morning and decided to visit a local church. As he entered the door, no one greeted him; he had to find a seat for himself; the people sitting next to him did not speak to him or help him follow the service; and after the service the pastor offered only a perfunctory "Good morning" without an invitation to return.

In the parking lot he noticed that the man in the car next to him smiled and nodded his head. The salesman responded by saying, "Thank you for the smile. That's the first sign of friendliness I've had all morning. This isn't a very warm church. What is it that you folks believe?" The man replied grimly, "Oh, we believe in doing what's right and bearing our crosses until Christ returns." The salesman looked at the man and thought of the indifferent worship, the cold reception, and the uncaring people and said, "Friend, let me tell you something. If he's ever visited this church, he ain't ever comin' back."

That story lifts up the need for the people of our churches to be

Robert I. Rhoads was born in the parsonage of Immanuel United Church of Christ, Shillington, Pennsylvania, where his father, T.W. Rhoads, began his ministry in 1927. The son served as associate pastor with his father (1960–1969) and is now senior pastor at Immanuel.

more sensitive to the "stranger in our midst," more intentional about practicing hospitality toward one another within the life of the congregation.

As an introduction to this essay, I want to share some reasons why I have chosen the topic of hospitality as a contributing factor to church growth.

In the late 1970s, I wrote my doctor of ministry dissertation on the subject of church growth and decline. The main questions in the survey were, "Why are people attracted to a church? and "Why do people leave a church?" Survey questionnaires were designed, various churches were selected, surveys were taken, and the results were analyzed. The overwhelming evidence pointed to the "care" factor expressed by the simple test question, "Did this church care about me?" The question was asked about the pastoral leadership, the preaching and worship, the program and mission, and the members. Where the responses were positive, people were attracted to the church, eventually joined it, and were assimilated into active membership. In other words, church growth took place.

Since completing this project and learning about the importance of the "care" factor, I have tried to apply this concern to all aspects of our church's life.

It is one thing, however, for a pastor to know the importance of caring and another to motivate the membership to the same kind of concern, whereby they become intentional about caring. This was a very special challenge in a large, well-established church with a rather strong ethnic character and with all the natural tendencies to avoid change.

In Saint Paul's letter to the Romans, he counsels the people to "practice hospitality." Paul understood hospitality as a gift of the Spirit and therefore as something to be nurtured. Of course, no one was more hospitable, more caring than Jesus. His compassion, his gracious nature, and his loving concern for people, which was at the very heart of his parables, supremely reflected God's own hospitable nature. For Jesus, the ultimate judgment upon our lives and ministry would be whether we cared about feeding the hungry, giving drink to the thirsty, clothing the naked, visiting the sick and imprisoned, and welcoming the stranger.

The dictionary defines hospitality as caring and a hospital as a place of caring. With this understanding, I have chosen to write about creative caring in a growing church.

226

The Church

Before we begin to describe our procedures and program, it might be helpful to give some idea of where we are and who we are.

The Setting

Immanuel United Church of Christ, Shillington, Pennsylvania, is a typical suburban church possessed of new, beautiful facilities for worship, learning, and fellowship with an estimated value of $2.5 million. It is located on four acres of land almost completely surrounded by several acres of campus of the local junior and senior high schools. There are ample parking facilities around the buildings, and there is an unpaved overflow lot across the street. The new facilities were built in 1959.

Residential development over the years has continued at a steady pace, transforming the area from an essentially rural community to a residential one. When the church was constructed, it was located on the fringe of town, but the area has been developed since into a small residential village with several apartments and town houses. New construction of homes on the other side of town has nearly doubled the population of the suburbs.

Although the community is a residential suburb, it has some commercial and a number of small industrial establishments that offer an opportunity for local employment. Several large department stores, a shopping center, and some smaller shops are located within a half mile of the church. There is a large Lutheran church and an Evangelical Congregational church in the community, as well as four smaller churches of various denominations.

The People

The church was founded in 1874 as a mission church of German Reformed people attached to a six-unit charge. Subsequently the charge was reduced to only two churches, of which this church was one. In 1953 the church began a life of its own.

The membership has consistently grown over the years. At the close of its first pastorate in 1926, membership was three hundred. By 1953, it had grown to 1,100 and today it is above 1,700. For the past several years the church has added an average of eighty-five new members and lost an average of fifty members for a net gain of thirty-five members annually.

The majority of the people native to this area are Pennsylvania Germans, known as Pennsylvania Dutch. Their characteristics can be summarized in one of their favorite phrases, "We see whatcha mean, and we know whatcha mean, but we've always done it this way." They are, for the most part, reluctant to change; they are also clannish, suspicious of strangers, and pessimistic in their outlook. They are very unwilling to move toward a stranger, to extend a hand, and offer a "Good morning, it's nice to see you" or "I'm glad you're worshiping with us." Such a move would be considered improper or "pushy."

Most of those born and raised in this area have already established their social friends and have no desire to make new ones. When new people were flocking to the church, many of the long-time members were disturbed and were heard to say, "What do we want with so many new members? We have enough." New members threatened to "take over," break familiar friendship circles, disrupt adult church-school classes, and destroy set ways of doing things.

The long-time people of this church are spiritually conservative, which at times is said to be another name for a compound of prejudice and stubbornness with a little religion thrown in for flavor. "It was good enough for papa, it was good enough for mama, and it's good enough for me." They are shrewd and thrifty but also honest and truthful. When the Pennsylvania Dutch eventually learn to trust someone, by a process hard to explain, they are extremely warm, kind, and hospitable. They will go out of their way to care for others, especially the sick and needy. There are very few people native to this area on public welfare; they always pay their debts, because above all else, they never want to be beholden to another, for that would be considered sinful.

Since about 1970 the majority of the members are no longer native-born but newcomers from outside this area. New residential developments, industries, and consolidated school districts have attracted people to this part of Pennsylvania. Our church's up-to-date facilities, the emphasis on an ecumenical outlook, and a community spirit have served as a magnet for people from outside the area and from other denominations. Hence, we have in our membership former Presbyterians, Methodists, Episcopalians, and some Baptists; the majority of Lutherans remain loyal Lutherans, and Evangelical people join the several Evangelical churches of the area.

In a recent survey of the reasons the newest one hundred members were attracted to the church, the results were overwhelmingly due to feelings of warmth and friendliness and the experience of inspiring and uplifting worship that included positive, helpful sermons, great music, and a creative, meaningful liturgy. People who have visited here and joined the church have said that they were impressed by the attention and care given to visitors.

Gladys

Gladys is a lovely, gracious lady who always goes out of her way to care for others' welfare. She makes the stranger feel welcome, and to the new member she gives a sense of belonging. She is alert and sensitive to potential trouble. On a particular Sunday morning, minutes before worship began, the organist was playing the prelude. A baby's cry broke the solemnity of the moment. Heads turned toward the baby's parents and people offered sour glances. The young parents, obviously aware of the commotion they were causing, stood up and walked down the aisle toward the exit. Gladys, who had observed the scene, met the couple at the door. "Would you like to bring the baby to our nursery?" she inquired. The parents hesitated for a moment, but Gladys reassured them. "Come, I'll take you there," she offered, "and you may return to worship or remain in the nursery. You will be able to hear the service on the P.A. system." That young couple later joined the church and confessed that if it had not been for Gladys' kindness, they would have left the service that morning and not returned.

Visitors and new members are Gladys' special interest. She has the gift of hospitality and is often referred to as the gatekeeper. Very few members of a large church have the courage to be vulnerable to the point of saying to someone, "Hi! I believe you're visiting with us for the first time" or to another, "I think you have visited with us before." Gladys would go beyond that greeting to direct them to the visitors' center to register their names and addresses in the guest book, fill out their name tags, introduce them to an usher for seating, and offer the parting words, "I'll look for you at the fellowship hour." At that time she would attempt to draw out the visitors' "life story" and introduce them to others and finally to the pastor with a word or two about them. Needless to say, Gladys was the major reason so many people returned to worship and eventually joined the church.

Gladys also inspired others to be more caring. Her influence and concern were felt in the work of the consistory, boards, and committees, and they have had tremendous impact upon this church in challenging it to be more creative in its caring and more intentional about its growth.

The First Approach

One of the responsibilities of our hospitality committee is to take "A Caring Inventory," focusing upon the "strangers in our midst." The committee meets in a series of brainstorming sessions. They try to think of the church as if they were a first-time visitor. Following are the specific topics they evaluate and review regularly. The basic first topic is our sign, "Visitors Welcome." These next topics all concern the question, Do we mean it?

Where We Are

All publicity and promotion about the church—newspaper advertisements, Yellow Pages, brochures—includes a simple map indicating streets, highways, and landmarks, for easy location of the church. Street markers are well placed and maintained in neat and legible condition.

Who We Are

The church brochure is simple, readable, contemporary, and creative. It says briefly (with ecumenical and community emphasis) who we are, where we came from, what our mission is, what we have to offer, and times of services. We have learned that wordy brochures are not read. In addition to placing them in local hotels, motels, restaurants, and realtors' offices, we distribute them to all visitors and, if possible, to all new residents in the community.

We have printed signs to hang on doorknobs with the words, "Come and celebrate with us!" and distributed them in several nearby apartment complexes.

What a Visitor Sees First

Before even entering the building, a visitor can determine whether this is a caring congregation. So we ask such questions as Are the grounds and gardens well kept? Are the sidewalks, steps, and parking lots well maintained? Are the grounds free of litter and debris? Is the outdoor bulletin board readable by those who drive by? Is it up-to-date, well lighted, and well maintained? Is there a special bulletin board listing weekly activities? Is the church clearly marked as being accessible for persons with disabilities? Are there well-marked, wide parking spaces, ramps, and curb cuts? Is the church's accessibility noted in all publicity and promotion? What services are available for the hearing impaired and persons who are mentally retarded?

Are the buildings well marked? Are there signs indicating doors for worship, fellowship, education, church-school classes, pastor's study, office, day care, preschool? Are there directional signs? Parking signs? Special signs indicating parking for visitors?

Stepping Inside

Once visitors have stepped across our threshhold, a number of procedures to make them feel welcome go into effect.

Welcoming Visitors to Worship

All worshipers enter the church by way of two doors, where they are met by *greeters*, who offer a word of welcome and a bulletin for the service. The greeters are selected from the membership each week by a chair of greeters. They wear name tags and their names are placed in the bulletin and on a small display bulletin board beside them at the doors.

Visitors are directed toward the center of the narthex, where stands our *visitors' center*, a writing table on a podium (an old-fashioned desk-secretary). On the slightly slanted writing desk is the visitors' book with a chain-mounted pen. The flat top of the writing desk is used by the person hosting the center to inscribe the visitor's name tag. At the back of the desk and on the top are slots for the insertion of two signs— "Visitors," for worship, and "Guests," for funerals and weddings. The slanted writing desk is hinged so that the name tags, the signs, and the book may be stored inside.

The person or persons hosting the visitors' center wear name tags, are listed in the bulletin, and are responsible for the following: (1) being alert for visitors, (2) welcoming visitors, (3) having the visitors' book signed, (4) filling out name tags, (5) introducing visitors to ushers, (6) inviting visitors to meet them again at fellowship hour, (7) introducing the visitors to others at fellowship hour, (8) answering inquiries. The hosts are chosen for their special gift of hospitality.

Our ushers are positioned at all doorways. They wear large name tags. A list of "Courtesy Concerns for Caring Ushers" is distributed to all ushers along with their ushering schedules.

We list the following concerns:

Special care for visitors. We urge ushers to be attentive to people who appear uncertain, to people wearing name tags, and to those introduced by the hospitality host(s).

Infants and nursery care. We urge ushers to be extremely sensitive to people entering worship with infants and small children. Ushers are tactfully to suggest that parents place children in the various child-care areas provided or that they be seated in the rear of the nave.

Children. Our ushers are aware that we provide children's worship so they may direct young children to their worship areas. With regard to children, the following note is placed in the worship bulletin: "We care about our children. . . . That is why we provide excellent nursery and child care during worship so that parents and others may enjoy a meaningful and meditative worship experience."

Disabled persons. Our ushers give special attention and care to those in wheelchairs, those in need of hearing aids, and the mentally retarded.

Procedures for illness and other emergencies. Instructions are listed for the locations of oxygen, first-aid kits, a litter, and blankets and wheelchairs. Emergency telephone numbers for physicians and nurses are provided. Procedures are given for removal and care of persons taken ill during worship.

It is important to have an occasional evening of ushers' training, because they are such an essential element in creating a caring mood. The training manual *Hospitality in a Growing Church* from the UCBHM Division of Evangelism and Local Church Development is very useful.

Welcoming Visitors to Church School

We have roaming greeters for the children's department and youth department of the church school. These are persons who are alert for people entering the educational building who appear to be looking for direction. Visitors are then taken to their respective classes and introduced to the head teacher and, if possible, to class members.

Inside the educational building there are directional signs, and all classrooms, resource rooms, audiovisual areas, and lavatories are well marked.

Our adult seminar, the largest adult class, meets in the large fellowship hall. Here there are special caring people who have been enlisted to be greeters and welcomers. They invite visitors to the coffee and tea area, introduce them to the class whenever possible, and invite them to worship.

Taking Their Seats for Worship

Perhaps our congregation's most noticeable display of creative caring is revealed through its worship. As I mentioned earlier, the reason most frequently given by new members for joining our church was the church's worship experience, which included positive preaching, inspiring music, and a celebrative, positive liturgy. Visitors see our caring during worship.

The Pew Partner Folder

On each pew at the center aisle is placed a pew partner folder. Inside this folder on the left is a visitor's brochure upon which there is a small chenille replica of the church with a gummed back. This is to be worn by the visitor to indicate his or her status as such. (Some churches use ribbons for that purpose.) On the right side of the folder is a pad of paper called "pew partners." After signing the pad, each person is to pass it along the pew and back again to the center aisle. In addition to places for visitors to indicate addresses and home church affiliations, there is a place for comments, celebrations, and concerns and a place to indicate that a person is interested in uniting with the church. There is also a reminder in the bulletin to "Please pass the pew partner folder."

The Bulletin

We believe the bulletin also conveys a caring attitude toward worshipers. We asked ourselves how easy it is for a visitor to follow the liturgy. To facilitate that, we mark all page numbers, print the words to responses, and indicate where the responses may be found. Should several staff persons be participating in a given worship service, their names are also in the bulletin. Everything that is done in the service is printed so that nothing may be assumed to be for "members only." We have the same caring approach to the announcements in the bulletin.

A moment of concern is included in worship. These moments are most frequently special emphases for missions, outreach, and activities; they are usually presented by lay people.

Children's Worship and Child Care

We also offer, in the chapel areas of the fellowship hall, children's worship during the last service. It is open to all children in grades one through six. This worship service is conducted by our associate pastor and provides an opportunity for children to learn how to participate in worship at their own developmental level. Children's worship has been a big factor in the increase of young adults in worship attendance. The children have been so enthusiastic about participation in worship that they are responsible for their parents' attendance.

Nursery care is provided for infants and child care for children ages two through five years.

Recognition of Visitors

All visitors are welcomed and asked to stand. Sometimes they are introduced to the congregation if they are special to a member family, have come from a great distance, or are visiting clergy. Special recognition is always given to the families of children baptized during the service and to parents and godparents of confirmands who are visiting for these special occasions.

There are from time to time celebrations where we recognize anniversaries, birthdays, milestones, special-offering goals met, and other achievements and accomplishments. Near the close of worship we observe a moment of fellowship, in which we turn and greet one another. On some occasions, the pastors will bring a greeting and acknowledgment of a special visitor, a vocal soloist, an instrumentalist, the choir, a minister of music, or a lay reader. At this time the visitor is invited to join us at the fellowship hour following our service. Directions are given, and members are asked to bring visitors. Soft organ music signals the close of this moment and prepares the congregation for the commission and benediction.

Leaving Worship for the Fellowship Hour

Our church is ideally suited for the fellowship hour. It is held in the parlor, a large room that extends from the nave and narthex of the church and has a kitchenette in a room adjacent. In the parlor are two tables on which are coffee, tea, fruit punch, and plates of donated cookies. Members of the hospitality committee are responsible for preparing and hosting this hour.

It is essential that it be stated from time to time that the main purpose of this hour is to greet visitors. The person hosting the visitors' center for the day will be responsible for introductions during this time. It is also an excellent opportunity for members of a large church to come to know one another. Unfortunately, it is difficult to program people or encourage them to move toward others. Many will remain in family or friendship groups. An extroverted host or hostess will often invade these tight groups and intentionally introduce visitors and new people.

Sometimes the person(s) hosting our visitors' center will invite visitors to lunch in the host's home or in a local restaurant. Other times the person visiting will meet an old friend or acquaintance and will be invited to lunch. This happens on rare occasions, but it has happened. This is, of course, the very best of hospitality.

What We Do Monday

We must constantly work with both our members and our visitors to insure an ever present spirit of caring. The groups and programs discussed below are additional ways we stay "caring-conscious."

Visitors Follow-up

On the day following worship, a church office clerk will collect names from the pew partner folders and the visitors' book. Members' attendance is posted in the computer, and visitors are also entered into the computer file. First-time visitors are sent a handwritten note extending appreciation for their visit. Second-time visitors are also sent a letter acknowledging their return and informing them of procedures for becoming a member.

The names, addresses, and telephone numbers of visitors indicating a desire to unite with the church are listed and given to the membership chair. These people are then called by telephone, and a mailing is sent informing them of the schedule for the next new-member orientation. New members are received when there are approximately twelve people. They are asked about the status of their present church affiliation and whether they will be received by letter of transfer, by profession of faith, or by confirmation.

A note is sent to people with a local address (within a three-mile radius) who have visited the church two or more times but who have not returned: "We were happy to have you visit and worship with us. We are sorry you have not returned. We miss you. Would you be kind enough to tell us what we were missing? How can we serve you?"

Membership-and-Growth Committee

The membership-and-growth committee has four major areas of responsibility. The first is creative thinking about ways of attracting new members:

1. promotion and publicity
2. visitors' relations
3. worship concerns and celebrations
4. community relations
5. all areas of evangelism

The second area is orientation of new members, which involves

1. preparation of agenda for new-member classes
2. lectures on "Who We Are," "What We Believe," and "What We Do"
3. a tour of all the church buildings
4. explanations of symbols in stained glass and other art forms
5. a study of denominational and local church history and polity
6. introduction of key leaders, who tell of their concerns such as music, stewardship, property, fellowship, and Christian education

The third is preparing new-member packets. These include the following:

1. membership and pictorial directories
2. church brochure
3. common courtesies in our church

4 a pamphlet about the United Church of Christ

5. a map of all facilities

6. a booklet, *Inquiring and Exploring: The Meaning of Membership in the United Church of Christ*

7. a copy of the constitution and bylaws of the church

Finally, the membership committee is responsible for the assimilation of new members. It does so by

1. distribution of names and interests to appropriate leaders

2. monitoring of membership statistics and trends

3. use and evaluation of survey and profile sheets

Care-and-Concern Committee

The care-and-concern committee is sometimes called the PLP (People Loving People). Its major responsibilities are listed below:

1. to visit, send cards to, and telephone the sick, shut-in, and elderly, whose names, addresses, telephone numbers, and other pertinent information are given to the committee

2. to prepare casseroles, desserts, or perhaps meals to distribute to members in need following illness, hospitalization, death in the family, or birth

3. to send congratulations to new parents and silk roses to mothers and to place the birth announcement in the worship bulletin and a fresh carnation in the sanctuary

4. to prepare altar flowers and distribute them after the service to the sick, shut-in, and elderly

5. to prepare and distribute audio tapes and videotapes of services, special programs, events, and celebrations to the sick, shut-in, and elderly

6. to provide to members in need transportation to all church events

7. to do sunshine mailings such as notes of cheer and birthday wishes to the sick, shut-in, and elderly

Care Bearers' Program

The care bearers is the present name for what was formerly the undershepherd program. It was established as a means of increasing caring communications between pastors and leaders and the members of the congregation.

Each care captain enlists ten care bearers to serve for a period of one year. The congregation is divided into zones and neighborhoods, with a care bearer assigned for each neighborhood of approximately ten members. This information is entered into the computer with each member assigned a zone and neighborhood locator number for easy retrieval.

Each care bearer makes approximately five telephone calls each year. A letter to the care bearers includes tips on what to say and how to listen! Some people are willing to visit in person. These calls are to remind people of communion services, special events, and certain stewardship or mission emphases. In turn, the care bearers report to the pastors or the office the names of those in need of pastoral services, births and other celebrations, concerns, and persons who move out as well as new residents who move in.

The care captains check on their care bearers periodically to encourage them, to learn of their concerns, and to enlist new people.

The care bearers have been the most effective innovation in recent years. The calls have produced a noticeable increase in attendance and contributions, but most important, they have increased the level of trust and feelings of genuine personal care.

Good-Neighbor Network

The good-neighbor network brings people of a neighborhood together for "caring and sharing." A host or hostess will invite to his or her house all the church members in the neighborhood. The main purposes of this evening meeting are to become acquainted, deepen friendships, share mutual concerns, and promote spiritual growth. A list of "good neighbors" in each network is distributed. This network connects with the care-and-concern committee and the care bearers' program. In a large church, few people know that their neighbors are members of the same church. Meeting those neighbors, sharing transportation, making new friends, and worshiping together are all wonderful things that have helped to make this new program another effective means of caring. This program shows great possibilities for the future.

Spiritual Council

The spiritual council, the elders of the church, have the responsibility for the "discipline" of the membership. They are primarily concerned with the inactive members. This is always the most difficult task for church leaders to perform, for we are all reluctant to evaluate another person's membership status and even more reluctant to remove that person from the church's active rolls. Nevertheless, it is a task that must be done. We at Immanuel Church believe it can be done "care-fully."

The spiritual council reviews the membership rolls quarterly and sends members letters on their status annually and other letters when necessary.

Just as we are interested to learn why people are attracted to a church, we are also interested to learn why they leave a church. For this reason we send letters to those who leave our membership by moving, by erasure, or by letter of transfer and ask them to return the profile sheet. The responses we have received have been interesting and helpful. Sample letters are below.

LETTER NO. 1
Sent to members who have been inactive for one year

We miss you and your support at Immanuel Church. According to our records, you have not been communing or worshiping with us and we have not received a contribution from you during the past year. Are our records correct?

We are very reluctant to place anyone's name on our inactive roll. We should prefer to keep you as an active, supporting member. We hope you will want to remain so.

So, may we hear from you? And will you state your intention concerning your relationship to the church? Please check your intention below and return this letter in the enclosed envelope within one month from the above date. If we do not hear from you by this date, we shall consider your membership as inactive.

I desire _____ to fulfill my vows and will worship with, commune
                   with, and support, the church.
          _____ to have the pastor call
          _____ to transfer my membership
          _____ to be erased from the roll

LETTER NO. 2
Sent to members who have been inactive for two years.

According to our records, you have not communed with or contributed to the church for at least *two years*. We are very reluctant to place anyone's name on the inactive role, and even more so to erase it from the church roll.

So, may we hear from you and have you state your intention about your relationship to Immanuel Church? Please check your intention below and return this letter in the enclosed envelope within one month from the above date.

I desire _____ to fulfill my vows and will worship with, commune with, and support, the church

_____ to have the Pastor call

_____ to be erased from the roll

Bylaw V, Section D, of Immanuel Church states: "If a member shall neglect to partake of Holy Communion, or refuse to contribute to the support of the church, or continuously absent himself from the public worship for one year, such conduct shall be deemed worthy of censure and shall be admonished by the Pastor or Elders.

"If after admonition he continues in such neglect of duty for another year, the Spiritual Council shall notify him that he is no longer in good and regular standing, and his name shall be removed from the church rolls."

LETTER NO. 3
Notice of erasure

It is with deep regret that we are notifying you that you are no longer an active member of Immanuel Church. According to our records, you have not communed with or contributed to the church for at least two years. We are very reluctant to place anyone's name on the inactive roll and even more so to erase it from the church roll.

However, you leave us no other choice at this time. Due to your negligence, your name has been removed from our roll as of the above date.

If, some time in the future, you should desire to be reinstated to full membership, demonstrating your willingness to honor your church vows, and to join in the privileges of the church, we shall be happy to assist you.

Bylaw V, Section D, of Immanuel Church states: "If a member shall neglect to partake of Holy Communion, or refuse to contribute to the support of the church, or continuously absent himself from the public worship for one year, such conduct shall be deemed worthy of censure, and shall be admonished by the Pastor or Elders.

"If after admonition he continues in such neglect of duty for another

240

year, the Spiritual Council shall notify him that he is no longer in good and regular standing, and his name shall be removed from the Church rolls."

LETTER NO. 4
Sent to those who have moved from the community (See UCC·Movers Program)

We have been missing you at Immanuel Church since *you've moved*! Our records indicate that you have not made a contribution during the past year.

We are very reluctant to place anyone's name on the inactive roll and even more so to erase it from the roll of the church. We should prefer that you become an active member of the church in your community. We hope you will do so!

So, may we hear from you and have you state your intention concerning your relationship to Immanuel Church? Please check your intention below and return the letter in the enclosed envelope.

_____ I would like to retain my membership and will

contribute to its life and mission.

_____ Please transfer my membership to:

Name of church_____

Address:_____ _____

Article III, Section C, of Immanuel Church Bylaws states: "Members who have permanently changed their residence to other cities or communities shall be urged by the Pastor to obtain letters of transfer as soon as possible and unite with another congregation."

LETTER NO. 5
Sent to inactive students and service personnel

In reviewing our membership roll, we noted that your membership status has been that of a student. It has been our policy in the past to consider all students and service personnel as active members of Immanuel Church. We fully appreciate the fact that while you are in school it is difficult to fulfill the obligations and enjoy the privileges of church membership.

However, we do feel that some expression of desire should be forthcoming from you. According to our records, you have not been communing or worshiping with us and we have not received a contribution from you during the past year. Are our records correct?

In order that we might know how we may best serve you and how you consider your relationship to Immanuel Church, we are asking you to respond to the following options within one month from the above date.

_____ I desire to fulfill my obligations and will worship with,

commune with, and support the church.

_____ I desire to be transferred to_____
(church name & address)

_____ I desire to be erased.

_____ I have transferred my membership to_____.
(church name & address)

_____ I am presently a student.

Further comments: (new address, change in status, etc.)

_____

_____

If we do not receive a reply within this one-month period, we shall consider that you desire to be removed from the active membership of Immanuel Church.

Hoping to be able to serve you in the best way, we remain,

The Revolving Door

Church membership has been compared to a revolving door: there are those entering and those leaving the membership. A caring spiritual council, or committee by some other name, will want to review this parade from time to time in order to understand the factors involved and to see what is really happening.

Leaving-Church-Membership Profile

One way to do so is to send former members a "Leaving-Church-Membership Profile."

LEAVING-CHURCH-MEMBERSHIP PROFILE

The purpose of this form is to build a profile for each of our former members. This information will help our leaders serve members' needs, design meaningful programs, assimilate new members into the life and work of the church, and plan more effective ministries for the future.

Last name   Date

Address   Telephone

Full Name   ☐ Male   ☐ Female (include maiden name if married)

Date of joining this church

How did you enter membership in this church (confirmation, letter of transfer, renewal of faith)?

What was the name and denomination of your church before you joined this church?

Please indicate method of leaving membership in this church (letter of transfer, erasure).

Name and denomination of new church

Address of new church

Please state briefly why you left this church (moved, conflict, unmet needs, different beliefs, or other).

Please make any suggestions to the leadership of this church that would be helpful in meeting the needs of its members (pastoral service, visitation, programs, style of worship, meaningful tasks, or other).

THANK YOU

Main Bulletin Board

The main church bulletin board that has the most traffic passing by offers great possibilities for introducing members and encouraging a caring congregation. Pictures of graduating seniors, college and military personnel, most recent new members, and members who are ill, hospitalized, or deceased (taken from the pictorial directory) are posted on this board. So are pictures of members celebrating anniversaries, promotions, or new births and newspaper articles pertaining to members.

Breaking Bread Together

Meals have proven to be excellent means of bringing people together, of becoming acquainted, and of raising the level of caring. We have discovered that one of the greatest ways of attracting people to an event in our church is to serve a meal. We have had tremendous success with breakfasts served by various groups. The confirmation class has served a Mother's Day breakfast, the consistory has served the annual congregational meeting breakfast, and young boys have served the men's communion breakfast. We have had luncheons and dinners to promote stewardship, "simple meals" for One Great Hour of Sharing, and "soup and sandwich" meals for a Lenten study.

Most recently we have held "Old Fashioned Church Suppers" for three nights in the fall of the year. The program for these evening meals has been a VCR presentation of the highlights of our congregational life and work throughout the year and a presentation of our program, mission, and financial goals for the coming year. An old fashioned sing-along helps to create an atmosphere of fun and fellowship.

Visitors' Ribbons

A clever idea that really worked was special ribbons that celebrated both our visitors and those members who brought them. The ribbons were made in our church's colors, either blue or gold, and were four inches long and one inch wide with a gummed top for easy attachment. On the blue ribbon were the words (reading from top to bottom), "MEMBER—I BROUGHT A VISITOR" and on the gold ribbon, VISITOR—HERE I AM." We learned that many members coveted those ribbons and therefore worked extra hard to bring a visitor. Naturally, we celebrated and recognized both members and visitors during the service. We continue to have these ribbons available.

Other Ways to Raise the Level of Caring

One of the keys to a growing church is to find creative ways to raise the level of caring among the members of a congregation.

Here are some ideas and suggestions:

Sermons can contain illustrations of what it means to care for the needy, accept the "different" and the "outsider," and be sensitive to the disabled. Sermons can also tell stories about what it means to be an "outsider," how it feels to be "different," when I was a visitor, and who is the "stranger in our midst"?

Newsletters can include a "Care Column" listing

1. those in need of a telephone call, a visit, or a card
2. those in hospitals and nursing homes
3. recent weddings, funerals, and baptisms
4. birthdays, anniversaries, and celebrations.

It can also print a "Visitors' Column" listing:

1. names and addresses of recent visitors
2. remarks or comments about their visit
3. reasons why they selected this church
4. names of members or friends responsible for their visit

Another helpful addition to the newsletter can be a list of "Common Courtesies in Our Church," covering

1. what to say to a stranger
2. how we welcome a visitor
3. how we serve communion
4. when to call the pastor
5. what to do in the fellowship hour
6. how to be more sensitive to the disabled

Still other efforts include encouraging creative caring in all committees and reminding all gatherings that we recognize and celebrate our visitors. Say it . . do it . . . over and over, "I was a stranger and you welcomed me."

Every group sponsoring a fellowship event in the church is responsible for welcoming visitors. Those persons in charge of the event are reminded to be alert for visitors and to be intentional about making them welcome. It is the goal that no stranger can visit our church and not know that he or she has found God's love in the care and concern of our membership. We have one hour to represent God's love, so we try to make every minute count.

The Power of the
Worship Experience
in a Growing Church

St. Paul's United Church of Christ, Chicago

THOMAS R. HENRY

I t is 9 A.M. on Sunday morning, and the church door opens and then bangs shut, then again, and then again. The children's choir members, with their parents, are arriving for rehearsal. The choir directors and pastors are on the scene, too. Everyone has a bit of the Sunday morning syndrome, signs of which are yawning, eye rubbing, or staring into space. But once the music begins, tiredness fades and energy flows. It is Sunday morning at St. Paul's Church, Chicago. This is the day which the Lord has made, and this day is the focus of our mission and ministry.

At this same hour, in another part of the church building, there are also services of worship in the German language, a reminder of our own particular church heritage, which continues to influence who we are. This service is attended primarily by older members of the congregation who came to this country from Germany from the 1920s through the 1950s, but the service continues a St. Paul's tradition that goes back to the founding of the church.

Thomas R. Henry is the senior pastor of St. Paul's United Church of Christ in Chicago. The church, which has a German heritage, now has a widely diverse congregation and has doubled its membership in seven years. Henry received an honorary doctorate in 1989 from Chicago Theological Seminary in recognition of excellence in parish ministry.

By 9:45, the adult choir is finding its way to the coffee pot and then on to the rehearsal room; the church-school teachers are taking a last deep breath before the children descend upon them; and the adult forums have begun. Some people, parents of church-school children and others not involved in music or education activities, circle about the coffee pot, reading the Sunday paper and talking to one another, waiting for the 11 o'clock service of worship. There are also a few people who arrive about 10:20 and go directly to their pew and listen to the choir rehearse in the chancel. In this way they can hear the worship music twice! They also have the opportunity to enjoy the sense of humor of our organist-choir-master, who entertains the choir even as he directs them in their task of leading us musically in worship. We are into Sunday morning once again as we focus thought, prayer, resources, and preparation on our mission, which is *making a joyful sound in the city.*

Our Mission, Then and Now

"Making a joyful sound in the city" is a piece of poetic prose paraphrased from the psalms. But it is much more than that for the members of St. Paul's United Church of Christ. It is the goal of our ministry in Chicago. This phrase gathers up in its few words our history as well as our present statement of mission.

Our Statement of Mission

In our mission statement we define St. Paul's Church in this way:

St. Paul's Church, as a congregation of the United Church of Christ, is a community of Christian faith. We attempt to make a joyful sound in the city through worship, fellowship, education, and service. We affirm the uniqueness of each person as a gift of God with us, and encourage personal growth and dedicated involvement in the ministry of the church. We believe our heritage in the United Church of Christ calls us to serve and witness as good stewards in our neighborhood, city, and world.

Our Mission in History

St. Paul's history goes back to 1843 and the immigration of German people to Chicago. The death of one of those immigrants and the absence of a German-speaking pastor of his tradition in Chicago led nine families to found St. Paul's Kirche. On Reformation Sunday in 1843, they worshiped in their first church building, a log structure on the Near North Side of Chicago.

A later brick church building on the same site was destroyed in 1871 in the Great Chicago Fire, along with the homes of most of the members of the church. These members sold the land on which their homes had been set. That land had become more valuable after the fire as the city development moved north. They purchased cheaper land in the farming community called Lincoln Park, which was farther north in the city, and gave the profit they made to the rebuilding of a new St. Paul's Kirche in 1872 on the foundations of the burned-out structure. The importance of ministry in the city had already become a part of the identity of St. Paul's, and it continued as the church built again in 1898. This time the building was in the Lincoln Park area, where most of the church members had moved after the Great Chicago Fire. However, this 1898 structure was destroyed by yet another fire on Christmas night in 1955. Making a commitment to ministry in the city was demanded again. Even though many churches were moving to the suburbs in the mid-1950s, St. Paul's voted to stay in the city and to rebuild one more time.

Within ten years of that rebuilding, however, Chicago was facing serious urban problems, and these problems affected churches. Membership in city churches was declining dramatically, while the expenses of buildings and ministries grew. By the early 1970s the church had to make some decisions once more concerning its commitment to its urban ministry. These decisions were made, with prayer and some degree of struggle within the congregation, and St. Paul's continued to put its human and financial resources behind a mission that would make a joyful sound in the city. The decisions were faith decisions made with a trust that God still had work for St. Paul's Church to do in the community in which we were located. The decisions were followed with plans for doing that work, but we often found ourselves running in many directions at one time, using resources to respond to every request that came our way. The results were mixed. So in 1982, we launched a strategic-planning process, which included objectives for church growth in our area of the city, an area that included both promise and problems.

Our Mission Today

St. Paul's Church is located in a neighborhood that has undergone regentrification; that is, older houses and apartment buildings have been reclaimed from decay. This process has slowed the move to the suburbs and in some cases reversed that trend. Married people and singles, couples and families have moved in to purchase or rent these dwellings. Most of these people are young, urban professionals; some are people returning to the city after their children have grown and left home. In a study of the neighborhood by the local churches, we discovered that most of these people had a positive response to organized religion but were apathetic about church attendance and actual support. In this setting, the church is just one part of a supermarket of activities and opportunities for the use of a person's time and talents. So, the church-growth question became for us, How do we overcome apathy and elicit a commitment? An additional but just as difficult question was: How do we attract these new people but in a way that continues to recognize the important place of long-term members of our congregation and therefore does not alienate current active members?

We have found some ways to answer these questions. We are not without our problems, but we have grown significantly in strength and in membership. We have done this by entering into a strategic-planning process, and through that process we have found our place in the supermarket of activity and opportunity in which our neighborhood people find themselves, as they shop around for something of value in which to invest their lives.

St. Paul's Church has found its place in people's lives in its worship services. In worship, we have our niche in the value market. Finding a "niche in the market" is a business concept that directs a company in seeking out some particular needs of people and then in developing its product to fill those needs. While business concepts and techniques should not be uncritically adopted by churches, this concept has some importance, particularly for a church that is seeking to attract new people to its ministry but finds itself with limited resources for doing so.

Through our long-range strategic-planning process, we discovered our resources and began to work within our limitations. This provided the impetus for us to develop our own church personality and our niche in the market of activities and options for the investment of people's time and energies. Even though there is a strong appeal to being all things to all people, we realized that no one church can ever accomplish that and be a good steward of the resources entrusted to it. Being all things to all people can cause a church to go in many directions at once, using up resources in a haphazard manner and burning-out its members. When people see no results from all their activity, they tend to give up. When there is no plan or focus for the ministry of a congregation, there are few results that can be celebrated.

There are many ways of being the church in the world. Some congregations emphasize fellowship, small groups, and the close sharing of members one with another; some are focused almost completely on their mission outreach; and some build their ministry around education because they have the resources for doing so. At St. Paul's we found that our building, our staff, our cultural setting, and the particular needs of potential new members in our area led us to finding our niche in worship. It is the service of worship that holds us together as a very diverse congregation in the midst of growth and change. The worship of God is the focus of our life together and the inspiration for our lives apart from one another. Our active worshiping members range in age from thirteen to ninety-three; they are mostly white, but there is a growing racial mixture; they are married, single, widowed, and divorced; some are gay; and some are in families. They are professionals, tradespeople, laborers, and students from nearby universities, and they come from church backgrounds in Roman Catholicism and in all of the Protestant denominations. Because of the great diversity of our membership and because our average worship attendance is currently 400 (with a membership of 835 and a sanctuary that can seat almost 1,000), we are strongly committed to keeping one Sunday morning worship service, at 11 A.M., rather than dividing the congregation into more than one service. Those who attend the twice-monthly German-language service also worship with the full congregation at 11 A.M. It is the worship service, then that is our one unifying factor. Recognizing that as a church we need to have a unifying factor in our life, to prevent our becoming a conglomerate of interest groups with no common purpose and ministry, we worship together as one body.

A Sunday Morning Church

Sunday morning is the one and only time that we can be all together in one place at one time. This makes us a Sunday-morning-centered congregation, which places limitations on our ministry. But it is a fact of life for us. We learned that either we work with this fact of life or expend our energy fighting against it. Beside needing a focus and unifying factor in their lives, churches also need to accept and work within their limitations. This does not mean giving in apathetically to those limitations, using them as excuses for failure, but it does mean finding ways to incorporate limitations into the life and ministry of the church so that they, in fact, add to the uniqueness of that particular church and give it its own personality.

St. Paul's younger members are active in many things. Almost all are employed full-time in demanding jobs. Some travel extensively in their work. They do not have time or energy for many weekday or weeknight meetings or activities. Our older members have the time available, but many of them find transportation a problem, and most choose not to go out at night. So, while there are week-day and evening education, fellowship, mission, and church-com-mittee activities at St. Paul's, our focus for the priority of our time and energy is Sunday morning before, after, and during the wor-ship hour. The church is a lively place of activity on Sunday morn-ing, as the congregation gathers for education, fellowship, and worship. It is this time together that also provides our membership with the impetus for congregational care, service, and mission. This does put a particular burden on Sunday morning, but it is something we have learned to work with in developing our church's place in the neighborhood and in the city.

We have found some ways that Sunday morning can bear the burden placed upon it, and we have discovered that an intentional focus on the Sunday worship hour can attract new people to the mission and ministry of the church. There is little mystery to what we have found. It is a matter of conscious effort—finding the niche and then developing and enriching our contribution, being willing to experiment, celebrating successes and risking some failures.

The Sunday morning worship service at St. Paul's has evolved as the congregation has grown and undergone change. Part of its evolution was also prompted by recognizing the place of the ser-vice in our ministry, in which we are consciously seeking to wel-come new people into our church, people who come from a variety of backgrounds.

Being at Home: The Security of Tradition

We have a traditional Protestant structure to our worship, with elements of praise, confession, pardon, affirmation of faith, scrip-ture, preaching, prayer, thanksgiving, intercession, and offering. This traditional structure is consciously maintained because it pro-vides security and stability. These are as necessary for young people who are leading fast-paced and hectic lives as they are for

252

older adults who find that most of their world is changing around them and little seems familiar anymore. The traditional structure also imparts a sense of "being at home" to people coming from the variety of denominational backgrounds. We have found this important even for those who were disenchanted with the institutional church during high school or college-age years. Stability and familiarity are very much a part of the attraction for new people. Attempting to make everything new and different in the worship service all the time adds to the frenzy of the lives people are living. St. Paul's, along with many other churches, was tempted to do this in the mid-1970s. There seemed to be an "audience" for ever changing worship services, but it proved to be a fickle audience, and the experiment, though necessary, was short-lived. The important questions any church leadership must ask itself as it focuses its resources on the worship service are these:

- What will help new people to "be at home" in the worship service?

- What elements of worship can provide some degree of commonality for people from a variety of denominational backgrounds?

- Does my church have a particular worship tradition or traditions that can be researched and explored and then celebrated in our worship service?

At St. Paul's Church we still feel the influence of the German heritage. In addition to the regular German-language worship service, there are also ways in which we draw the German heritage into the worship life of the full congregation. For example, Reformation Sunday is a festival service for us, and we continue to celebrate *Totenfest* on the last Sunday of the church liturgical year (which is the Sunday before the first Sunday in Advent). This is a service of memorial and thanksgiving for the lives of all those in the congregation who died during the last year.

A worship service that helps new people feel at home and yet highlights particular traditions of a certain church gives to that service a blend of commonality and uniqueness. Because the United Church of Christ is a "united and uniting church," any of its congregations already have some of the qualities of belief and structure that appeal to those who come from a variety of church backgrounds. What can be added to that commonality is the uniqueness of the individual congregation. And there is no better place to highlight the blending of commonality and uniqueness than in the worship service.

While young adults will be repelled by worship that has no life in it and reminded of all that they disliked about the church when they were growing up, they nevertheless are attracted by worship that is rooted in tradition. For many young adults, who are separated from their families and their own heritages, putting down roots in a new community is extremely important. The church can be a place that gives them some roots, and the worship service can be the means of finding those roots in the Christian faith and in a community of faith.

Sunday Morning Surprises

Saying all of this, however, is not to promote uncreative liturgy and unconscious worship. A traditional worship structure need not be dull. In our worship we attempt to have tradition with surprises! Tradition is reinterpreted in order to give it some new meaning or to recover some old meaning that has been lost. The surprises elicit interest from week to week and assist the congregation in interpreting the meaning of the elements of worship. They also help to keep pastors and lay leaders fresh and alert. This, too, is important in attracting new people.

At St. Paul's we plan for some surprises in Sunday morning worship to awaken interest and attention to the praise of God and the offering of our lives to God's will and purpose, but we also make room for unplanned surprises of the Holy Spirit working with us and among us. Our worship, though structured, is not tightly controlled. At times this looseness has challenged pastors, musicians, and lay leaders to be improvisational. Our organist-choirmaster, Sam Hill, is also a jazz musician who is accomplished in the art of improvisation. He has helped all of us to move with a spirit that picks up on what is happening at the moment and directs it toward the enhancement of our worship experience. This sense of improvisation and openness to unplanned surprises has brought to our worship service some humorous moments that kept us from taking ourselves too seriously, and it has also given us some deeply moving experiences. One such moment occurred on a Sunday morning when our organist-choirmaster walked away from the organ as we were singing a hymn and directed the congregation in singing that hymn without accompaniment. The full congregation became the choir, and the singing was followed by a powerful silence and time of reflection. On an Easter Sunday morning, a loaf of communion bread, forgotten in the freezer until minutes before the service, provided one of the humorous moments for us. Frozen bread does not break easily, if at all. After the snickers from the congregation subsided, and the pastor regained some composure, there was a moment of insight into how difficult it can be at times to break bread in communion with others. We as a body of Christ can be frozen in prejudice, resentment, and unwillingness to change. Structured worship can have moments of surprises that bring it alive. It requires a trusting relationship among the worship leaders, an attention to what is happening at the moment, and an attention to the presence of the Spirit of God.

Walking Through a Sunday Morning Service

The best way to gain a sense of the structure-with-surprises in St. Paul's Sunday morning worship service is to "walk through" a service, noting the blending of commonality and uniqueness.

Prelude

As in most traditional worship services, our worship begins with a prelude. This is usually an organ prelude and is most often played by our organist-choirmaster. But it is also a place when other musicians can offer their talents in the worship of God. The prelude is a particularly good place to involve those who may be somewhat inexperienced and shaky before a gathering of people. Since this is the time when people are gathering, the musician is not the object of complete attention. This relieves some of the anxiety. Having musicians in the congregation offer their talents in playing a prelude also gives an immediate impression to new people coming for worship that the talents of members of the congregation are welcomed at this church.

Welcome

At St. Paul's, the prelude is followed by the welcome, which has three parts to it. First, all people are welcomed and invited to the coffee hour after the worship service. Directions to the social hall for the coffee hour are given in the welcome, and they are also included as part of a regular series of announcements printed on the back of the bulletin. Newcomers are invited to fill out a visitor card and drop it in the offering plate or mail it to the church. Every one of these cards is followed up by a pastor with a note or telephone call. Those who indicate a desire to be on the mailing list of the church are sent a current newsletter, and their names are put on the list.

The welcome is also the time when important information is given to the worshiping congregation. If it is a communion Sunday, it is announced that we have an open communion and that a person need not be a member of our congregation to participate. A bulletin announcement also indicates this and informs the new worshiper that we serve communion in the pew (except for special occasions, announced in the welcome, when the congregation comes forward to the table). The announcement also indicates that children may be served communion if they are seated with a parent or other responsible adult who wishes them to be served. We announce that the trays contain both wine and grape juice and that we have both bread and wafers in the plates. Again, all of this is done to make it possible for a variety of people to "be at home" and not to feel like a stranger in the midst of people who know what is going on without having to be told. If we wish to attract first-time worshipers back again, we must never overlook the importance of worship instruction, done orally and in bulletin announcements. New people often arrive early for worship in order to find a back pew and take time to read through the service and the announcements. They do this in order to acquaint themselves with the church and to ease some of their anxieties about being a stranger in a strange land. An uneasy worshiper who feels left out and embarrassed that he or she does not know local customs likely will not return.

A second part of our welcome includes other announcements of the life of the congregation. We do this at the very beginning of the service at St. Paul's for two reasons: (1) There is less of a break in the flow of the worship service by making announcements at this point. The announcements are necessary and valuable, but they can disrupt a service at a later point, calling more attention to ourselves and our programs than to the worship of God. (2) Having the announcements at the very beginning gives another immediate impression to the new worshiper as to the life of the congregation. Both pastors and lay persons make these announcements at St. Paul's.

A third portion of the welcome is the greeting of one another. All worshipers are invited to stand and to introduce themselves to those around them. In this way, visitors are not singled out for attention, but they have a way of meeting other people, giving their name, and telling someone that they are a visitor. The greeting is important for many reasons. It gives worshipers an opportunity to come face-to-face with those around them and to realize that worship is more than "me and my God." We are a community of faith together in worship. The greeting lets newcomers become a little more familiar with their surroundings. And members of the church who meet new persons often invite them to the coffee hour. Because people tend to sit in the same place for worship each week, the visitors begin to "know" some other people around them as they return to worship week after week.

Children and the Call to Worship

After the informality of the welcome and greeting, establishing a sense of "homeyness" in the middle of a formal church sanctuary, there is a shift in mood and feeling. The greeting is followed by a choral introit by the choir from the rear balcony of the church, and the congregation is led in a call to worship. There is a processional hymn as the pastors, choir, acolytes, and communion servers (on communion Sundays) come forward to the chancel. We come into God's presence with praise. But even here, there are some surprises to newcomers to a fairly large congregation worshiping in a formal space according to a traditional structure. The call to worship is led by a child each week. Children are participants in our worship service from the time they are in the first grade in school. In the fall in which the child goes into first grade, he or she is welcomed from the child-care program into the worshiping community and presented with a Bible. This is done on World Communion Sunday each year. The children are not just with us; they are part of us and who we are as a church. We have worship activity packets for the children. They are called "Just for You" packets and they are prepared each week with activities related to the scripture reading for the day. In these packets we also include the children's activity sheets that come with One Great Hour of Sharing and Neighbors in Need offering materials.

The children worship with us, and they also lead us in worship. It is a part of our Christian education program to have children grow up at St. Paul's learning to be worship leaders. In first-grade church-school classes they learn about our worship service and the meanings of the parts of the service. They begin to sing in the children's choir in first grade. Acolytes are fourth graders and older, and they light candles and receive the offering from the ushers and take it to the altar. By the time children reach sixth grade, they can lead in the call to worship. Thus, there is a regular procedure for including the children of the church with increasing responsibility and opportunity as they grow older.

To young parents who are newcomers to the church, the inclusion of children in the leadership of worship marks the church as one that welcomes children and accepts the offering of their talents, too. Sometimes even before these parents discover our church school, they gain a sense that St. Paul's is a place for children. Again, with the worship service as our focus and our niche, we concentrate attention on each element of the service and what it communicates to new people and what it says about our identity and personality as a church. How we worship God communicates to newcomers what we believe about God and about ourselves as a people of God.

Confession and Pardon

We continue our worship with a prayer of confession and assurance of pardon and with the reading of scripture by a lay person. The name of the scripture reader is listed in the worship bulletin along with the names of all the worship leaders for that day: ushers, greeters, acolytes, call-to-worship leader, communion servers, child-care workers, and coffee-hour hosts. In this way, names and faces can be connected providing another means for settings to know one another.

Music

Our worship music is drawn from classical pieces to gospel songs (again recognizing the variety in church backgrounds in the congregation and the resources available to us in our church musicians). Our church choir is made up of singers who are members of professional choruses and people who just like to sing. We use instrumentalists in our congregation who are of junior high age along with members of the Chicago Symphony. Whatever the level of ability, they are all of one mind, to give of their best in the worship of God.

Sermon

For us the sermon can be the focal point of a worship service, or it can be that which points to another portion of the service, helping to interpret that portion. There are times in our worship at St. Paul's when the liturgy is built around the sermon, and there are times when music becomes the center of the Sunday worship. At these times, the sermon can be used to put the music into a context of worship. Once a year we have a Sunday when we celebrate the place of gospel music in the Christian tradition. Because gospel music is not our standard music for worship, we make use of the sermon and other parts of the liturgy also to interpret what we are doing and why. If a church is serious about attracting new people, it must always be conscious of the need to interpret and communicate its message clearly, never assuming that everyone in the congregation speaks the same language of worship.

Because we have three pastors on our staff and other clergy who are available to the church, we make use of the sermon as a resource in church growth, making it possible for clergy other than the senior pastor to preach regularly. There are a variety of gifts in preaching. Making use of different styles and themes in preaching can add to the element of surprise and keep worship fresh.

Offering and Prayer

The final portion of our worship is offering and prayer. As an integral part of the prayer of the church we have the joys and concerns of the congregation. Preceding prayer, worshipers are invited to stand and bring their joy or concern before the congregation. This part of the liturgy also communicates an attention to the lives of the members of the congregation. It is often the impetus for congregational and pastoral care. A person who would feel it an imposition upon the time of a busy pastor to call him or her to tell of a seemingly insignificant concern, may stand and voice that concern in worship. This provides the opportunity for the pastor as well as the other members of the church to make contact with that person.

Within the context of a formal, traditional worship structure, voicing joys and concerns becomes a moment of informality as worshipers come to know one another through the joys and concerns of their lives.

The joys and concerns of the congregation is an element of worship that came directly from the congregation. On a laity Sunday seven years ago, the group of members in charge of that service first introduced this element. Pastors and lay leaders alike were cautious and even skeptical. There were many objections. Some felt that older members would not like it; others said that people would be too intimidated to stand up in that large space with so many others around them; and most believed that, in a large space even if people stood, they would not be heard.

While all of these objections had merit, we decided to experiment. It is now seven years later, and even though the joys and concerns can become lengthy and sometimes trivialized, they are now an integral part of our service. Older members stand and voice joys and concerns as much as younger ones. The belief that other members of the congregation care seems to have overcome the intimidation of the large, formal worship space for most people. We have dealt with the hearing problem by having the pastor who is leading in the joys and concerns repeat each joy or concern from the microphone at the front of the congregation. The pastor also repeats the name of the person bringing the joy or concern. In this way, also, newcomers and members of the congregation come to know one another by name. This is another way that even formal traditional worship can be made less anonymous and generic.

All of the joys and concerns are gathered up as prayers to God. They are prayers of intercession, praise, and thanksgiving. We bring ourselves and our world before God in prayer as we close another Sunday morning at St. Paul's Church, going back into the world on a hymn of praise.

Special Worship Celebrations

Special services of worship can become occasions for testing some of the surprises. The occasion can be a laity Sunday (the time when we tested joys and concerns); it can be a Christmas Eve service or a Good Friday service; it can be a service of communion or baptism or reception of new members. Not everything that is tried and tested works. Some things appear gimmicky and trivial once they are tried, but it often takes trying them to see this. Other things are skeptically given a chance (like our joys and concerns) and prove to be just what is needed to help the congregation in its corporate worship of God.

If worship is to be the focus of a church's ministry and the center of its program for membership growth, then testing is very important, and attention to all details is necessary. Even the informal elements (joys and concerns or welcome and announcements) take care and planning. The corporate worship of a congregation is a complex mix of theology and art. Nothing in the service should be taken lightly. Every element should in some way direct the worshiper toward God in praise, confession, prayer, hearing the call of God, and offering oneself in God's service. The elements and style of worship should not in the first place serve as means to church growth, but they can lead to church growth when worshipers experience a powerful and meaningful presence of God, when they can see and hear and feel something of worth to which they can give their lives and in which they can invest their time and talents. When new worshipers feel that some important ministry is happening in a church, that this ministry is expressed clearly in worship, and that they as new people are welcomed and invited into that ministry, they will return to become a part of the church's life. And with each new member, the church gains in quality as well as in quantity. For every active member of a congregation is a unique gift of God and adds something to the personality of the church.

Building the
Beloved Community

Colonial Church of Edina, Edina, Minnesota

ARTHUR A. ROUNER JR.

The "Colonial company," as its people call it, is a family of about 3,800 adult members gathered, we believe, by the Spirit, in equal parts from the suburban city of Edina, Minnesota, the Twin Cities of Minneapolis and St. Paul, the western and southern suburbs of Minneapolis, and a few out-lying communities. Between thirteen hundred and fifteen hundred people assemble for worship on most Sundays for services at 8:30 and 11:15, with a "gathering hour" for everyone in the period between.

About 250 new members are received annually, including from 60 to 80 ninth-grade confirmation youngsters. The net gain has held steady at about a hundred throughout the forty years of the church's life. More than 2,700 single, mostly divorced people, are members of Singles All Together, with 400 to 700 of them meeting weekly. The high school ministry peaked in the mid 1970s at four hundred young people gathering each Sunday evening. Ten or twelve support groups for the bereaved, for women, for divorced and divorcing persons, for parents of anorexic and bulemic children, and for those in job transition give character to the church's

Arthur A. Rouner Jr. is senior minister of Colonial Church of Edina, Edina, Minnesota. He travels annually to Africa and has raised more than $800,000 in Colonial Church to fight African famine. Rouner has published ten books, lectured at North Park Seminary, Chicago, and preached at Harvard and at Park Street Church in Boston. Religious Heritage of America chose him Clergyman of the Year for 1987.

life. One hundred and twenty-five people sing each Sunday in the Colonial Chorale and give endless hours to Lenten productions of the Last Supper and the Triumph of Christ and the Christmas programs *King of Love*, Christmas hymn sing, and service of lessons and carols.

Physically, the Colonial company is housed in a "New England village" of gray-stained clapboard with white trim, dominated by a graceful, free-standing spire and bell tower, and a "meetinghouse." The meetinghouse holds a thousand people gathered on three sides around a high, center pulpit and wide platform holding a simple table and benches for the deacons. A three-sided balcony wraps round the room to bring the whole congregation close to the center of worship. The "Common," a room named for the Pilgrims' first governor, John Carver, dominated by a great fireplace, is crowded after each service with people in close conversation. They are trying also to be on the lookout for new people who have come to visit.

Building Bridges

Colonial Church was founded in 1946 by Kenneth E. Seim, who remained its pastor for fourteen years and was followed by a two-year interim pastor. Colonial in the early 1960s was a church of high potential, but its fifteen hundred members were greatly troubled. They had been full of anger over polity. When the United Church of Christ was formed, more than eight hundred people had voted on whether to join the merger. Many had feared that joining would mean a loss of independence, an issue that resulted in much politicking and many residual wounds, after the decision not to join had been reached. The church had sought a minister who would be clearly a Congregationalist, a lover of the Pilgrim way, but who would also have sufficient breadth of spirit to work with, love, and engage the large number who had voted for the merger and lost.

I arrived in 1962, a young minister of thirty-three. My background was New England Congregationalist—as a Congregationalist minister's son in Portsmouth, New Hampshire; a product of New England schools and colleges, as well as Union Theological Seminary in New York; and a minister in two New England churches. So I came to Colonial as a Congregationalist with a mandate to heal the wounds and build a "new" Colonial Church—in spirit, unity, and hope.

We chose a road of independence from both the United Church and the National Association of Congregational Christian Churches, but we continued membership in the Minnesota Conference, which later joined the UCC, and we joined the Minnesota Fellowship of Congregationalists. I asked that I be sent to the NACCC's annual meeting and the UCC's General Synod as a visible and personal bridge. This policy was our effort to keep in touch with the two modern houses of historic Congregationalism in the United States. It gave us room to grow and respond as the Spirit might lead us in the next twenty years. We hoped to have influence on both groups and to show our good faith by making reasonable, if not proportional, gifts to both of them.

In the course of time, we became a bridge church in other ways. We were a bridge between theological conservatives and theological liberals. We were a bridge between white and black and between rich and poor. In the mid '60s I wrote a book called *The Free Church Today: A New Life for the Whole Church* to offer the principle of the gathered church as a radically different basis for denominational relationship. Bishop Gerald Kennedy wrote the foreword, and it was published by the YMCA's Association Press. We were trying to offer ourselves as an ecumenical bridge not only between the UCC and the NACCC but also as a home for seekers of many denominations and no denominations. As time has gone on, Colonial has received a number of street people and ex-prisoners (resulting particularly from our three prison ministries). We receive an increasing number of former Roman Catholics as well as many people who have not been part of any church for ten to twenty years.

Responding to National Issues and Community Need

Church polity was not the only issue troubling Colonial Church in those years. The 1950s, marked by the postwar growth of suburbs and the deceptive growth of churches, were over. In the tumultuous, wrenching 1960s, the "torch handed to a new generation of Americans" was soon consumed in the conflagrations in the streets where the younger brothers and sisters of that generation fought to bend America's institutions toward justice and mercy. The ecumenical movement in its race to organize Protestantism into one great monolithic church was scuttled in those same streets. The reason was that as black and white, priests and ministers, young and old marched together at Selma and registered voters in Hattiesburg, the denominations were together. The Holy Spirit brought them together. They didn't need the organizing of the ecumenical diplomats. Something else, rending and creative, was happening.

For Colonial Church, the heart of it all was Jesus. Whatever else we needed, we knew we needed that. In addition, I felt a moral claim personally and a strategic and spiritual necessity ecclesiastically, for Colonial as an institution to respond to the painful issues of that increasingly tense and finally violent decade.

National Issues

We struggled publicly with the assassination of President John Kennedy, conducting a memorial service that evening in October of 1963. Later we did the same for Robert Kennedy. We prayed publicly, and some felt, interminably, for Mrs. Kennedy and her children.

On the day after Martin Luther King Jr. was assassinated, the superintendent of schools wanted to have a high school assembly to acknowledge the awful thing that had happened. He called me to come and say a word because he knew I cared; he knew where Colonial stood.

When the local Council of Churches bid congregations join in a newspaper advertisement declaring our churches racially open, Colonial took the suggestion to church meeting and lost. A year later it was brought to a vote, and Colonial unanimously declared itself an open church in fellowship and membership to people of all races. In the summer of 1968 we deliberately invited a black minister from Memphis, who had participated in the sanitation workers' strike that climaxed in brother Martin's death, to come and live in our parsonage and be our summer preacher for a month. We lost only two families over that issue, and we gained wide community respect.

As I began accompanying first one and then another young man to the draft board to testify for conscientious objector status, the church—again in open church meeting, according to the Congregational way, which we were struggling to recover and live out—declared unanimously its support spiritually for these young men as well as for those who chose to do military service.

We cried out against the United States invasion of Cambodia during Richard Nixon's presidency. When the University of Minnesota went on strike, a whole corps of striking students were invited by Colonial's trustees to set up an office in our building as a headquarters from which they could fan out two by two to teach and witness to the suburban people of power about their deep concerns for their country.

Later, when the high school went on strike for a day to protest the invasion of Cambodia, the students invited me to address them at their rally on the football field because they knew where Colonial and I stood. It didn't make the chairman of the school board, a member of Colonial Church, very happy, but hundreds of young people knew that Colonial Church was on their side and cared about the issues of the world and, more important for our growth, cared about young people.

The vision of mission was born with the work of the Viet Nam doctor James Turpin and Project Concern, in whose Walk for Mankind I participate still, as an annual rite of spring. Twenty-five percent of our budget annually was committed to mission, and this figure has been increased to 30 percent. So we grew from a few thousand dollars to about $600,000 annually.

In 1981 the World Vision relief organization said, "People are dying in the Horn of Africa. Will you come over and help us?" Through controversy and struggle the decision was made to go. Five churches, represented by sixteen people, made the journey in early February of 1982 to a remote area of Kenya known as West Pokot. In the village of Kiwawa, famine had stalked silently through the hills. A thousand people were fed daily in the little mission of Dick and Jane Hamilton of the Associated Christian Churches of Kenya. We were challenged to raise $250,000 in our suburb, and after forming our own corporation, Christian Volunteers of Minnesota, the five churches raised on Easter Sunday 1982, $369,000. Each year thereafter we have raised another $200,000. Colonial's share each year has been about $100,000.

The second year our Edina team went into northern Ethiopia before the depth of the famine became as dramatically known as it did suddenly, in the fall of 1984.

"Africa" has become a matter of high identity and deep heart for Colonial Church. The team's return each year, with their pictures of themselves ministering in those far places created the sense that Africa was ours—our people, our land, our mission. And more and more people dream of themselves going.

Our heeding of the "call from Macedonia" to respond to the need of the dying in the famine in Africa has had a deeply renewing effect on the life of Colonial Church. It has also brought us into a closer relationship with our sister churches of other denominations in town that have shared with us in that vision and venture. I am trying to share that abroad, in a book in progress titled *African Hunger: Journey of the Heart*.

The fact that Colonial dared to reach out beyond itself and its suburb to the Third World to the extent of going to Africa each year and raising about $100,000 each Easter for the famine and for development projects, has conveyed a message to visitors that we are not bound by the mind-set of affluence and of safety in the suburbs. It has made Colonial yet again controversial but at the same time intriguing and compelling. Those who have seen our beautiful New England village from their cars on the Crosstown Highway and wanted to visit us may have feared we might be exclusive and forbidding. But they have found us trying to be a people of love with a heart for the whole world and especially for Jesus' "least of these."

Community Needs

Colonial Church has been concerned about the local community as well as the wider world. When I arrived in 1962, all manner of community organizations held regular meetings in Colonial's facilities. The nursery school was in full swing, and the Boy Scouts, Girl Scouts, and Cub Scouts, as well as the Garden Club flower show, used Colonial's building.

As the streets of our own city erupted in the '60's we tried to respond—very much along the lines of Gibson Winter's proposal of pie-shaped sectors in *The Suburban Captivity of the Churches*. We actively campaigned in 1963 for the Minneapolis City Hospital to become a county hospital, with the suburbs helping to pay for the care of "all those drunks." When the juvenile court judge declared teenage girls' delinquency as a major problem that churches should address with housing, Colonial worked on a project in cooperation with the Volunteers of America and the State Corrections Department to buy and establish The Colonial Residence for Girls.

We gradually established a weekly prison ministry in our federal prison and two local monthly prison ministries. Street people began coming to Colonial. A half-dozen ex-prisoners are members of our church now. To meet the problem of rebelling youth, we gave the first funding for the City, a street academy. Our youngsters opened a high school teen center, held junior high dances at the church, and developed the Colony, a drop-in center for junior high students. Out of that came the Reborn Group—a teenage Alcoholics Anonymous for more than two hundred young alcoholics and drug addicts. We funded for an inner-city UCC church the first interracial nursery school, which still functions. We helped fund Wayside House for alcoholic women. We established the self-help Lower Sioux Indian Pottery project. We established a sister relationship with an inner-city black church, one of whose members has now become chancellor of the New York City public school system. Our deacons met with their deacons. We became friends. We were known by Hennepin County Welfare as a company sincerely ready to help them, which we still do.

Closer even than the community is the home. One of the most painful issues we address concerns the family—especially the areas of sex and marriage. These areas have come up continually in my counseling and care for the flock. In the 1970s I tried to articulate Colonial's and my views of marriage and its sanctity in *Marryin' Sam Speaks Out*, a little book written partly in protest against what the sexual revolution was doing to all of us and our society. It was followed by *How to Love* and *Struggling with Sex*. These books are an attempt to share our concerns and what we see as the answer for the sexual struggles of all people and especially single people today.

Spiritual Growth

Colonial Church has developed inwardly as well as outwardly. Our worship and common life together have continually called people to personal commitment to Christ and to a covenant relationship with the local congregation as a family of faith. The fellowship is critical to us, and we ask people to make that commitment very seriously. My book of sermons, *Master of Men*, with a foreword by Robert McCracken of Riverside Church, New York, my former teacher, was an attempt to show a picture of the relationship that followers can have with Jesus as it is revealed in the New Testament.

Prayer has long been a high commitment in Colonial's life. As our support groups and counseling ministry grew, we held regular "schools of prayer." We formed a prayer chain that has functioned every weekday for twenty years, and we named people in prayers of intercession each Sunday. I shared our different kinds of prayers in a book called *Someone's Praying, Lord*, for which James S. Steward of Scotland, my New Testament teacher and friend, wrote the foreword. We hold healing services. In my book *Healing Your Hurts*, I try to offer mainline churches an avenue into the ministry of Christian healing, which has become a vital part of Colonial's ministry. Sunday morning and evening we give altar calls for commitment to Christ, and we celebrate Pentecost by speaking in tongues. The Cursillo, Bible Study Fellowship, and Young Life movements have touched hundreds of our people.

In the early 1970s the Pentecostal-Charismatic revival came to Colonial through my own baptism with the Holy Spirit at the hands of a Lutheran minister at a Catholic university. My sabbatical journey of 1972 was a seeking of the Spirit—a kind of follow-up to the breakthrough into love that had been happening to Colonial as a Christian company since the summer of 1968.

Summer preachers came and influenced our life: Howard Thurman, George Buttrick, John Bennett, James Cleveland, David Torrance, and a cluster of English ministers.

A series of lectureships through the years has brought Robert Lee, Father John Powell, Bruce Larson, William Stringfellow, Henri Nowen, and M. Scott Peck, who have shared in molding the vision and mission of this Colonial company.

From early in my ministry the Holy Spirit has been a deep concern for me. Pitney VanDusen at Union Seminary once told me he viewed it as the most neglected doctrine of twentieth-century Christianity. Precisely that has been the growing edge of Christian renewal in the late '50s and early '60s and in all the years since. My book *Receiving the Spirit at Old First Church* was a description of Colonial's and my spiritual journey toward the baptism of the Holy Spirit and the advent of a conscious opening to all the gifts of the Holy Spirit and the whole renewal of the church that Colonial had experienced.

In every way we can, we are trying to help people be open to the miraculous, to the invading power of God, and to the infinite possibilities for the spiritual renewal of churches. We have tried to witness to the possibility and reality of any church becoming a live church.

A Growing Church

Constant increase in the membership of Colonial Church, in program ministries, and in maturity as a Christian body has come out of our philosophy of church life and mission. At no time have we been very successful in mounting campaigns for programs designed specifically to increase church membership or to win the community to Christ or to Colonial. No evangelism explosions, or door-to-door witnessing, or worship services in public places have been part of the annual arrival of about 250 people in Colonial's life.

Clearly, Colonial was formed originally by a canvass of the community and by personal invitations to people to join this church that was being established according to the free tradition of the Congregational way. That freedom itself was a powerful attraction to a fair number of strongly independent, professional, corporate people who became the early members. Very early on, a commitment was made to be a community church and to serve the community.

A Caring Church

In the early 1960s it seemed very important that Colonial, as a church, clearly establish itself as an institution that cared about people. That meant first, that in preaching we began to deal very directly with the great human issues of those tumultuous years. We began praying aloud for individuals, by name, in the public prayers. We prayed for world and national leaders, for politicians and protestors.

I preached about issues—racial justice, peace and conscientious objection to war, greed, suburban responsibility for the city. Some of us worked actively in the movement to make the Minneapolis city hospital a county hospital. My sermon about suburban responsibility, "Behold the City," referring to Jesus weeping over Jerusalem, was circulated downtown in that campaign. Our city's management was horrified that the new, young minister over at Colonial was working so obviously against the interest of our suburb.

But we dwelt on the theme "of him who hath, much shall be required." We were the privileged, the poor of the city were not, and we were obliged—having taken our wealth out of the city—to invest in the city in human compassion. We could do no less as Christians.

I worked very hard at being the pastor to this flock. I tried to be wherever I could intercept people at their work and in their homes. I made clear in sermons and our schools of prayer that I believed the sick could be healed through prayer. But particularly, I made it clear that the hospital ministry was critically important and that I would do it. In the early years I visited all our sick members in hospitals all across the Twin Cities three days a week. As our staff grew, I shared that role with one other person so that I went out, as I still do, on Monday and Friday afternoons, and another staff person—now our director of pastoral care (our "Mother Superior" and chief "lover")—went on Wednesday afternoons. A handful of five women who had once been deacons visited our hospital people every Thursday afternoon. So we have reached people at a critical time of pain and fear. It began to be noised about that Colonial cared about the sick.

For years I tried to go visiting nursing homes each Tuesday afternoon. That is done now entirely by women deacons. Every shut-in or nursing-home patient is visited once a month.

On Thursdays I called ahead and went to visit business people in their offices about town in the afternoon. It was just a quick call, but they felt complimented that their minister would actually come to their office. They would proudly show me around. Often, we'd have a prayer before I left.

We worked hard at funerals and at caring for people in grief. I still try to go to every home after a death has come, whether we have done the service or not.

I also tried to pay attention to people after church—to pray for them on the spot if they needed it, what one woman called "Colonial curbside service." Today, in Lent we invite people to come forward at the end of worship for personal prayer.

We try to go when there is a crisis. We did much more going out to people in the early years, for example, our many projects in the inner city and our work with youth. Now people wander into the church all the time, and we have many opportunities to help them. If there is a human need that we can fill, we try to do it, as our response to the call of Christ to minister "to the least of these, My brothers."

Our rate of growth has never seemed to change through the years. During the most disruptive period of social change we tried consistently to address the issues in our public worship together, in preaching and in prayer, and to take action where we could. To our surprise, we began to realize we were growing because of our honest dealing with the issues, not in spite of it. There was often controversy and even dire threats. But if people left the church over one issue or other, more people came because they learned that we cared. That perception has been one of the strongest elements in Colonial's gradual creating of a persona, first in Edina, then across the Twin Cities and the state, and now far beyond.

But I believe that the reason for our steady growth, particularly during those tumultuous years of the '60s and early '70s, was that we clearly proclaimed and tried to live an evangelical theology centered on the love of a personal Christ who could be known and served. I suppose we became a genteel version of the Jesus movement. We even went through a period of long hair and beads, with the local minister being identified by the local police as "the hippie minister."

Clearly, people long to be loved. With emphasis in worship on the Person of Jesus and his call to love, a curious late '60s breakthrough came in Colonial's life, a breakthrough into a widely felt sense of community, of being a people of love. New members testified that on the first day they walked through Colonial's front door they felt an atmosphere of love.

We began to symbolize that feeling in the later '60s by making a custom of holding hands as an entire congregation during the benediction at each service. Like the Puritans, we created a noisy interlude early in the service of people turning about and greeting one another with a hug and even a "holy kiss." We clapped. We introduced visitors. We prayed with the laying on of hands for anyone going out on mission from our midst. After 1972 and my own search for the Spirit and baptism with the Holy Spirit, on each Sunday, we have invited the people to stand, as the early New England Puritans did, with hands raised, during the opening prayer and while the Great Bell was being rung. So Colonial was not only a social-justice church, but it became more and more evidently both an evangelical and a Pentecostal or charismatic "Spirit" church. I did a great deal of teaching about the Holy Spirit to try to help that experience be naturally incorporated into our life.

More and more, Colonial came to be know and experienced as a place where people would be loved. It was a place to cry, a place where a great deal of pain and hurt were felt, but where those pains and hurts were dealt with, both in the spirit of the church and in the specific offer of healing through prayer and care.

A Confessional Style

In the late 1960s there was a significant break in my own life as the minister—a period of struggle and pain that significantly changed my ministry. I had to face my own darkness and seek repentance and healing. Out of that experience came a much more confessional style of preaching. To be honest with myself and with

God I had to tell the truth about all of life more bravely. I had to dare to run risks in my teaching and preaching and lifting up of concerns and proposing directions for the church. And I had to make it clear that I preached to myself first: that I knew myself to be a sinner like my brothers and sisters and that I had no claim or presumption on "high and mightiness" or, if you will, the "magisterial ministry." I was a sinner among sinners, and I had to let people know that and know that I was coming to them in a spirit of confession and humility and need for them.

I found, in fact, that I was better able to love them and heal them. Suddenly, I much better knew their hearts.

So, our healing ministry became deeper. The offers of healing and requests for healing became much more obvious. During the season of Lent it is a regular custom to invite any who seek personal prayer to come forward at the conclusion of the morning worship services and receive prayer with the laying on of hands. The tears and the offer of prayer are perfectly obvious to the rest of the congregation and are widely accepted as part of what our ministry is about. Deacons often hover near to hug or hold or join in prayers or at least offer Kleenex to dry the tears. A woman visitor observed recently: "They don't play church here, do they?"

Since my own experience of the baptism with the Holy Spirit, I have felt it important to celebrate Pentecost Sunday with free expressions of the Spirit including speaking in tongues and physical movement. At times it has seemed right to make speaking in tongues a part of Sunday morning's pastoral prayer. Far from being an offense, it is often noted as a point of inspiration and beauty.

Growing Ministries

Over the years our ministries have flourished and increased. One of the city magazines included us a few years ago as one of those places of "Super Worship" in the Twin Cities. Our worship resembles the appearance and spirit of early Puritan worship with the ministers in academic robes and Geneva bands. Besides the ringing of the Great Bell early in the service and the greeting of one another with hugs and kisses and kindly words, we invite everyone to reach out during the benediction and take hands with, or fling an arm around, the person on either side. Everyone does. It has become a mark of our life.

For a decade our ministry with young people was known in many parts of the country—four hundred high school youngsters showed up each Sunday evening for Pilgrim Fellowship. It was a pioneer mission and service that attracted scores of teenagers from every religious tradition or none at all. Today that ministry attracts perhaps eighty teenagers on a Sunday evening. But other specialty ministries have developed.

The ministry to singles has boomed. Five hundred to seven hundred single people come to our village each Thursday evening. Another 75 to 125 come on Sunday evenings for a program conducted on a more spiritual foundation.

We have support groups including a counseling center staffed by three full-time, trained counselors, and two spiritual directors are a feature of our doubled building space. Added to the program is now the first National Childhood Grief Institute.

Beneath all this is the reality of the church felt and experienced as the "beloved community." That spirit pervades all else that we do, and it has had as much as anything to do with the continuing growth of the Colonial Church.

The New Land and the New Church

Since 1982 Colonial Church has grown in numbers, mission, and spirit in an unusual way because of sense of being a new church in a new land.

After a ten-year struggle of plans, preparation, and long, agonizing church meetings, the Colonial company, in January 1979, left its Georgian building on Wooddale Avenue near the earliest beginnings of Edina's life. We departed after the third service of the morning carrying the Pulpit Bible, communion ware, covenant, other documents, and our own small "Plymouth Rock" (hand-carried by one of our members from Plymouth, Massachusetts). Singing as we went, we walked a thousand strong, the two and one half miles across town to our own "new land" at Tracy by the Pond, 1,000 feet from the geographical center of Edina and strategically placed on the northwest corner of the major intersection formed by Crosstown Highway and Tracy Avenue.

After being taken to Boston and Cape Cod to see the meetinghouse form of church architecture, our architect finally said, "I will build for you what the Pilgrims would have built if they were alive today." We said, "We are." And he did. The West Parish Church in West Barnstable, a 1717 Puritan meetinghouse of exquisite proportion, was the inspiration for Colonial's double-truss-and-beam gray-stained clapboard set of five buildings and a free-standing bell tower and spire. The complex later won an honor award of the American Institute of Architects and appeared on the cover of *Time* and *U.S. News and World Report*.

Another three hundred people awaited us when we arrived in the new land that January Sunday. A horse-drawn haywagon with a crowd of children and the sacred documents concluded a procession led by Paul Revere on horseback, the ministers in academic gowns, and members of Pilgrim Fellowship carrying flags. Speeches in the Governor John Carver Common and a picnic lunch in the South Common were followed by our first communion service in mid-afternoon. A prayer vigil had prepared us for the journey, and another was held before our official dedication.

The new spaces were beautiful and the buildings "worked." The architect's New England village made an immediate impact on the community of Edina and became a landmark in the Twin Cities. At last we had been given a cathedral setting for a ministry that had become more and more a cathedral ministry with a metropolitan influence. The setting was now appropriate to what we were really doing—to our inner city concerns, our missionary enterprise, our ministry to diverse people, our building of theological, economic, social, and racial bridges.

And yet, despite the looming majesty of the buildings that took the community by storm, Colonial Church more and more clearly became known as a place of love. This church's most dramatic growth has come since 1981.

I believe because we didn't give up on our African mission and have continued to care about the people of Kenya and Ethiopia, God has blessed our whole life as a church. Suddenly, our support groups were drawing people from all over the Twin Cities. The huge Singles All Together group, founded a decade earlier, reached its present immense size. Our first full-time music minister came to us, and a choir of 125 voices sings regularly. The youth ministry spawned other ministries all over our community. Two summer camps were established. Healings happened in the weekly Sunday evening sunset healing service.

Increasingly the Holy Spirit was understood, welcomed, and claimed, and many lives were changed. Our Bible studies drew people from across the community. And always the mission went out. Since the 1960s the church has given 25 percent of its working budget each year to missions. Colonial knows itself to be a world church, which is to say, the people think in world terms and seek in their prayers and concern to embrace the world.

The community itself sees us now as a different kind of asset. Though a thorn in its side in spiritual and moral challenges, we have become a force for good and a place of grace and beauty. Many people look to Colonial for their worship on the high holidays. Our Pilgrim historic recall services on Thanksgiving are always captured on local television news, and the community comes in increasing numbers. It is a day on which Colonial teaches the community about America's roots in the Pilgrim-Puritan ethos.

Our Independence Day services, with flags and bunting, brass band and reading of the Declaration of Independence, is another day for teaching our heritage. Our Christmas Eve candlelight service and Easter sunrise service on the hill are other ways Colonial serves the community.

With encouragement from the UCC's Board for Homeland Ministries, a television ministry has fought for a place in our life, and two thirteen-week series of half-hour programs have reached out to late-night people on television, bringing an even more widely diverse group into our life.

Many groups want to come and be sheltered under Colonial's wing. The great evangelical movements of our time have crossed and recrossed Colonial's life and left their mark upon us: the Cursillo movement, the Bible Study Fellowship movement, Youth Life, Campus Crusade, InterVarsity Christian Fellowship, the Youth Conflict Seminars, Marriage Enrichment, the Church Growth movement.

And so this Congregational church has grown, consciously seeing itself as fulfilling in its own time the original seventeenth-century Puritan vision of the "Errand into the Wilderness." We see ourselves as planted strategically in the center of the American wilderness today—in the spiritual wilderness of our time, and in what easterners might think of as the physical wilderness of a cold, northern climate, next to the Canadian border where the Chinooks come through and the prairie is bleak. It is, in fact, a beautiful land of pristine lakes and pines, where the determined will of the down Maine pioneers and the lively faith of the hardy immigrants from Sweden, Norway, and Germany who followed them have made this place a creative confluence of forces for good. The ideal of service and of sharing runs high here. And Edina is set in the center of that creativity: a suburb of people of great energy, education, wealth, and ability, who love to be first.

The challenge of Colonial Church is in the appeal to them to be first in doing good, in serving others, in changing the world for

God. Colonial lives in a strange counterpoint with this community. It is physically a beautiful gem in the community, and yet it is a witness to the love of Jesus that in many ways stands over against the community. Colonial calls people to the inner city, to the prisons, to the marketplace, to Africa—now even, to South Africa.

We fought for that role. In the early years it made the community uncomfortable. But Colonial has not gone away. It has been consistent. Many trust us now. And still people come: hurting people, lonely people, seeking people, some young families. Our nature is changing. But we are growing.

We believe we live in a day beyond denominations. Those loyalties mean little to the people of this age of "do it yourself" religion. These are not good days for bishops and prayer books and church law. They are very good days for congregations that are whole and alive, who proclaim Jesus, love one another, and serve the world. People go where they find help. Local churches are called to embrace all these people, to take them seriously, and to give them a home, and a relationship, and a family, and a purpose. And, most of all, a Lord to serve and love.

The people coming now want Jesus and an open spirit and the reality of love. They want the Bible. And they want justice and service to others and passion. And probably, they want in their church, independence. They want authority and direction and leadership and teaching and decision to be right there among them, not handed down from headquarters. Without knowing it, these people are essential Congregationalists. The UCC has a wonderful heritage to offer them—of independence, of evangelical beginnings in Puritanism, and of the social passion that has always characterized the Congregational way.

The Homeland Board in its Project Proclamation said essentially, "The local church is the front line. It is here that an impact is going to be made locally." That is the right direction. It goes back to the Congregational genius of making the people responsible for doing ministry or mission themselves and for being attuned together to the leading of God in mission. Ours is a great missionary heritage. Keeping that alive is a way of keeping the church growing.

What we need in Colonial Church is a heart of daring, the ability to evangelize unashamedly: to do just what the political workers do—call people up and ask them to be interested in their candidates. We could do the same, for Jesus. We're going to try. It will reach many and heal them. It will also reach them for Jesus.

278

The hope, for churches of our way, is that we reclaim our Pilgrim and Puritan heritage of democracy and personal responsibility and offer American a new and vital faith, a new seriousness about Jesus, a new reality in prayer, a new power in proclamation, a new commitment to serve the world, and a new power to love all people. Under that vision, we all will grow again.

Growing by Giving Yourself Away

Church of the Beatitudes, Phoenix, Arizona

CULVER H. NELSON

"Explosive" is the only word by which to describe the beginnings of Church of the Beatitudes in Phoenix. After World War II, the desert country of the Southwest was flooded with war-weary Easterners escaping the Snowbelt. They regarded Phoenix as a sort of new Jerusalem. The First Congregational Church and Encanto Community Church established a mission church to serve the burgeoning population on the northern edge of town. From the day of that church's gathering in 1954, and for two years thereafter, twelve persons were received into membership every Sunday morning. It was a heady experience for a young pastor. As well, it shaped the character of the church's methods and ministry.

This church has been able to adapt quickly and easily to new circumstances. It has never resisted experimentation with new programs. It has generally been prompt in integrating new members. And an attitude has grown that suggests that: we never fail at anything! We merely discover something now and then that doesn't work, and we learn from the discovery.

Culver H. Nelson is founding minister and senior minister of Church of the Beatitudes, Phoenix, Arizona. He has taught at the Pacific School of Religion, Berkeley, California, and been an officer for the Southwest Conference of the United Church of Christ. He helped organize the interfaith North Phoenix Corporate Ministry and has served as a director of many community organizations. Nelson has written many articles and a book.

"Serendipity," Horace Walpole called it! "Predestination," Calvin insisted! "Fate," concluded Marcus Aurelius, who added, "Whatever happens at all happens as it should." I'm no doctrinaire Calvinist, much less a fatalist, but it is uncanny how often in the life of this church things "have happened as they should."

Church of the Beatitudes is a history of good timing, of a satisfying match between pastor and people, and of a highly visible relationship between the church and the community. If one, therefore, must give credit for what has happened here, other than to the good Lord, it must be shared among all these "timely" elements.

A Good Place to Begin

Six years in an earlier pastorate shaped my own readiness to accept the bewildering cognomen, "founding minister." And, the advance work and friendly welcome afforded by Fred Barnhill, then pastor of First Congregational Church, shaped the readiness of the neighborhood area into which our church was to come. Barnhill not only offered many of the resources of First Church but encouraged about a dozen of its families to form a ready nucleus for the new congregation. A three-and-a-half acre site in a prime location had been purchased, which meant the new church would be highly visible in a growing neighborhood. What is now the Board for Homeland Ministries provided the necessary loan.

I was not the first minister to be considered for this task. Another had declined the invitation, explaining that "there's no potential in such a desert community." I recall telling my friends that he may have been right. In Phoenix, no one is afraid of dying and going to hell in the summer; and no one wants to die and go to heaven in the winter! This "product vulnerability," however, did not at all handicap our growth.

I had spent the previous five years in Pacoima in the San Fernando Valley, where I had built a congregation of about fifteen to more than six hundred and relocated and built a new church plant. That was incredible preparation for tackling a new-church start in Phoenix.

Pacoima was a working-class area in a drab Los Angeles suburb: Phoenix was a dynamic, middle-class community of business and professional people. Pacoima was a transition community: Phoenix was a community in transition. In Pacoima people wanted to get a start and leave; in Phoenix they wanted to become established and stay! Nothing could have better prepared me for the task of "handling change and transition" comfortably.

My wife and I arrived in August 1954. Everything was hot, including the prospects for a new church. I was invited to preach in two local congregations as a way of giving visibility to the idea of a new church. I was given freedom to recruit laity from First Church, who would conduct a door-to-door neighborhood survey, mostly just asking people their religious preference, and leaving a throw-away announcement of the new church.

From the results of that survey, I called on every unattached family of our approximate religious persuasion in the area. A month later, on the first Sunday in October, we held our first worship service with a hundred in attendance; and fifty-four joined the church.

If a building can take credit for a church's growth, Bud Brown's Barn is that building! Brown and his wife joined the church that first Sunday and, as well, gave us the free use of their "Barn," really a museum of Western memorabilia, where frontier dinners and square dances were held. In this colorful setting, we created a house of worship every Sunday morning. We worshiped there for sixteen months and held church-school class under the largest branding iron collection in the world, neatly suspended from the ceiling. Children often dragged their parents to church—it was that kind of place—and the biblical notion came true that a little child led them.

From October to January, the emphasis was on visibility and growth. The openness to new ideas and new ways of doing things began then and has remained ever since. I visited all potential new members in their homes. A choir was organized under my wife's skilled musical leadership—she become our minister of music and continued so over many years. A small board of trustees was created, mostly by pastoral fiat, until the church could be organized more formally. We were hesitant to create a constitution. We decided instead to create the church and then describe what it was we were doing and call that the constitution. Not a bad idea.

Energetic Visibility

Our emphasis was simple: energetic visibility! Each new member was given some task to do. And each person was assigned a neighbor or friend to bring to worship: each one reach one!

I enlisted the laity in one more task—to help me as pastor to become visible. They did, and I spoke or prayed at more community gatherings that winter and spring than seems possible in retrospect: Parent Teachers' Association, Boy Scouts, Girl Scouts, Camp Fire Girls, Rotary, Kiwanis, Women's Club, neighborhood gatherings, a political meeting, and an educational conference. I gave book reviews and banquet talks, and anyone who wanted a minister got one! I even blessed a new post office. The church members clearly understood what this was all about and made it possible; by the end of my first year, I was a reasonably well-known minister in Phoenix.

There are those who make fun of what has been called the "preacher's barrel," his or her backlog of sermons preached earlier. There are those who insist a minister should not rely upon this barrel. The fact is, my backlog of both preaching and teaching materials from my earlier pastorate was invaluable. Of course, I revised and edited, but I used these earlier materials in my first two years in Phoenix. And this gave me added time to pursue organizational needs, visit people's homes, and be available for the visibility every new-church pastor should seek. Finally, of inestimable importance: my wife, Dee, not only served as minister of music but gave me the support and freedom to pursue an eighty-hour week . . . for a while!

Minimal Organization

In the earliest phase of our church's development, we deliberately kept organizational structure simple. Decision making was never prolonged, and, as pastor, I was given wide latitude. Pastor and people develop creative organization out of mutual trust, and nothing can take the place of that primary relationship.

For our first few years, we concentrated on function not office. No one was interested in creating a committee unless there was a specific task to be done. Committees too often "make work." No one, or almost no one, was concerned about rules but only about relationships. That mood continues to this day.

But we had to close the charter and enter the lists of the Congregational fellowship. We did so in January 1955, about four months after our first worship service. Two months later, on Palm Sunday, and six months into the life of our church, we received our three hundredth church member.

I had chosen to receive new members every Sunday morning. It kept me alert, no less than the congregation, to our need for constant growth in the beginning. It also kept spirits high. And within four years we were a congregation of a thousand members and still growing rapidly.

This is why I have placed an absolute priority upon worship! This is why I spend fully twenty hours a week, direct or indirect, in sermon preparation. I have never been content with excuses for mediocrity in worship. However, I do not consider "administration" a dirty word, as some pastors have tended to do. Good administration becomes good pastoral work, and in my experience, a well-run church tends to produce a healthy and imaginative congregation. A church is not a business but ought to be run in a businesslike way. Nor need this requirement, in any way, inhibit a congregation's passion for social justice and community involvement.

Settling In and Building

Fifteen months after we had begun in Bud Brown's Barn, we called an associate pastor, and a long, collegial relationship was begun. The month following, we moved into the first unit of our new church home at Seventh Avenue and Glendale, an all-purpose hall, which served as our sanctuary. A month later, we built an additional small wing as a kind of youth facility. Within two more years, we were ready to build again—the North Wing. Thus a pattern was set for development in which our members have never felt, "At last, we've arrived!" Even in our pattern of building, there was a mentality of openness to continued growth and development, a kind of a "pilgrim" thing!

Our very first unit was financed with a loan from what is now the Board for Homeland Ministries after a successful pledge effort among our own members. Thereafter, our church has successfully sought community financing. Further, we had a special building-fund campaign in the spring of our first year, but thereafter by constant emphasis, we built three further phases of our church plant by depending only on enhanced regular giving. Only when we came to our sanctuary did we again have a special building-fund campaign.

In the late 1950s we continued with new construction, erecting a large, two-story building for education. In the late 1960s we built a home for the elderly (described below) and enlarged our fellowship hall to accommodate a growing congregation on Sundays and community groups during the week.

In 1972, after years of planning and fund raising, we completed our house of worship. This spare, dignified santuary was built on the assumption that we would have two worship services on Sundays, and it seats, depending on the occasion, from seven hundred to one thousand. Our fellowship hall, so long used for every sort of gathering, was now converted to its original purpose. It was named Nelson Hall, for the founding pastor on the twenty-fifth anniversary of our church.

A dramatic fire in 1980, the largest in Phoenix that year, destroyed the fellowship hall. That year the congregation raised nearly $500,000; which, added to insurance monies, made possible the rebuilding of Nelson Hall and the offices and ancillary rooms, at a total cost of nearly $1.5 million. The buildings were dedicated in 1982. During the year of reconstruction, the church gave $25,000 to the Southwest Conference New Initiatives in Church Development campaign.

In the late 1980s the church underwent a complete renovation, as did the home for the elderly. The church plant was brought closer to completion by the addition of a major building for youth, for our own groups and others. A major intergenerational day-care center was scheduled to be completed in 1990.

Reaching Out to Others

Upon the completion of our first facilities, we immediately adopted a policy of "reaching out" in offering them to community groups. We did so partly out of generous concern to serve the community and partly as a way of making this church a "visible presence" within the community.

Most churches do this sort of thing. We made it a conscious effort: Scout groups began to meet in our buildings, also Alcoholics Anonymous, a musical group or two, and a women's group, in addition to our own programs, which were increasing. As soon as we finished our education building, we made it available on week days for the Maricopa County school for brain-injured children. Our church continued to house the school for the next nine years. Eventually, the Phoenix Symphony, the Junior League, the Assistance League, and the community election boards were meeting on our premises.

Giving Ourselves Away

All this time our membership was growing. From 1955 through 1958, we received an average of more than three hundred new members each year and developed a program for integrating them quickly into some group activity within the church. I was becoming aware of a reality with which we had to deal. We were no longer "a congregation" but a series of overlapping congregations—one church but several congregations. We dealt with this situation by creating staff, both paid and volunteer, to relate to each such group and by devising programs aimed at the particular needs of the various groupings. As part of this effort, we called a third minister to join the pastoral team, whose ordination was the first of many subsequent ones.

Membership growth in the years 1951 to 1961 was 275 new members a year. But the city's growth was beyond the reach of our one congregation. It was time for us to give ourselves away. We offered to give leadership in initiating two new congregations: Shepherd of the Hills in eastern Phoenix and the United Church of Sun City. We negotiated the purchase of properties, provided lay leadership from our church, did the bookkeeping in the beginning, and generally offered every support. Shortly after that, we joined with others in assisting with a new church, First Congregational, in Scottsdale. In 1973 Church of the Beatitudes again assisted in initiating a new congregation, Shadow Rock Congregational Church in Phoenix.

We gave ourself away in other ways too. In 1959, we created the first full-time psychological counseling service attached to a church anywhere in the state. This, too, was a hint of things to come. Our counseling service was phased into a much enlarged ecumenical program, housed in our church as Phoenix Interfaith Counseling Service.

Also in 1959 we created a two-week summer mission experience for our high school teenagers. We began taking thirty young persons each summer to Guadalajara, Mexico, so that they would become better acquainted with the Hispanic culture that we live close to here in Arizona. In Mexico every day they worked, in the morning building and painting in our denomination's social-service center, spent another half day in educational sight-seeing, and used the evening to become acquainted with Mexican youth from our Congregational Church in that city. This program continued for the next fifteen years and eventually included youth from neigh-

287

boring congregations. Since then, owing to increased costs and unfavorable travel conditions in Mexico, our church has had to substitute similar projects within the United States or in immediate border towns in California and Arizona. The program greatly enhanced our visibility among young people and strengthened the loyalty of both the participants and their parents.

Still another aspect of giving ourselves away was to provide leadership in creating The North Phoenix Corporate Ministry, an ecumenical consortium of five Protestant, one Roman Catholic, and two Jewish congregations. The offices for this consortium were in our church and a Catholic nun became its first full-time director. It began adult education programs in common, held occasional worship services, developed a clothing bank for the city's needy, and produced forums that addressed community problems and concerns.

In the 1980s, Church of the Beatitudes helped create Interfaith Cooperative Ministries, an inner-city ministry to the indigent and homeless. It now serves more than 100,000 people a year. We also endowed the Clelland Lectureship, in honor of a distinguished seminary professor and member of the church, to bring significant religious voices to the community. We created and endowed the Fox Festival, honoring a woman whose family has been active in the church, to provide programs in the fine arts with an emphasis on music.

Engaging Our Youth

Ever since our settling-in years, we have made a conscious effort aimed toward youth. Phoenix was a young community then, and we created a vigorous program for young people: the typical youth groups, several children's choirs, a summer camping program, and the previously mentioned mission travel program.

If there was a special emphasis in the years between 1967 and 1971, beyond continuing what we had begun, it was toward encouraging our ablest young people to listen for a call to ministry. We created a program expressly aimed at making professional ministry a vocational choice. Church leaders created a policy to pay the full seminary tuition of any young person who felt called to the ministry. He or she signs an agreement to enter the ministry and stay for six years or pay back the money. We developed resources for working with high school and college-age young persons. Within the next three years, three young persons were ordained in our church, two men and one woman. Eventually, by our thirty-seventh year, this church celebrated the ordination of seventeen men and women. We have had an ordination in our church about every other year. We consider these ordinations among our greatest accomplishments.

Caring for the Elderly

Between 1962 and 1966, church growth continued with an average accession of 250 each year. Over the next three years, the church grew to an active membership of more than 2,500. We were still receiving two hundred new members each year, but the area was being "overpopulated" by other churches, and the area of the city where we served most prominently were rapidly being "filled in." But a dramatic new development was about to transpire in our church's life. We had always focused on finding a new challenge and meeting it!

Phoenix was becoming known as a mecca for persons of retirement years, and there were simply no facilities for the elderly of modest incomes. Further, nursing homes were uniformly inadequate. Our church decided to do something about this situation. After two years of intensive research and study, the congregation voted to build a home for the elderly.

This home would be owned and administered by the church, as other of her ministries are. It would accommodate persons of moderate incomes. It would provide full service without an entry fee but on a fee-for-service basis. The church made contributions in leadership and monies and created a borrowing capacity toward property purchase and building. Twenty-five acres were obtained, and in 1964, our first high-rise structures were completed.

This was only a hint of what was to come. Under church management and leadership, over the next several years, more facilities were added until the Beatitudes Campus of Care provided quarters for 750 residents. It also included a 160-bed medical unit, two kitchens, two dining rooms, a library, a pharmacy, a branch bank, a gift shop, and, as stipulated in lieu of one staff psychiatrist, three beauty parlors!

By 1969, our Beatitudes Campus of Care was virtually complete. From the women's group of our church, we created an auxiliary and rapidly expanded it to include persons of the wider community; very soon it was giving well over twenty thousand hours of volunteer service a year. We created numerous auxiliary programs on our Beatitudes Campus, including a choir, a chaplaincy program, educational programs, and a Kiwanis service club. We initiated a "scholarship fund" for those elderly who could not afford full costs in the home or who, after becoming residents, might find inflation had eaten away their ability to be fully self-supporting. In the 1980s we added a Life Center, including a chapel.

The Beatitudes Campus has been a modest source of members for the church, but that is not why we founded it. We encourage residents to remain loyal to their own congregations or religious traditions. In addition, we provide opportunity for occasional denominational services on our campus or bus service for congregations who wish to use it. Church of the Beatitudes, however, retains the authority to direct the program; the senior minister serves as chief executive officer, and a member of the pastoral team serves as chief operating officer.

In the 1970s we began a new ministry for the elderly, Center DOAR (Developing Older Adult Resources), under the leadership of a newly added staff member. It has expanded into a service to reach the frail and homebound adult. Through a creation of our church, Volunteer Interfaith Caregivers Program (VICaP) was born. It provides training and support for seventy partnered congregations throughout the Phoenix area, in which some 1,500 volunteers are trained, and in-service to thousands of the homebound.

And On and On

How does one sum up a generation and more of church growth and development? There are the statistics, of course. Church of the Beatitudes has had a total accession in excess of six thousand members in its first thirty-seven years, with a present active membership of more than three thousand. By now, the minimal organizational pattern that served so well in our early years has given way to a far more complex structure involving separate incorporated ministries under church control and direction. There have been seventeen ordinations into the ministry. The church has assisted in initiating four new congregations beside itself and is now funding, as a satellite new congregation, still another in Scottsdale. The church buildings, including property, have a replacement value of about $9 million, and the Beatitudes Campus has a replacement value of perhaps $45 million.

What really counts, though, are the people who have served and been served, the ministries that have been created and are ministering still: the Beatitudes Campus, Center DOAR, VICaP, Interfaith Counseling, Interfaith Cooperative Ministries in the inner city, ecumenical relationships, and one of the most successful arts programs in the city.

At the heart of it all is worship, the weekly celebration of our faith. And our faith is this: God has made the Divine Presence known in human form, supremely in Jesus, but as well, in every one of us. At the heart of it all has been a dream, an inspiration, an ability to remember not just the past but the future!

"Thy kingdom come!"

Miracle of Renewal

Mt. Zwingli United Church of Christ, Wadsworth, Ohio

JERALD W. BAKER

n my thirty-odd years of pastoral experience, I have made a specialty of building and remodeling churches. Budgets ranged from a few thousand dollars to nearly half a million. I was part of the United Church of Christ's original task force pioneering the New Initiatives in Church Development program, which used experienced pastors to lead in new-church and church-renewal projects. Never did I think I would soon be among them myself! Yet, it happened; and now, looking back, I must say that it was a most fortunate circumstance that I was as well prepared as I was to take on such demanding work.

I view Mt. Zwingli Church, Wadsworth, Ohio, as the highlight of my entire ministry. It has been demanding, frustrating, frightening, and satisfying—not necessarily in that order; but having achieved what we have in such short time, I cherish the entire experience. Not only did I bring experience and learning to this project, which aided our process immeasurably, but I learned much from a congregation unusually dedicated to the realization of their dreams. And I learned that with the Lord behind us, we are more than able to contend against challenges before us.

I hope that what I share in this account will be of support and help to others as the principles of church growth and development carry this denomination forward into the future.

Jerald W. Baker is pastor of Mt. Zwingli United Church of Christ in Wadsworth, Ohio. He was formerly a two-term president of the United Church Board for Homeland Ministries and served on the New Church Task Force, which initiated New Initiatives in Church Development. Before that he pastored churches in Wisconsin, Florida, and Ohio.

The Early History of Mt. Zwingli

The story of Mt. Zwingli United Church of Christ began in April 1859, when J. Schlosser, an itinerant missionary of the Sandusky Classis of Ohio in the Reformed Church in America, gathered a small group of farmers in a local schoolhouse. By December 1859, he had a committed group of seventeen people, who were chartered as Mt. Zwingli Reformed Church.

After ten years of worshiping in the schoolhouse and holding their meetings in members' homes, members erected a wooden church building on land given by one of them beside a community cemetery. It was the center of many community activities until 1909, when it was struck by lightning and burned to the ground. The devoted and energetic congregation, still small in numbers but vigorous, constructed a stone church on the same site; and that building remains as an historic building utilized as a chapel by the present congregation.

The little country church flourished until World War I. Visiting pastors, itinerant revivalists, and lay preachers kept the congregation going; although throughout its history, Mt. Zwingli has been a church run by the laity. After World War I, however, farmers were leaving the land for city jobs. The automobile allowed a mobility not previously enjoyed. Returning soldiers went to the nearby towns and cities to work and live. The little church fell on hard times.

In the late 1920s and early 1930s, it was practically closed. The only use of the building was for Fourth of July picnics, Thanksgiving services, and other special events. Sunday school was sporadic, and at times even that was impossible to maintain.

In 1936, however, the lay pastor P. E. Stover restored and reorganized the congregation and renewed ties with what was then the Evangelical and Reformed Church. He succeeded in having Mt. Zwingli yoked with other and stronger churches nearby, giving them regular pastoral attention and weekly worship experiences. Slowly but surely, new life came back to Mt. Zwingli.

All early church records were destroyed in the 1909 fire, but from a number of other sources we know that the congregation was always small, numbering in the dozens only. In the 1950s, however, a surge of growth in the area, coupled with good pastoral leadership, combined to bring attendance and membership near the hundred mark. At the same time, concerned about handicapped children in the area having no facilities to serve them in any way, pastor and congregation decided to do something positive to help fill that need. In 1959 they purchased additional land adjacent to the church and constructed a building to house a summer Bible school and community camping program for the handicapped and retarded. The program proved so successful it became too large for such a small congregation to handle. The University of Akron took over the program and moved it to another site. Giving away their major community program combined with several changes in pastoral leadership led to some congregational regression over the next few years. Nevertheless, the new building, now available for congregational use, became the church's fellowship hall and helped increase local church activities.

In the mid-1970s, contemplating another population surge in the community, and having enjoyed some small gains in membership, congregational leaders and an energetic pastor, Eddie Bray, began dreaming of a new church building, something they knew they needed to compete for new members and expand their congregational life. The old church had no rest room facilities and no classrooms. The new hall had both, but the buildings were about 100 yards apart, and winter made it difficult to go from one to the other. Further, the hall was primarily that: a hall full of noise and confusion, not a place conducive to good experiences in Christian education. In 1979, hearing rumors about a new UCC program to be known as New Initiatives in Church Development (NICD), Bray and consistory leaders sought the advice of association staff in eastern Ohio. Their enthusiasm carried over, and soon, that office and the Ohio Conference began to do some careful study preliminary to having the church apply to become a project. Fred Atwood-Lyon, associate association minister, assumed leadership responsibility for the research and, by winter of 1980–81, had compiled an impressive case for Mt. Zwingli to become Ohio's first renewal project, one of the earliest on the NICD schedule.

Studied, reviewed, evaluated, and accepted by the covenantal parties involved, Mt. Zwingli, it was determined, (1) would cease to be a yoked church and go on her own, (2) would seek a new, full-time pastor, and (3) would begin the new working relationship as of September 1, 1981.

I was called to Mt. Zwingli in July 1981. I accepted and began work as the church's first full-time pastor in 122 years. It was agreed that the Board for Homeland Ministries and the conference together would subsidize the project in the amount of $16,000 per year for three years, with an option left open for further and reduced support for an additional two years if it was deemed wise. On that basis, Mt. Zwingli began an era of renewal.

Era of Renewal

Here is a more complete picture of our circumstances in 1981. The stone church, built in 1909, seated eighty in the pews. It was a one-room structure with a dirt basement housing a furnace and some lawn equipment. The fellowship hall, approximately 100 yards away, was being used during the winter months for *all* church activities owing to lack of funds to pay heating costs for both buildings. It consisted of a large hall for general activities, a very nice kitchen, two Sunday school classrooms, and rest rooms. Additional land purchased when the hall was being constructed amounted to a total of four acres. Membership at the start of the era of renewal was 112 on the roll, with approximately 75 to 80 truly active people. Attendance averaged in the sixties throughout the best months of any year. There was no office. The only office equipment was a portable electric typewriter and a small mimeograph allowing production of bulletins and a monthly newsletter, both produced and authored by volunteers. Our financial obligations were for local church expenses and benevolence only, plus some responsibility for the pastor's salary and housing shared with the larger church to which we had been yoked. Our total budget in 1980 was $19,100. There was no indebtedness, and a housing allowance enabled the new pastor to purchase his own home, since the church had no parsonage.

Things "broke loose" very quickly. The next five years were almost unbelievable!

The First Steps

On September 1, 1981, Mt. Zwingli's ministry began with worship, meetings, and putting our house in order. One of the two Sunday school rooms in the fellowship hall was taken over for an office. With a budget of $300 for setting up an office, we went to auctions and bought a desk, four office chairs, filing cabinets, and basic supplies. Concrete blocks and planks became bookshelves. Donations of curtains (adjusted and hung by my wife, Rachel), paper products, and other small items were accepted gratefully. Rachel and I repainted the room at night. Volunteers offered to serve as part-time secretarial help.

We designated special workdays (Saturdays and Sundays),

which brought out two or three dozen people to clean, paint, repair, and put all cemetery and lawn areas in first-class condition. Volunteers constructed a huge sign announcing who we were and what we were about and erected it near the roadside, in front of the area where we hoped to construct a new church building.

Our worship attendance had jumped from 65 to 75 to an average of 125 between September and November. Apparently, the arrival of their own pastor and an accompanying excitement stirred the congregation to prod friends and neighbors to "come and see!" Worship lasted one hour, began and ended on time, and was designed to incorporate congregational participation as much as possible. We celebrated birthdays and anniversaries during our services and went all out to interest and hold children's attention by means of weekly object sermons. We found the greatest drawing card to be pets, ranging from white mice to a Shetland pony, for a lengthy series based on "What We Can Learn from Pets God Has Given Us." A "singing church," we sang those hymns and gospel songs people loved most, even having occasional "Favorite Hymn Sundays," when singing occupied most of worship time. It all worked, and we were gearing up for a super Christmas.

On December 31, 1981, we looked back on an astounding Christmas season: two services on Christmas Eve had brought out a total of 265 persons. In that little sanctuary seating 80 in the pews, we had 155 on Christmas Sunday—people in chairs in the aisles, in tiny rear rooms with doors kept open, out in the narthex, and sitting on a step in front of the chancel.

By then, we knew that our stewardship drive, begun in November but lingering, had been a huge success, going from the previous year's budget of $19,100 to the challenge of $42,250 in 1982. The pastor and consistory had agreed that we had to double our previous year's giving. Although we could rely on that $16,000 subsidy to aid us, we had other things to do: buy equipment, make some major repairs, and build a reserve in the bank to pay for any forthcoming building studies and an architect to help us. Our fund-raising campaign was very simple: a special one-page explanation and plea in the November newsletter; a single mailing of the budget, a pastoral letter, and pledge cards; and four weeks of personal appeals by laity leaders from the pulpit in advance of Stewardship Sunday. It had worked! We now knew we were at least $5,000 beyond our basic needs for the new year. That fact, plus our being so crowded, had everyone rejoicing, hardly able to wait for the annual meeting.

At the annual meeting, January 24, 1982, final reports for 1981 were presented, elections held, and honors bestowed, as usual. Different this time were two proposals. The first was that in view of crowded conditions and the surge in membership (eighteen since September), we should establish both a building-study committee and a constitutional-revision committee. The former would assess our possibilities, visit other building projects, do a lot of thinking about the future, consider potential architects (hiring one by the hour when needed), and draw up some recommendations. The latter would study our strengths and weaknesses as a structured congregation, assess the patterns we should follow as we grew (with an eye on involving newer members in the leadership of the church), and draw up a new constitution. The second proposal was that both committees should come to the next annual meeting fully prepared to recommend action by the congregation, having kept everyone informed as to progress or problems throughout the year. It was the most exciting annual meeting in the history of the church, or so we thought.

At Easter the numbers amazed us—106 at the sunrise service, 124 for breakfast in the hall, 165 at the celebration service (some were outside the church, standing on the porch). Such attendance pushed morale to an all-time high. It also put more pressure on the committees to get on with their tasks.

That summer we joined a local softball league involving six other churches; Mt. Zwingli was ready to play ball! Announcing the league as a good opportunity for fellowship, whether playing or cheering, the pastor was astounded when forty-five persons signed up to play. That was too many for one team, so we organized two, found two coaches, and ended up with an adult team for those beyond college age, and a youth team for junior high, senior high, and college ages. Enthusiasm was so high that several people suggested capitalizing on the teams for advertising; thus, we bought T-shirts and caps reading "Mt. Zwingli" and "Mt. Z" respectively. Sold for a bit more than cost, they even gave us funds for softballs! At our first outing, the shock of opposing teams was both visible and audible as we trooped over to the playing field: two teams with forty-one of the forty-three present to play, accompanied by thirty-eight in the cheering section. Said one member of the opposing teams, "Did you bring the whole church?" and we said, "Yes, why not?" Our sense of unity and common interest overwhelmed the community; it even astounded us.

New Building

December 1982 found us with nearly identical attendance figures to those of the previous year; but we saw signs of diminishing returns. Despite the continuing surge in membership and influx of visitors, we heard people say, when asked why they were absent, "Well, you can't get inside if you are late, anyway." Or, "Yes, we have been away for awhile, but we felt it was better to make room for some of the others." Excuses? Perhaps, but signals that it was no longer "funny" to be overcrowded, sitting on a step instead of a chair or in a pew. Besides, there was no more room! We knew we had to do something fast.

At the annual meeting in January 1983, those anticipated reports from the two committees dominated everything else. The results? A unanimous vote to proceed with building plans as presented, to hire the architect by contract now, instead of by the hour, to seek fund-raising help from the Board for Homeland Ministries' Office for Church Building and their Church Finance Advisory Service (CFAS), and to alter our structure of operations as a congregation through an updated and renewed constitution that would allow rapid and wider involvement of members.

In April we began a building-fund drive based on assumed needs of $60,000 over a two-year period to add to a $220,000 loan from BHM. Our success left us stunned: $97,000 raised or pledged! The initial goal of $60,000 was met with pledges totaling $77,000 in a campaign led by Richard Whitney from New York. The other $20,000 came from a variety of sources. An all-church auction open to the public and with a professional auctioneer, featuring donations from throughout the community, netted us $6,800. A generous couple in Florida sent us a very special gift of $10,000 to "do what you could not do otherwise!" The remainder came from special gifts from neighboring churches, and a large gift from the Eastern Ohio Association. It seemed that everybody wanted to be part of the action at Mount Zwingli!

In June 1983 we held a special congregational meeting to discuss and approve the architect's plans, to hear other committee reports or recommendations, and to make a final decision to proceed. A packed church voted unanimously to hire contractors immediately and move ahead.

That same June at the Fourteenth General Synod in Pittsburgh, Mt. Zwingli received the Biennial Membership Growth Award, as the fastest-growing church-renewal project of the original list of NICD projects. How thrilled we were, and how grateful! The dreams and the prayers were being fulfilled.

Groundbreaking on July 15 was an historic occasion with the church packed beyond capacity and the front porch full of standing individuals. A parade led by our oldest members moved us from the old church to the new site, an event that we photographed and videotaped for future memory.

On August 6 earth began to move as bulldozers went to work. Equipment and supplies piled up, and in a few days actual construction began on a building based on a pole-barn design chosen for its cost-effectiveness and ease of construction. An old idea resurrected and refined by our architect, it promised us the most building for the dollars at our disposal.

November 23, 1983, we held the first service in the new sanctuary, a community-wide Thanksgiving Eve service, because so many people throughout this community had taken part in our development. Metal chairs, some dust, and some confusion did not deter from the joy and thrill of that historic occasion.

On Christmas Eve—with pews in place at last, seating 300 adults—our first Christmas candlelight service brought out 243 persons. Momentum was picking up again, and just in time. Now, the new building and "our fantastic story " were combining to bring in the curious, visitors from great distances, and family members from afar.

February 26, 1984, was the long-awaited Day of Dedication of our new building and other facilities; Mt. Zwingli entered its 125th year celebrating its renewal.

In June 1986 the last of five annual reports read to the Ohio Conference began with a letter from BHM's Division of Evangelism and Church Development citing Mt. Zwingli to be "*the* Renewal Project of the United Church of Christ." The delegates responded with a great ovation. The last of all subsidy funds was received in August. Mt. Zwingli was henceforth a strong, self-supporting congregation of 246.

Since then I and key laity leaders have told the story of Mt. Zwingli in many different places and different ways—groups of small-church pastors, training schools for pastors of new and renewed churches, single churches embarking on their own building programs, association and conference workshops.

The Things That Made It Happen

The fact that this project succeeded so rapidly and to such an extent has left the congregation and its pastor awed. There have been elements of the miraculous from start to finish, and we can only give credit to the Holy Spirit for much that took place.

What is a miracle? Webster says "an event or effect in the physical world deviating from the known laws of nature . . . an extraordinary . . . event brought about by superhuman agency." It is not an overstatement to use that definition to describe this project.

Numerous inexplicable and astounding events contributed to the story of Mt. Zwingli. While ideas and actions came from our human minds and endeavors, surely the Spirit inspired and fulfilled them. Let this be known!

At the outset in the fall of 1981, so much was bleak and unpromising that I was haunted by apprehension, even despair. Three major problems presented themselves, two of them quite unexpected.

The first was the anticipated dearth of finances, but we had foreseen that problem and planned to attack it with a fund-raising campaign. The other two problems were much more threatening, even devastating: (1) an unexpected recession across the country, which had a dire impact on northeastern Ohio, especially on the real estate and building markets, and (2) a severe economic crisis in this area, leading to massive layoffs and joblessness. At the beginning of our first real growth, the area was number three in the nation in percentage of population out of work, partly the result of too much dependence on the steel and auto industries. Ripple effects helped make our area part of the Rust Belt crisis. All this meant that the anticipated population growth was curtailed or postponed. We lost anticipated financial support from both existing members and those new members we planned to gain.

What to do? With a lot of discussion and prayer, dedicated leaders determined that this project was surely God's will and therefore nothing could or would deter our moving ahead. Somehow we would overcome! Thus our project became a project of faith. Enthusiasm actually flourished in view of these severe problems and perhaps (with hindsight) because of them.

Obviously, if we could not count on population growth in the area, we had to capitalize on existent people, so we decided to do that precisely and with vigor. We would activate those who had fallen away, and we would reach out to everyone available in the widest perimeter possible.

Outstanding Activities

The first thing to do, then, was to make existing and new activities at Mt. Zwingli absolutely outstanding. Worship was never more carefully crafted or executed. Fellowship events were billed as community-wide events to which were invited family members, friends, neighbors, and anyone else showing the slightest interest. I called on current members and visitors, and they were encouraged and brought into involvement by every means at our command.

Never having enjoyed full-time pastoral care before, the little congregation was hungry for it and extremely appreciative of it. The result was a surge of grateful response of self-giving. Volunteers labored to put existing facilities into attractive and first-rate condition, based on the premise that, if we failed to show interest and concern for who and what we were, it was unlikely that we would excite others by our own indifference and slovenliness. Volunteers were recruited to invite other people, to involve them in what we were doing, and to come and see the new life being generated.

In short order we recognized a large number of people who were either unchurched entirely or disenchanted Christians who had fallen away from their own churches. Excited by all the activity and encouraged and welcomed warmly, an astounding number were brought into our church family.

That, in fact, was our main theme: Mt. Zwingli was, and would increasingly become, one of the warmest, friendliest family churches ever! It was no idle notion. People were welcomed, accepted lovingly, and integrated into our common life as rapidly as they would accept involvement. Some newcomers were already ushering, greeting, serving refreshments, and working on internal projects before they were received formally as members. A number were elected to consistory or committees within one or two months after taking membership vows.

As the momentum grew and a new worship building became an obvious essential in the near future, we advertised for anyone who wanted to be part of a unique church-renewal project to come and join us in the exciting venture. We stated openly that we needed and welcomed "builders" who liked a challenge. The result was the winning of several skilled and enthusiastic members from other congregations in the vicinity in which they felt unneeded, ignored, or bored. A number did not transfer membership but attended, supported, and participated fully in our project, and to some of these we remain most indebted. This phenomenon continues, although nearly all those originally involving themselves have finally joined. It was too good a fellowship not to become a full partner in it.

Presenting ourselves as a superior example of an extended family, we included everyone in everything, especially the children! Morning worship services included (and still do) a special children's object sermon that was as carefully prepared (if not more so) as the sermon for adults. One summer series on "God's Gifts to Us in Pets," ranging from mice to a pony, brought out unbelievable numbers of families with children. These object sermons, along with programs, parties, plays, and other all-church activities, attracted many of the younger families in the area. We noted that "a little child shall lead them" is a fact to reckon with.

Adult classes, formerly ill attended, were eventually scrapped for a single pastor's class with topics ranging from old-fashioned Bible study to life-situation problems. Eventually, this class turned into a talkback session, using the day's sermon and prepared study questions as the basis for group discussion. This session, attended by thirty to forty persons, remains a provocative and useful part of our Sunday morning experience.

Fellowship events, long significant in the life of the congregation, were increased and fine-tuned to draw people by answering needs in their lives. Among those at the top of the list were family-night dinners and celebrations designed to interest every age group but particularly young people. These included hayrides and wiener roasts; father-son and mother-daughter banquets with programs ranging from video presentations to high school singing groups, science programs, and patriotic themes; scavenger hunts; softball games; and homecomings. Our goal was to make Christian fellowship at Mt. Zwingli the center of personal and family life insofar as possible, and we have succeeded.

Youth activities proved to be our greatest challenge, especially in view of the fact that at least seven junior high schools and senior high schools are in our area. Regardless of the day or night selected for an event, we could be sure of conflicting with programs at at least half of these schools. Thus, because we were small in numbers and faced so much division of interest or loyalty, we decided to focus youth work on Sunday mornings in two classes, one junior high and the other senior high, but for other activities, we combined the two into one. Yes, there were (and are) some problems with such wide age differences, but combining them worked to our advantage in that it cemented ties among the young people and gave us the benefit of larger numbers involved in projects. The formation of a youth softball team playing eight games in an adult league in the summer has been the most effective and long-lasting activity, resulting in members forming bonds that have helped the total church program throughout the year. We usually held a special event each month, and while that has been less of a total program than we desired, it has been effective under the circumstances. Those events have included a workday visit to one of our conference camps; a car-and-dog wash to raise funds for youth activities; overnights at the church; picking apples to make cider to sell, for the benefit of the church building fund, and other fundraising activities to support Church World Service projects, including participation in several CROP-walks.

Sacrificial Giving

Perhaps the most astounding and awesome element early in this enterprise was the response of the congregation (members and visitors alike) to the call for sacrificial giving. Having endured a few years of perilous financial conditions prior to becoming a renewal project, we had made every effort simply to pay the bills, especially for heat. Although the congregation knew the arrival of a full-time pastor would necessitate greater giving, I am sure they were not prepared for the challenges that came to them once I arrived on the scene. Although NICD subsidy payments covered the base salary of the pastor for three years, other expenses such as benefits, office expenses, auto expenses, and anticipated expenses from sheer growth in numbers were congregational responsibilities that necessitated large increases in the budget. Thus, the first stewardship campaign, in the fall of 1981, was accompanied by a call to everyone to double his or her previous giving, regardless of what it had been. The response? They did more than that!

During informal moments on Sunday mornings, and by letters mailed to everyone on the mailing list, details of projected needs were shared. Every item was explained thoroughly, and if ever a congregation knew the facts about the budget, this one did. The covenant between the local church, the conference, and UCBHM in every new-church or renewed-church project includes an agreement that 10 percent of all local monies raised is to be given to Our Church's World Mission (OCWM), but the consistory agreed with me that we should at the least tithe our entire income, including subsidies and gifts received! Thus, when our first-year gifts and subsidies amounted to $18,000, it meant that right off the top we tithed $1,800 for "mission purposes" as a matter of course; and we never received a negative comment! It meant raising that extra amount locally, but that seemed a small response to so much caring shown by others toward us.

What all this did was build a morale; a kind of spiritual feeling permeated all our efforts from that time onward. It was amazing how many individuals came forward "to help out" in the structuring of our first church office, to help us obtain needed equipment, and to provide items for which there was no budgeted source. Typewriters were purchased or received as gifts. A copy machine came as a gift from a new member, a medical doctor, who replaced the one in his office and gave the old one to us rather than trade it in. Worship and office supplies came by the same route, and somehow, every time we truly needed something, the means was there to accomplish.

Fund Raising

In the spring of 1983, just a year and a half later, contemplating a building project so essential to our continued rise, I told the congregation that we did not have the slightest chance of accomplishing our goal unless all of us "doubled our giving again!" And they did it! It was absolutely essential in order to facilitate repayment of a building loan from UCBHM.

At this point, I must give great credit to the UCBHM's Office of Church Building and CFAS. As we began contemplating building costs, we became certain that we needed professional help in achieving our financial goals for the building itself. Asking people to "double their giving again" is one thing; bolstering morale and enthusiasm with planning and professional skills is another.

Our call for help from CFAS brought Richard Whitney to Mt. Zwingli, and it is his guidance and spiritual counsel that we credit for much of our success. Letters of appeal went to all church members and friends long before his arrival, and that motivation, coupled with his program of information and challenge, brought profound results! Going after an essential $60,000 over a two-year period, we ended the campaign with a victory banquet announcement of having achieved over $77,000! To that sum we added $6,800 netted from a super public auction held as a building fund raiser in May. Excited by our enthusiasm, "friends of the church" or friends of the pastor from former parishes sent us additional sums as gifts so that we wound up with a grand total of $97,000!

Obviously, we found approximately $13,000 in what might be called "outside money," from friends and strangers. What motivated them, I asked, and the reply was, "We want to be part of a program that involves such dedication and enthusiasm," or "We like to be part of a winning team!" One thing we learned throughout this process was that enthusiasm and devotion to a cause are contagious. If a congregation not only tells but shows by high visibility how serious about their purposes and goals they are, the entire community will respond in support, and the "outside resources" will simply amaze everyone!

I do not want to overemphasize fund raising, but it has proved to be a blessing here in various ways; there is no understanding of our success without careful attention being paid to it. Regarding the wide community support, let me share something about the super public auction to give evidence and explain more fully what I mean.

Several years ago in another parish where we had a building program with inadequate funds, I decided to hold a public auction complete with a professional auctioneer and items donated or consigned by members of the church and community. We borrowed a huge tent to cover us in case of inclement weather but also to draw the attention of passersby. It was a monumental effort, but the result was a profit of $5,000 and wide news coverage by major state papers because it was both new and successful. That started me on a hobby that has grown with the years, how to manage an auction effectively.

At Mt. Zwingli, we were dealing with a much smaller congregation, which meant fewer resources for items to sell, so we promoted our auction as a community-wide affair, inviting any people who might want to help us succeed in our building efforts to participate in any way they could. The result was a generous outpouring of help from Catholics, Baptists, Lutherans, Methodists, and many others who gave approximately 70 percent of the items we had to sell! The auctioneer, one of the best in the area, donated his time and that of his support staff. The women of Mt. Zwingli offered an all-day lunch at a reasonable but profitable price, and on the side we ran a rummage sale. Altogether, we realized that $6,800.

Fine-tuning the process every two years, reaching for a wider circle of consignments, and advertising over television and radio and in local newspapers, we just finished our third auction in May, 1987, netting the amazing amount of $10,300! It is a project with appeal, and it works!

One thing more about auctions and similar fund-raising events: we announce honestly and openly that "every dollar goes into the building mortgage fund," and that our only expense items are advertising and food supplies. Everything else is donated or consigned, with our receiving a percentage on major items. The fact that everybody is "donating" items and/or talents is its own drawing card.

Serving public dinners on occasion and dinners for specific agencies or groups has been another means of raising funds. All our organizations—youth groups, adult groups, women's guild, and others—pledge generously in every building or building-mortgage campaign. They raise their funds through such events as mentioned or by serving lunch at other local auctions, holding some occasional raffles, and hosting events for small outside groups.

I repeat: while the dollars realized in these ventures are crucial to our success in the building venture (none of these events raise any funds for the local church or mission), of equal value and importance is the fellowship they generate. Meals served to the public in large numbers (three hundred or more served) require careful planning, purchasing supplies, donations of food, and finding many people to prepare and serve them. That means three or four dozens of people are involved in every event; and, because we always feature them as all-church events, donations and services involve dozens more!

For something as big as the public auctions, our efforts begin a year ahead of time, not just planning, but securing semi-trailers for storage, crews with pickup trucks to haul items to the trailers, a strategy group to prepare the all-day luncheons to be offered, and handling crews to aid the auctioneers and their staff. Literally dozens of people must be involved and dedicated to their tasks in order for the auction to succeed. Were I pressed to indicate the major factor in assimilating new people, creating a stronger family bond within the congregation, and giving them a sense of ownership in their church's life, I would have to say these fund-raising activities rate as number one! People who work together on projects learn how to relate despite foibles and eccentricities. And, when success is enjoyed after long and hard labor, they share common joy.

Yes, these activities require forethought, planning, and organization, but, as I say, there is a double-edged benefit: we accomplish necessary tasks to keep our facilities in first-rate condition or to raise needed funds, and the process puts people side by side in work conditions that allow them to talk about their backgrounds or church concerns and thus form binding ties. There is no substitute for working at a common task, especially one that uses talents that almost anyone owns, to create friendships. These events and happenings have helped make this the warmest, friendliest congregation I have ever served.

Evangelism

Little or nothing has been said about evangelism thus far, although evangelism is implied or attached to much I have already said. Frankly, we have not done the usual things characteristic of a good evangelistic program: widespread paid newspaper advertising, door-to-door visitation by persons or teams, or having the pastor regularly pounding the pavements doing "cold calling" on a massive scale. What has worked for us instead?

I have already noted the existing congregation offered a variety of pastoral needs that the church has met and continues to meet. We have paid to advertise for special holy days and unique services appealing to the wider community, but we have learned how to use newspapers, radio stations, and television studios at critical times to gain free advertising! All the media in our area seek items for their "community calendars." The religion editors are hungry for items dealing with special projects and events; and, if you make every attempt to be unusual or distinctive in projects or programs, your request for a "plug" is received gratefully. Our organist and choir directors also teach music lessons on the side, which means their pupils give "recitals" every year. We announce them beforehand, and with a bit of encouragement, newspapers will even send photographers to tell the story later in a pictorial review. The same is true for quilting bees, unusual work projects and special events such as the dedication of handbells. We have tried to keep the community aware that something special is always happening at Mt. Zwingli! And that stirs commentary.

Consequently, we have found that the most effective advertising is that done by word of mouth and that same word of mouth is our most effective evangelistic tool. At bridge clubs, service club meetings, local restaurants and barbershops, and across back fences, people talk up that strange and exciting bunch of people out on County Line Road who are always so active in all kinds of projects. Curiosity, intrigue, whetted interest—these have worked beautifully for us. Every new member received hears the same plea as those who were here when this renewal project began in 1981: "Please help us grow by bringing others with you!" Not everybody does, but most do, and we attribute the bulk of our growth to having people take seriously the concept of "each one win another!" Of course, this conclusion substantiates national research done on why and how people choose churches; the bulk of them are brought or invited by a friend or a neighbor. Once there, the atmosphere and program must sell themselves.

I should explain that part of our reticence in using the proved evangelism methods mentioned above is due to a simple but real lack of time, not because we reject their validity. As a pastor, one cannot do everything, and I have opted from the start to "do all I can, but do it well!" The congregation has been more than gracious in responding to calls for help in dozens of projects, in giving at record levels, and in attendance and participation. As anyone acquainted with a small church knows, some individuals tend to be in everything and have to be for things to succeed. The same people are on consistory or committees who sing in choir or play handbells, support every effort attempted, attend Sunday worship, teach in church school, or lead organizations. There is a limit to endurance and that has been taken into account. Again, we do what we do to the limits of our vision, knowledge, and ability; and what cannot be incorporated is postponed or laid aside.

Now that the building process is ended and most physical projects are completed, we intend to turn to some of the more traditional methods to advertise and evangelize. Yet to this point, what I have cited has worked well.

Pastoral Leadership

Finally, I want to say a word about pastoral leadership technique, because it cannot be ignored in determining why this project has succeeded. Every leader has his or her own style, but one thing we all have in common—or should have—is that we show the way by personal example. When it comes to work and sacrifice, the leader must be out in front, not as a pusher but as a puller. Throughout the five years of Mt. Zwingli's renewal project, the vast majority of weeks have been seven-day weeks, and some days have been fifteen- or sixteen-hour days. Although I have frequently been charged with being a workaholic, in fact I have not enjoyed such a demanding schedule and have often resented it. But I maintained it for two reasons: (1) For at least the first three years, if it was to be pushed through, I had to push it; if I had waited for a volunteer or some committee action, progress would have been thwarted. (2) When I set such a rapid pace, no one could refuse to do his or her part when the time came. Indeed, I played on that theme often, saying, "I will never ask you to do what I am not doing myself." Thus, I gave of my time on personal days off; I shared time that should have been vacation; I forced myself to do tasks that are often considered beneath one who has spent eight or ten years to be properly educated, to fill a certain role. This effort on my part brought tremendous response and discipleship. We have shared the concept that "you can get too big for God to use, but you are never too little!" Every task, however small or humble, is visualized as part of the whole, and none of us is above anything that needs to be done: taking out the trash, hauling garbage, cleaning rest rooms, raking gravel, singing in a choir, teaching a class, working, or playing. The ultimate result is a sense of comradeship unique between pastor and people, and I count on that to keep momentum and morale high for years to come.

Some clergy have been urged, even taught, to do nothing that could be done by a lay person, to stay apart from or above "little stuff"; but in this congregation, that kind of behavior would be seen as lamentable ignorance or laziness, neither of which belongs in a family, where we are all for one and one for all.

What We Learned

A number of significant truths emerged from our experience of church renewal.

The Mood of the Congregation

It was agreed between this congregation and me that never would we hesitate or vote down any proposal simply because "we never did it that way before." No one has ever broken that agreement, and much of the credit for this venture is due the congregation for maintaining a spirit of openness, a pioneering attitude, and a unique willingness to run risks as well as change quickly.

Naturally, I have compared notes with others leading in similar situations, and this freedom of spirit has proved to be critical. It is akin to starting over without any blueprint or heritage on which to rely, but that kind of freedom is absolutely essential for success in growth and development.

Why? Every church, including this one, has a heritage, a routine, or a blueprint of operations; and, while elements may be retained if they work well, the very concept of renewal implies that something needs changing or something new should happen.

As a result of this freedom here, changes were made ever so easily in Sunday worship, in having new people actively involved, in trying new programs or projects, and in allowing change to take place without friction.

One thing I have noted, however, is that while the older members accepted such a concept and willingly encouraged it, those who were reared in the church as children or youth, and who are now in the twenties or thirties, were those most unnerved by all the changes. In other words, having Mother or Grandma relieved of their long-held positions did not bother Mother or Grandma; it was irksome and uncomfortable for Daughter or Granddaughter!

Further, it remains true in a new or renewed-church project as it is in any other church setting: once a change has been made and in place, that becomes "our traditional way" in extremely short order. Maintaining the freedom of spirit becomes an ongoing challenge in ever so short a time.

The Pastor's Changing Mood—to Be Expected

Before arriving on the scene and becoming thoroughly involved, a pastor is almost certain to be on an enthusiastic emotional high; filled with anticipation, hope, and great energy, and armed with research data indicating the project will be a sure success, he or she arrives all ready to "make it happen" momentarily!

Reality, however, seldom measures up to anticipation; and swings of mood are almost inevitable. There is a period of "crash" as the realities of the situation become evident: inadequate funds, poor or nonexistent facilities, lack of competent help (in comparison with previous staff), and hesitancy of people to offer their services owing to a long-standing, low self-image.

311

What is required is a do-or-die, bedrock conviction that this will succeed, regardless of odds against you! A strong conviction that this is God's will and that the power behind you is greater than any obstacles before you, is the essential foundation if you are to avoid depression and total despair. Prayer and meditation must be constant; but even then, you need companionship in the form of support persons or groups to emerge from what are certain to be very difficult slumps.

Assessment of what you have to work with, especially people, is critical; it results in uplift more often than not, because there is a reservoir of laity talent "out there" everywhere, just waiting to be recognized and tapped. Once the laity can believe in you and know that you believe in them, volunteers of capacity and competence appear without invitation; and your mood is improved!

A glimmer of success excites your personal morale, which is catching; people are quick to note your positivism or negativism. If you can surmount what is depressing, maintaining confidence in the face of great odds or threats, the people will carry you along.

Humility helps, and remembering that God has called you to be faithful, not necessarily successful, keeps your personal morale stable; and in due course, you realize that success may come despite dubious leadership. After all, this *is* God's work, is it not? Let the Holy Spirit work in and through you however dim the vision may become. Amazingly, God does use . . . even you and me!

General Advice

Dream big dreams! Numerous authorities claim that the limits of accomplishment are determined by the scope of our dreams or ambitions, and it is true, especially in these NICD projects. One can be foolish, of course; but it is amazing to find how church people share your visions and may even go beyond you!

Don't be afraid to ask! Frequently in this experience, I have been overwhelmed by the response of individuals and couples to great challenges. From the most unexpected persons and places came remarkable gifts of money, talent, or other resources. A quiet farmer, but a most devoted Christian, provided (on his own initiative, since I assumed it an impossibility) an outstanding sound system paid for completely by himself and his wife, a gift of major of proportions. Our building contractors, impressed with our imagination and positivism, gave the church air conditioning as a gift; while the architect gave a beautiful chancel cross as his own contribution. All it took was a listing and a sharing of our needs, indicating that if someone could provide this, we could have it; otherwise not. Many are waiting to have an opportunity "to do their thing for the Lord."

Give thanks and celebrate! I speak here of thanking people, of noting and announcing their special deeds or services, of celebrating their life's great experience or moments . . . just as we do in our homes and families. If a congregation is to be what it says it wants to be, a family, live like it. As Jesus said, "Rejoice with those who rejoice, weep with those who weep."

Set priorities and stick with them! Pastor and congregation simply *must* live within their means: both financially, and in terms of energy and time. The danger of being spread too thin, of trying to do everything that everyone wants of you, of being overwhelmed to the point of doing all things poorly—is real! A pastor cannot be on all kinds of community, association, and conference committees and still be effective in doing all that needs to be done on a church-renewal project. It requires all the energy, vision, and activity any one leader can give. And a congregation has limits of focus, energy, and time; to ignore this is foolish.

Children are evangelists! Not every location has the resource of children, but most do; so focus on and address your children. If they feel loved, wanted, and included, they will bring their parents and grandparents, aunts and uncles. Who can refuse a child having part in a play, a choir, a program, a party at the church? Let children lead and minister insofar as they are able, and the results will astound. We worry about teaching them; but the truth is, they can teach us! Without fanfare or title, they can and do excite church involvement.

Accent others' trust in us. A new or renewed-church project exists only because other Christian friends believe in our goals and ambitions enough to provide funds, put themselves out, and share as they can in our dreams. Holding that imagery before yourself and your congregation gives strong motivation; with so many others behind us we dare not fail! Later, once we have accomplished our goals, this outside support becomes an ongoing motivation for mission giving and doing—to enable others as we have been enabled.

Laugh off any failures. Let no one assume everything we have tried has been of great consequence; numerous ideas proved futile, and some events we thought would work, failed miserably. But the other side of running risks and winning is running risks and losing. It is a wise church family that learns to laugh at itself and individuals to laugh with each other when embarrassed. Laughter has great healing powers.

Humor is vital. Whether one realizes success or failure, perhaps the second great virtue is humor, right after faith. We believe that Jesus had to be a warm and humorous person; otherwise, how can we explain the way children seemed to love him, and all kinds of persons followed him so ardently? Consequently, we laugh a lot and try to see the humorous side of any threats or obstacles. Don't take anyone or anything too seriously.

Use your resources. Tempted though we may be to go it alone, the Lone Ranger is just that: alone! Association, conference, and the UCBHM offer resources readily and freely. As cited in this essay, we owe all of them so much for what they have given and done for us. Use them! That is what a covenantal church is really all about.

The story of Mt. Zwingli as related in these pages is certainly in short form. Our task and purpose has been to relate the basics involved in the project from inception to completion, but many other factors, incidents, and experiences cannot be included under the limits of space. The invitation remains open to anyone wishing to explore details more completely, to write or telephone for additional information.

You should know that, as of this writing, Mt. Zwingli has succeeded in meeting both its local and mission budget and the building mortgage budget without any subsidies or outside support gifts since August 1, 1986. The first year was a challenge with respect to both budgets; but increased membership, the special fund-raising projects, and increased giving combined to ensure that we ended the fiscal year without deficit. The membership was at 285 with the expectation of going over 300 by the end of the year.

Much concern has been voiced within the congregation that we not lose the warmth and vitality of the small church; and currently, that is one of our priorities.

Most of the principles or strategies mentioned continue as our guidelines: constant changes in worship forms, the accent on children and the entire family circle, continued volunteer projects, and broadening the scope of membership involvement. The transition from a period in which the accent was on building and landscaping to one of more stable and normal church operations continues to be a challenge. Turning the direction of energies and activities toward greater spiritual development, wider mission interest, and an enlarged ministry to those in church and community, is an issue with which we deal daily, but it is happening and we shall proceed to achieve those goals.

If you are ever in this vicinity of Ohio, come and visit!

Beginning Ministry
in a New Parish

First Congregational Church, Appleton, Wisconsin

JOHN T. MCFADDEN

There is an abundance of resource material available to clergy beginning ministry in a new parish setting, much of it organized in a practical, step-by-step fashion. The reflections I offer here are of a very different nature; they are intended to complement these other resources by encouraging clergy to ponder broader issues of personal identity and the nature of their unique calling. I begin with the prejudice that the calling of the parish minister is to *upbuild the life of the church*, not to be a community's prophet in residence, not to build a personal "support community," not to serve one's own needs and pursue one's own spiritual growth. These may all be worthy goals for God's people, including parish clergy, but they are not our calling. God places us in parishes to upbuild Christ's church, to care for the saints and equip them for ministry. This exciting, terrifying task is why God calls us to local churches, and it must always be our highest priority.

I may at times sound harsh in my comments: please be assured that it is not my intent to judge fellow clergy. These comments

John T. McFadden is senior minister of First Congregational Church, Appleton, Wisconsin. Previously, at Glen Ridge Congregational Church in New Jersey, he was one of the youngest senior pastors in the denomination. McFadden has written articles for a variety of religious and secular magazines.

grow from my own experience, including experiences of pain and doubt, and from the experiences of valued friends and colleagues over the years.

I write from my own experience, which is obviously a male experience. I write also as one whose entire ministry has been in larger, multiple-staff churches. Those who minister in churches of other sizes may wish to bear this in mind as they read: some observations may be less applicable in such settings. I am also, perhaps, an eccentric person, or so I have been told. Some of my observations may therefore be eccentric.

I believe that many parish clergy are intimidated by the nature of their calling, expressing their anxieties through a variety of non-productive, even self-destructive, means. Some become flat-out lazy, running and hiding from their calling like latter-day Jonahs. They hide in homes or offices, shuffling papers and reading books and resource materials of no real relevance to their ministry. They fiddle with computers, designing elaborate and pointless spread-sheets. They swamp themselves with denominational, ecumenical, and community commitments, all less threatening than the local parish. They extend their visits to supportive members while pro-crastinating on making calls and doing tasks of real urgency. As they adopt a full array of avoidance techniques, the church suffers. I do not mean this criticism unkindly or judgmentally, and I have great respect for my local-church colleagues. But I believe we owe it to God, the church, and ourselves to be honest about our fears and doubts and the ways in which these have affected our ministry in the past. The parish ministry is a high and holy calling, and it is also the most frightening one I can imagine. It is not surprising that there should be so many parish clergy who crumble: to chemical dependence, to sexual misconduct, to despair, to avoidance, to self-deception. Recognizing this weakness, we clergy must vow to be honest about the ways in which our calling intimidates and overwhelms us. Accepting a call is a new beginning in Christ, and we should seek prayerful guidance at such a time in understanding ourselves and our ministry.

Preparation

We do not always have the luxury of choosing the timing of a change in parishes. Conflict, crisis, the needs of spouse or chil-dren—dozens of factors external to our own sense of calling—can dictate such a change. Still it is important to raise as an ideal that *preparation for a new parish should begin one to two years in advance of the move itself!* You may not even know where that new parish is likely to be, yet personal preparation does not need to be hampered. You should work on personal-identity issues. Put another way, you should "get your act together." If there are tensions or unresolved issues in marriage or family, the time to deal with them is *before* accepting a call. If you are struggling with matters that have a negative impact on your emotional or spiritual well-being, seek help *before* making a move. Put your house in order: take as little unhealthy or nonproductive baggage with you as possible.

If a church must suffer a certain amount of neglect while you work through personal matters, let it be the church where you are completing your ministry rather than the one where you are to begin. You will have better connections for counseling resources and support in the community you already know than in a new one, and you will be in a better position to ask others to take over certain tasks and functions while you explore these issues. I would go so far as to suggest that all parish clergy should enter into some form of meaningful therapy for at least a year before considering a call. Consolidate strengths, learn from mistakes, rebuild important relationships, strengthen one's base of ego-strength and self-esteem. Quite frankly, the first year of ministry in a new parish will not permit much time for such issues; *now* is the time to work on them! I would place a particular stress on marital and family issues. Your spouse may well have an equally demanding employment challenge waiting for him or her in the new community but also needs to be fully supportive of your new ministry in a church community eager to come to know you both. Beginning a new ministry faithfully will place great demands on your time and energy. If possible, begin from a position of strength rather than weakness.

In addition to examining personal issues, it would be well to explore vocational issues related to your calling. Your conference or association office will be able to alert you to clergy career centers or other resources to help you in an honest appraisal of your strengths and weaknesses. No parish minister is equally competent in all areas of church leadership; it is helpful to know which areas should receive your additional attention. No parish minister leaves a church without carrying wounds and grief; we need to seek healing and wholeness before engaging in a new ministry. Whether this ministry is to last five years or twenty, what is experienced during the first year will continue to have a profound effect on that ministry. With this in mind, do everything within your power to ensure that you are fully prepared to make the most of that first year!

Needless to say, moving itself can be a source of considerable stress. You may need to sell one home and buy another, pull children from a happy school experience, surrender relationships that nurture and support. It is often said that the ideal move comes in early summer, permitting more time before the new school year for all family members to adjust to their new setting. In my experience, few things in this life come in an ideal manner, but when possible such timing should be considered. Careful consideration of the complex dynamics of moving should be viewed as a part of the process of beginning a new ministry.

Priorities

As you start your ministry in a new parish, a great many things will claim your attention. You will need to set some priorities and hold to some basic rules.

Put Worship First

The first priority of the minister in a new parish must be *worship*! It is not only the central reality from which the rest of the church's life draws meaning, but it is the primary means by which you as the new minister will become known to your congregation. I would urge caution and restraint in making wholesale changes in the existing order of worship, as you have no way of knowing just how much local history and tradition is invested in that order. But make a vow to come each Sunday morning *fully prepared* for each element of the worship service. If you have a particular style or method for individual elements of worship, such as the sacrament of baptism or the reading of scripture, which has theological integrity and has been well received in the past, by all means include it in worship. Your goal is to present yourself as the person you are without "bulldozing" honored values of your new church.

Whether or not you perceive preaching to be one of the strengths of your ministry, it should receive special attention during this first year. I would go so far as to suggest that you consider preaching *every Sunday* for that year if possible. Granted, the purpose of preaching is to proclaim Christ and interpret scripture. But if you are one who approaches the task through the medium of your own vulnerability and experience, a most positive bonus will be that parishioners come to know who you are and what your values as a Christian lead you to proclaim. The importance of this cannot be overstated. If you have a "sermon barrel," use it sparingly, and always have the courtesy and integrity to rewrite with the local setting in mind. Whenever possible, draw images and illustrations from the present rather than the past; let the people know that you are now a part of *their* community of faith!

Let your pulpit presence be *positive!* No one wants to hear the minister whine and whimper each week about his or her pain and the terrible burden of lugging a cross around, yet that voice of ministerial self-pity rings from many pulpits. If the gospel is indeed good news, it should be shared with joy. Only you know what preaching style is effective for you, but I suspect that in this first year the informal preacher has an advantage over the more formal one, and the topical preacher may "click" more quickly than those who use the lectionary. Whatever your approach to preaching, bear in mind that it is primarily through this medium that people will come to know who you are. Share yourself, even as you share the message of faith.

Regard each Sunday morning as a final examination. Prepare the best sermon you can, one that speaks to the genuine needs of the congregation. Invest all of your ability in communicating that message effectively, in enabling the word of God to touch the lives of those with whom you worship. A minister ill-prepared for leading worship is an embarrassment to the church and the faith it proclaims, and he or she shows an utter lack of respect for the congregation. A minister who dwells on pet topics and personal perspectives is faithless to the gospel we are called to proclaim. Remember that during the first year of your ministry you will be "checked out" by your members, both active and inactive, and by community members as well. Most of them will give you but one chance: you cannot permit yourself the luxury of an "off week."

Reserve Judgement

When you arrive in your new setting, the only people you know may be the members of the search committee. You may regard them as being the most splendid Christian people upon the face of the earth, and they will be a source of invaluable support and guidance in the early stages of your ministry. But should committee members—or anyone else—begin to tell you what's wrong with the church, who will be a troublemaker, and other negative information, reserve your judgment. Talk to as many people as possible, inside and outside the church. Visit with the association minister and, if possible, the conference minister; hear their perspectives on the church. Meet with current and past lay leaders. Listen to their joys and concerns. Through it all, reserve judgment. It will be months, perhaps years, before you can begin to claim to understand the church. If you commit yourself too soon to a particular viewpoint, you may well find yourself painted into an uncomfortable corner. Practice active listening: ask questions, grieve with the sorrowful, commiserate with those who have been "done dirty," but resist being drawn into value statements. All good pastoral ministries are preceded by a time of listening and learning.

Learn the Local Resource Network

Take time to become acquainted with the chaplains and other staff members at hospitals where you will be calling. Learn the ins and outs of the local network of counselors and care providers. In particular, if there is a pastoral-counseling center in the area, take time to visit with the director. Learn which counselors are effective with various kinds of clients and issues and which agencies are equipped for third-party payments and special services. As time permits, arrange visits with the counselors and therapists. Visit ecumenical agencies and pastors of other churches. A major component of your pastoral care for the congregation will lie in creative and appropriate referrals, and the sooner you learn the ropes the sooner you will be able to provide this care.

Attend Every Meeting

If it is a larger church to which you have been called, the array of boards, committees, and commissions can be overwhelming. You will not be expected to attend each and every meeting, of course. But for the first few months you should. This may mean being out four or five evenings a week on top of long, six-day weeks. There are those who believe that parish clergy should take responsibility for modeling a sane and rational stewardship of time and not drive themselves this hard. I understand this position, but I respectfully suggest that for a new pastor there is no substitute for long hours and hard work. You will not have this first year to live over again, so use it fully and well. The new minister must demonstrate a genuine love for the church and show that it is his or her first priority.

Delay Staffing Decisions

If you are coming into a larger, multiple-staff church, there may be several staff vacancies that need to be filled. Wait. As the new minister, you are the spiritual leader of the congregation. Like it or not, the style of church life during your ministry will be very much shaped by your personality. The needs of the church cannot be clearly identified until the unique chemistry forged by your personal style in the setting to which you are called is established. Other staff members may well need to "balance" your style in various ways. If they are selected too soon, such balance is not likely to be achieved. Also, an understaffed church during your first year will speed the process whereby you become known to people. You will be a more active and visible presence, working in areas of church life that may be surrendered to other staff members in the future. Lay persons will need to be more fully involved while you are short of staff members, and their involvement too speeds the process of integration. Delay bringing other staff members into the church for a full year. This may sound masochistic, I know, but I believe that the long-term benefits justify the extra demands this delay imposes.

Build Good Staff Relations

Affirm and support your staff members, both those you inherit and those who ultimately come to join you in your ministry. Never speak ill of a staff member to another person. *Never!* Doubtless there will be issues that need to be worked through among staff members; you will be called to hold members of the staff accountable for their performance. All this dialogue should occur within the staff family itself. The bane of multiple-staff churches is friction among staff members that becomes a public issue. Express loyalty to your staff. Be an advocate for appropriate professional salaries for all staff members, lay and ordained. The church will only be as strong as its staff and only as harmonious as relationships amongst staff members.

Limit Your Counseling

Unless you have been called to a setting where pastoral counseling is a major component of your calling and is so identified by the congregation, you should do *no more* than five hours of counseling a week. If premarital and funeral-related grief counseling are factored out, even that five hours is quite high given the other matters demanding your attention. Too many parish clergy are seduced into heavy counseling caseloads, often including long-term work. Assuming your community has adequate counseling resources, this represents poor stewardship of time. It may not even serve the clients very well unless you have received extensive psychological training, and even then I am skeptical. Particularly for the new minister, the special "strokes" received in individual counseling may become a substitute for the friendships left behind, a dynamic that is not healthy for you or the members of the congregation seeking your help. Certainly a thoughtful and caring ministry of referral to appropriate counselors and agencies can express just as much support as can accepting these persons as clients yourself. I would suggest that the uncompensated counseling offered by a pastor is not as likely to be valued or effective as is counseling for which the client has contracted and is paying.

I do not mean to suggest hard and fast rules in this area. Certainly most parish clergy need to do *some* counseling to continue growing in their abilities. Consider doing joint counseling with professional counselors and psychologists to whom you refer members from time to time. It is a marvelous opportunity for growth, and it also enhances your ability to make creative and appropriate referrals. But your calling is to upbuild the *entire* body of Christ. To do so you must devote most of your time to broader issues affecting the overall life of the church while offering pastoral care to persons in need of the uniquely spiritual resources you are called to share. Unless the counseling you offer is somehow different from that offered by your secular counterparts, it is best to defer such situations to them.

Be Available

The church support staff and members of the congregation should always know when and where you can be found. At the least, you must keep regular office hours, something that a surprisingly high percentage of parish clergy seem to resist. Morale sags quickly in a church office where the secretary does not know what time the minister will wander in or where the minister goes when he or she wanders off. If you have not yet done so, build structure and discipline into your professional life. Maintain times during the week when you are generally available and interruptable; make it clear when such interruptions are not welcome. Try insofar as possible to be consistent in these things from week to week. More than most professions, ours is characterized by interruptions and the intrusion of the unexpected: all the more reason to claim such order out of the chaos as we can. Use an appointment calendar divided into the hours of the day, not the seasons of the church year. Ministers who drift from home to church to who-knows-where do not inspire confidence in staff or congregation.

If you have a full-time secretary, that secretary should *always* know where you can be reached. I can think of no excuse for a minister to arrive at the church office later than 10 A.M. most mornings; even that is late. Some clergy note that they need extra morning time to compensate for hours given to a church meeting the evening before. To the best of my knowledge, the employers of the lay persons who also attended that meeting still expect them to come to work on time.

Take Care of Your Own Needs

I am asking much of clergy entering into a new setting: fifty-to-sixty-hour weeks will be the norm during the first year. For this reason, establishing your needs for physical, emotional, and spiritual health and accepting responsibility for *meeting* these needs is critical. Our needs are as diverse as we are, so you must define these for yourself. Trial and error have taught me that I need a good physical workout—a five-mile run or game of tennis—most days, enough time with my family each week, and a day off disturbable only by Gabriel's trumpet, if I am to continue to function at the level required of me. Likewise vacation time is extremely important. Colleagues whom I value structure breaks into their days ranging from prayer and meditation to playing with a jazz quintet. Find your own rhythm of work and self-care and stay with it!

Decorate Your Office

I am convinced that effective parish clergy spend more time in their offices than in their homes. Claim that space as your own! Make it a comfortable and cheerful place for you to be. Many offices in church buildings contradict a Protestant theology that does not include the concept of purgatory. An office that lifts your spirits when you arrive in the morning is a marvelous ally in parish ministry.

Decide Upon a Strategy of Visitation

Many clergy arrive in a new church with the ideal of visiting all members in their homes within the first year. Certainly it is a lofty ideal; in some parish settings it may be an entirely appropriate use of your time. But in larger parishes, in particular, this kind of "calling for the sake of calling" becomes a Sisyphean task, one that is hard to abandon once begun because of the expectations it has generated. In many situations this time may be more profitably invested in administrative duties, worship preparation, and other challenges that address the needs of the entire body of Christ.

By all means be faithful in hospital visitation. Set aside a block of time each week for visiting shut-in members and those with special needs. But give careful thought as to whether the real needs of the church are met by establishing a pattern of routine visitation. My sense is that in most communities it is not particularly good stewardship of time, and may not even be welcome.

Set Limits to Outside Involvements

Clergy are, of course, fair game for recruitment to denominational and community boards and agencies. Such involvement can be a legitimate extension of your ministry and an expression of your commitment as a Christian. But in the first year of a new ministry, the parish should always have first claim upon your limited time. It may well be healthy for the church for you to be visible in public settings; certainly it can help with the mission of evangelism and church growth. Make these commitments with thought and care. Volunteer your services when doing so can aid the mission of the church or when you feel genuinely called to do so. Try not to be just an "easy touch," a reputation I fear most of us richly deserve.

Love the Congregation

Most persons will form their impressions of you based upon two areas of your ministry, your worship leadership and the manner in which you care for them in time of need. A parish minister who develops the reputation of not coming through for members in time of death, illness, or crisis might just as well dust off his or her résumé. Once credibility in this area is lost, it is not likely to be recovered. Likewise, if you are perceived as playing favorites, of caring for some members more than others, your ministry will be a short one. If you do not honestly love each and every person God has given to your pastoral care, your ministry has utterly lost its meaning and direction.

Honor Personal Boundaries

Some clergy can have deep personal friendships with members of the congregation, some cannot. Either way, you are not permitted to forget that you have been "set apart" in a special role as spiritual leader of the community of faith and must conduct yourself in a manner appropriate to that identity. Churches are deeply wounded when clergy permit themselves public behavior that is flippant, cynical, rude, hurtful, or—worst of all—sexually abusive or exploitive. If you have a "private side" that needs expression, do so in a setting removed from the congregation. If you are possessed of traits or patterns that are not compatible with your calling in Christ, seek help in reintegrating them in a healthy way. If you have an overwhelming need to be perceived by others as one who is frightfully witty, stunningly fashionable, and sexually irresistible, consider a career in the recording industry.

Do Not Be Passive in Your Leadership

True, it is best to refrain from sweeping changes in the structure of church life until you are integrated into the life of the church. But you have been called to *lead* the congregation, not simply to smile and nod your head. The "honeymoon" is a special grace period in which much might be accomplished. It is a particularly good time to give the stewardship program a significant boost, for example, and you should also consider campaigns to address significant capital needs of the church. The year after a new minister is called will generally be a period when the spirit of a congregation is strong and healthy: direct this "can do" spirit into meaningful accomplishments!

Recruiting and Assimilating New Members

A significant part of our calling lies in the task of revealing more of God by bringing more persons into the body of Christ. Recruiting and assimilating new members is something the church expects of us and we should expect from ourselves. This task should be integrated with your overall ministry from its inception.

There is a variety of good resource material available on styles of evangelism, and I will not reiterate these materials here. If you are not yet familiar with these resources, you should certainly become so: you will need to develop a strategy of evangelism appropriate to your new setting. Likewise, as the new minister, you may need to raise the consciousness of the congregation concerning the many things, large and small, that help visitors and guests to feel welcome and comfortable in the church.

I would like to offer here some ideas and reflections on the challenge of preparing persons for church membership. It is a key task and should be counted among the very highest priorities of your ministry. A colleague pricked my awareness of this some time ago with these words: "You are not responsible for the members you inherit. But God *does* hold you accountable for those who come into the church while you are minister!"

His words, which I believe to be quite accurate, are intimidating in the extreme. He was speaking of nothing less than the *quality of discipleship* of those we bring to church membership. Their worship participation, their stewardship, their level of involvement in church life, the very quality of the life they live unto God is in some sense the responsibility of the cleric who guides them into the decision of Christian commitment. What, then, could be more important than the work we do in preparing persons for this decision?

Teaching classes for new members is something you must do yourself. It should not be an assignment turned over to other staff members or lay persons. *You* are the minister, the spiritual leader of the congregation. The persons *you* bring into church membership should know you—and be known by you—better than any other group in the congregation. They should be the best informed, most active, most committed members of the congregation. If they are not, you have no excuses to present.

I suggest that you give one evening of the week, every week, to teaching new members. When one group enters into church membership, a new series of meetings should begin. Obviously this cannot be an inflexible rule; the size of the congregation and the number of prospective members interested in such classes will vary from church to church. But if you are faithful to your overall calling, particularly in offering worship experiences that truly feed people's spiritual hunger, there will always be persons interested in learning more. Give yourself to a special teaching and nurturing ministry for these persons.

The ideal size for a new-member group, I have found, is somewhere between ten and twenty. A smaller group can be threatening and intimidating to those participating, a larger one too impersonal. I am currently offering four sessions, lasting from an hour to an hour and a half, to each group. This means that approximately twelve to eighteen new members are received each month, somewhat above the "replacement" level for this congregation of 1,500 members. The four sessions I offer seem to me the bare minimum needed to share essential information and to meet other established goals, including building a sense of fellowship among those sharing the experience. At least one colleague, now retired, taught membership sessions lasting a full thirteen weeks! You will need to make your own decision about the length of the program, but be certain you do not shortchange this task.

It is hard within the United Church of Christ tradition to make anything an absolute requirement for those contemplating membership, but I try to make these sessions come very close to a requirement. There will of course be persons who wish or need to meet with you privately to discuss issues of importance to them, but that is not a proper substitute for the group experience. There have been instances where persons have chosen to join the church and then attend a series of classes later in the year for valid reasons, but attending the classes remains an important expectation. I suspect that one reason many of us hesitate to speak of "requirements" is that we are secretly uncertain that what we have to offer is of sufficient value to justify them. If these series are run faithfully and well, word of mouth should ultimately serve to make persons eager to participate.

The First Session

In my first session, we take a bit of time for becoming acquainted. In addition to names, I ask people to share how they came to this church and what church background they have experienced. Given the diversity of religious experiences that characterize members of UCC churches, it is helpful to prospective members to learn they are not unique in coming from a different tradition. I also find it an invaluable aid in preparing for future sessions in the series—particularly those dealing with theology—to learn what backgrounds characterize the members of the group. It is a good "getting acquainted" question for the group, avoiding the standard "Where do you work?" questions. Each session begins with sharing of names, and this first one involves wearing name tags as well.

One goal of the sessions, expressed each week, is that in the midst of a large congregation each person will be able to match names and faces with at least those persons sharing these new-member classes. Most of the time in this first evening is devoted to describing, insofar as it can be described, the United Church of Christ. The difference between hierarchical and congregational organizational structures is clearly explained, as is a polity that stresses freedom and respect for the integrity of the individual believer. Those coming from stricter, highly structured backgrounds tend to hear this as very good news! Participants are encouraged to relate this information to that which they have experienced in worship on Sunday mornings, to explore together what United Church polity implies for worship, the role of clergy, and other topics. Questions of all kinds are actively encouraged and are answered as fully and honestly as I possibly can. I suspect I am more "real" in this setting than any other, trying to speak in personal, rather than abstract, terms. I encourage an environment in which all questions are taken seriously and answered with honesty. My experience has been that the give and take in these evenings comes closer to the ideal of Christian community than any other aspect of church life.

The Second Session

The second week is devoted to the local church: a bit of history, an overview of organizational structure, an informal view of our values, our priorities, our style of life together. The evening concludes with a tour of the physical plant, accompanied by an interpretation of how the use of physical space speaks of our common life and mission. This session demands a full hour and a half, of which the participants are warned in advance. (I offer no child care or refreshments at these meetings. I am not trying to "woo" members; rather I invite persons to discipleship. I believe that offering services not available at, say, a church committee meeting undervalues the commitment of those who attend.)

The second session is in some ways the most enjoyable evening, because it gives me free reign to express my sense of the congregation's mission and ministry. It is also the most frustrating session, because so little of the total picture can be shared. Those who opt for a longer series may wish to consider the local congregation as a topic for expansion. Many programs for new members approach this section by bringing in lay leaders to speak of their areas of responsibility. Don't! There are other settings where this will be more appropriate, and one of the purposes of the series is to share yourself as well as information. Besides, my experience is that lay leaders speaking of their area of church life have a hard time avoiding recruitment talks.

The Third Session

The third session is given fully to theology, to stating what it is we profess as a Christian community. In a nondoctrinal denomination this is no easy task! Some groups arrive bursting with questions—questions often tinged with the pain of personal experience—while others need to be drawn into discussion. The most helpful method I have discovered to date is a compare-and-contrast format employing some of the backgrounds represented in the group. Particularly if there is a significant number of persons from a Roman Catholic background, comparing beliefs about the sacraments can be especially helpful. Needless to say, if you are not well versed in comparative Christian theology, you should address this subject. Understanding where people are coming from in their beliefs is essential to your ministry with them. In addition to the sacraments, attitudes about marriage and divorce is often a key area: many of our new members are divorced Roman Catholics. It is very important that you speak of other Christian traditions fairly and with respect. Contrasting beliefs does not imply judgment or condemnation.

This is a high-risk session, particularly if you are one who finds security in careful preparation; there is no way to be certain of the topics you will be addressing in advance. Here, above all, you must be honest and authentic about your faith. People often tell me that this is the single most helpful session for them; it can even serve to set individual spiritual journeys moving once again after years of stasis. You will doubtless find that it occasionally precipitates appointments with individuals who need to discuss some of these themes in private. Encourage this: one message you want to convey throughout the series is your availability as pastor.

The Fourth Session

The final session is in part a catchall, a time for wrapping up any unanswered questions from previous weeks. (Early in each session I inquire as to whether there is any unfinished business from the week before.) Most of the evening is devoted to the decision to join the church.

I speak of my expectations of church members. They include an emphasis on the meaning of Christian commitment in the world, on a renewal of one's determination to live one's life as a follower of Christ. I speak of service within the church and participation in its life. I emphasize the ministry of all believers and the role of the church in equipping all the saints for ministry in the world. This session is, year by year, evolving into a theology of church membership, with each class helping to shape a bit of that theology. I note that in our tradition the decision to join the church is not in itself what other traditions would term a "decision for Christ." Rather, it is a commitment to the community of faith, a learning, growing community of Christians working together toward a deeper experience of Christ in our lives, both corporately and personally.

I speak also of Christian stewardship. Bluntly. Many prospective members have had no training whatsoever in Christian stewardship, and the very basics need to be reviewed. In the course of the discussion I ask for a minimum financial commitment of 2 percent of income or $10 a week. I was frightened the first time I asked this, and I still fight a bit of fear each time I repeat the request. I explain the principle of Christian stewardship as fully and carefully as I can. I note that 2 percent is just about where most of us begin to "feel" our giving, but it is not so high that there is not room for growth in giving. I state my conviction that financial stewardship is one of the basic expressions of our Christian commitment in the world. It is to be hoped that the previous weeks have established my credibility in such a way that this statement is heard as honest pastoral concern rather than a plea for money. To date no one has balked at this request. Some new members do give less, particularly younger and single persons, but many also give far more. As a group, our new members are the church's strongest financial supporters, which is as it should be if these classes are meeting legitimate needs.

Membership Sunday and Sunday Brunch

Ideally, the group is received into church membership on the next Sunday morning. We meet a half hour before the service to have pictures taken and tend to other business. The group enters as a group and sits together, some candidates including their children and other family members. Each person stands in place when introduced; then all come forward as a group for the simple

332

rite of membership. Following the service, new members are greeted in the narthex by the congregation.

By the next Sunday, pictures taken of the members will be posted. Every other month, a Sunday brunch is offered to the last two classes. Also invited to this brunch are staff members and church officers. Now they are free to make recruitment speeches! Children are of course invited to the brunches, which are primarily designed to expand the base of relationships among new members. Within three months, each new member will be asked to accept a simple job—greeting at the door, serving coffee, perhaps—designed to increase visibility to the congregation. Fellowship groups will issue invitations, and expressions of particular interest in various church activities by the new members (taken from an interest inventory given to each) will be passed to church commissions. Further work is needed in the area of longer-term integration, but fewer new members have slid out the "backdoor" since this program was initiated.

I recognize that many of the particulars of a new-member teaching ministry will need to be tailored to your setting and individual style. But I urge you to give this matter serious consideration as a major component of your ministry. Your calling is to upbuild the life of the church and to equip its saints for Christian ministry. This calling encompasses all persons belonging to the fellowship of the church, but it speaks in a special way to your work with those making the decision of discipleship.

The most effective parish clergy will always demonstrate both faithfulness to the gospel and a high degree of professional competence. May God richly bless your new ministry, and may you continue to grow in this calling!

POSTSCRIPT

Y ou have just read an amazing collection of stories about congregations within the United Church of Christ that deserve recognition because they are gaining rather than declining in membership. From the point of view of the institutional church, this reversal of a trend within a mainline Protestant denomination is a "good news" story to be celebrated. Nevertheless, there is a haunting question that faithful Christians always need to ask when reflecting on their common life. In this instance the question goes like this: to what extent are these Good News stories? I say "extent" because the answer cannot be simply that they either are or are not Good News stories.

If we are to take seriously the principle of prophetic judgment, which is fundamental to Protestantism, a critical spirit needs to be brought to bear on every aspect of our common life as Christians so as to determine what is faithful and what is not faithful about our growth or decline. Of course, only a particular congregation can engage in this critical task, for only it has complete access to its own common life. What are presented here are stories, stories told by pastors. I suspect that if they were told by lay persons from the congregation, by a reporter from *Time*, or by a cultural anthropologist, they might be quite different stories.

The comments that follow, therefore, are in the form of a guide to critical reflection. They are not intended to judge congregations or their pastors but rather to provide an aid for all of us who are concerned about evangelism, the making of Christians, and the vitality and faithfulness of the church to evaluate our common life.

There are three processes involved in the making of Christians: namely, *formation* (the practice and experience of Christian faith and life), *education* (critical reflection on practice and experience in

335

the light of the Christian faith and life), and *instruction* (the acquisition of knowledge and skills useful to Christian faith and life).

What follows focuses on Christian education. Faithful congregations need to *be* an educational ministry rather than *have* an educational ministry insofar as they should be always examining honestly and reflecting critically on their life in the light of the Good News. Further, faithful congregations are those that take seriously the insights and implications of their reflection and continually re-form their life. This postscript, therefore, will contain a series of comments and questions that have evolved from my reading of these "good news" stories, comments and questions that, I hope, will stimulate critical reflection on church growth but are not intended as a criticism of any particular congregation. Indeed, many of the stories—in the light of these comments and questions—are about being faithful, and do exemplify Good News.

My basic approach to reflection on congregational life is first of all theological, but it is also anthropological. Cultural anthropology helps us to look below the surface of life and discover the "hidden curriculum," that is, what is really going on, or what people are really learning in contrast to what society believes it is teaching. It is one thing to write an aim, that is, a mission statement with goals for our common life that is faithful to the gospel, a mission statement that the community affirms and intends to achieve. It is another thing to see what that community's primary task is, what it is really doing. For example, a church may say that its mission is to proclaim the gospel in word and example, but what it may really be doing is working to survive as an institution. In any situation there is always a gap between aim and primary task, and a faithful community strives to name the gap and close it. The questions and comments that follow are intended to help you name the "hidden curriculum" in your congregation and thereby transform what may be "good news" stories into ever more faithful Good News stories.

Appropriately, worship played a central role in each of the stories found in this book. In 1925 Willard Sperry, a Congregational divine and dean of the Theological School in Harvard University, penned *Reality and Worship*. In that important book, he wrote,

> The conduct of public worship is the differentia of the church. . . . whenever and wherever men and women meet together avowedly to address themselves to the act of worship, there is the church, clearly and distinctively defined. . . . If it loses faith in the act of worship, is thoughtless in the order of worship, and careless in the

conduct of worship, it need not look to its avocations to save it, it is dead at its heart.

What the Church Is Communicating

In that regard, a primary question that comes to mind is what a church is communicating to people. What is a church really saying when it holds worship to an hour and worries about beginning and ending on time? Is it possible that it communicates that worship is really not the most essential and important aspect of people's lives? What do we really communicate to people when we try to attract them to our Christmas and Easter liturgies? Would not it be more faithful for Christians to play down Christmas and play up Epiphany? Has not Christmas become a Hallmark card day rather than a Christian celebration? Further, isn't it necessary for people to attend the Good Friday service if their presence at the Easter liturgy is to be faithful? When we avoid silence in the liturgy, is it not giving the impression that God does not speak and we do not need to listen to or meditate upon God's word? (People typically say God does not say anything, but if they treated other people the way they treat God, people wouldn't say anything either!) What does it mean when people's birthdays are celebrated in the church? Isn't a baptism day a more important occasion to remember? Should we be happy if people only come to church to "feel better"? Shouldn't people come to church to be converted and transformed?

Sperry also wrote, "A novel service of worship usually succeeds only in defeating its own ends." Margaret Mead warned that American culture was being secularized by the church's interest in novelty in worship. She pointed out that ritual calls for habit, redundancy, and repetition. She also pointed out that people like novelty because it provides escape and entertainment but does not form or transform their lives.

Sperry observed, "Unless the tradition of worship is to die out in Protestantism altogether and be replaced by lectures, forums, and the like, the Sunday liturgy must become 'the Mass of the Faithful,'" which is another way of saying the church ought to celebrate weekly eucharist. What does it mean when the church puts its total emphasis on preaching and expects preaching to become the focus of worship? Is it possible to maintain a community of faith unless the community participates in an act of worship comprised of both the proclamation of the word and the celebration of the eucharist?

Sperry also commented that "Protestantism has become too subjective in its interests and methods of worship." He pointed out that in most Protestant churches worship is addressed to the people rather than God, a sad reality that is typically symbolized by the fact that on a stormy winter Sunday some churches cancel their service of worship. What happens when the church worries about numbers at worship so as to build up morale? Isn't worship to be an end in itself? Do not worship and its environment need to focus the awareness of the community on the sacred, invite contemplation, offer a sense of the holy, and provide experience of the divine so that the otherness of the transcendent mystery of God can be made incarnate?

Of course the worship environment also needs to be a place where the stranger, the handicapped, the suffering, young and old, rich and poor, wise and simple can feel welcome without necessarily knowing one another personally. It needs to be hospitable space and the kind of worship where persons are encouraged to be actors rather than spectators engaged in the divine-human communal drama. But what happens when ministers focus concerns at worship primarily on the people and create the service with their human interests and needs in mind?

Sperry noted:

> Many churches recognize the presence of children with a children's sermon. This is a generous concession to childhood, but I am unclear that it belongs in public worship. If the sermon proper is so erudite that children can get nothing from it, it is a bad sermon which cannot be atoned for by a children's sermon.

Indeed, children's sermons may actually estrange children from the community. Can anyone feel that he or she is part of a community when he or she is set apart? Do we make children feel a part of a family by not permitting them to sit at the table with the adults and join in their conversation? Further, by offering children a different kind of sermon from those they will experience when they are adults, are we not rendering them unable to benefit from, enjoy, and be engaged by, sermons delivered to the adult community? Perhaps that policy explains in part why youth drop out and adults complain about sermons. What is the purpose of dialogue conversations with children that tend to make them vulnerable and turn them into a sideshow for adult entertainment?

338

Worse, do not these dialogues appeal primarily to the sort of child who is verbal, competitive, aggressive, extraverted, and individualistic—the very ones who rarely need public attention?

How Christianity Relates to Civilization

A second question that surfaces in reading these stories is what the relationship of Christianity is to civilization, the theme of H. Richard Niebuhr's book *Christ and Culture.* In that book, Niebuhr advocates a "Christ transforming culture" image for the church, an image of which the United Church of Christ, at least in its early years, was a prime example. Being in but not of the world, the United Church of Christ attempted to separate itself from the culture's ways and bring a prophetic judgment on this nation's values. (The journals *Colloquy* and *Youth* were examples.) The UCC advocated "Acts-Evangelism," and as might be expected, it upset a number of people who wanted a cultural Christianity, a "Christ of culture" image for the church, which supports secular understandings and ways. While there is a move toward a "Christ of culture" stance today, we need to ask whether the church can be faithful if it accommodates itself to culture. We know it is easy to attract people to the church if we give them what they want; namely, a blessing on, and support of, their way of life. By identifying Christ with culture, however, the church forms people who cannot differentiate between being a capitalist and being a Christian, between being a U.S. citizen and being a follower of Jesus. This does not necessarily mean, of course, that capitalists and citizens are not good, kind, loving people who care for the poor and advocate justice. But it does mean that they do so in ways that are consistent with the culture's beliefs, attitudes, and values, and they thereby manifest a popular expression of religion that cannot transform culture. Therefore, whenever a church becomes popular and begins to increase its membership, it needs critically to look at its "hidden curriculum" to see if it has sold its soul to the culture. More important, the church must be very careful that it does not use the culture's ways to attract people to the church, for when it does, it undermines its faith. We need to remember that how we communicate is what we communicate.

Consider some examples in some of these "good news" stories. American culture wants us to make a difference, but the gospel requires us to abide in the difference God has already made. Jesus, you will recall, was tempted in the desert to be relevant, spectacular, and powerful. He rejected those temptations in order to be present to the world in another way.

Further, the church sometimes permits sociological description of the way things are to become ecclesial prescriptions for how they should be. It is easy to forget that Paul in his letter to the church at Philippi makes very clear that our commonwealth is in heaven, that we are called to live as strangers in a strange land, that is, as resident aliens trying to stake out a living on someone else's turf. We always need to remember that when we are most faithful to our vocation, we may not be popular in society.

At least in its early years, the United Church of Christ understood its vocation to be apostolic, that is, to provide a sign of an alternative to the way the world lived and to be a witness in the world to God's judgment on society's ways. To what extent is that vocation diminished when we emphasize attracting an ever larger number of members?

How Large Churches Relate to the Making of Christians

Of course, American culture believes that bigger is better. But a third question arises. But what happens when Christians make the large church desirable and normative? When we do, doesn't the role of the clergy change from that of pastor and teacher to that of pastoral administrator, and then doesn't the pastor begin to function as if she or he should have earned an M.B.A. rather than a M.Div. degree? There may be a sense of belonging to something impressive and important when a church has more than three hundred members, and it may be able to offer opportunities no smaller church can provide, but what is the price of belonging to a church that is like a corporation?

Agreed that personal relationships between members can be formed around small groups, but ministry tends to become more formalized and impersonal. Isn't the church called to be a community of faith in which Christ's reconciling activity is made known, living, conscious, and active so that the church might become the body of Christ, Christ's reconciling presence in the world, to the end that all people are restored to unity with God and one another in Christ? Isn't a community of faith quite different from a large, institutional church? Doesn't the large church become more like a business and engulfed in bureaucracy? Doesn't church growth encourage a large institutional church to form around a charismatic leader? What happens when a congregation becomes identified with its pastor? As Sperry observed, "Liberalism is the belief that society can be safely founded and built on the self-directing power of a personality." It is sometimes difficult to remember that the church needs to be more concerned with the spirituality of its leader than with his or her personality or leadership and management skills. Growing churches can be a blessing; a church that has grown too large can become a curse. Is a concern for church growth the same as a concern for the making of Christians? Shouldn't the church be concerned about the conversion of adults to the gospel and the creation of communities in which they can be nurtured and enabled for ministry in daily life and work? Shouldn't a healthy church have less program every year and encourage people to spend as little time in church as possible? Wouldn't it be wise to ask every group that meets in the church: How has our time together contributed to God's reign? How is our community a better place because we have met?

A community of faith is united by covenant, a relationship based upon giving one another whatever love demands. A community of faith understands the worth of persons in terms of their being, and it governs its life by custom. An institutional, corporation church unites people in a contractual relationship, is governed by an increasing number of bylaws, and judges the worth of people in terms of their contribution and participation.

The point raised by some of these stories is simply this: in order for the church to grow, how far are we willing to go in adapting ourselves to society's understandings and ways of life? For example, should every denomination compete with every other for members and be aggressive in attracting individuals to join its fellowship?

Perhaps it is because the United Church of Christ was the last denomination to act on the ecumenical principle of a melting pot, but in a day when the move is toward denominations claiming a particular identity and character, what does it mean to desire growth? Perhaps some denominations should always be small because of their particular vocation; while they are essential to the whole body of the church, they may appeal to only a small number of persons. If all denominations make church growth their end, they may maintain a less distinctive communal identity and may in the long run have nothing to offer anyone.

Who the People Are Who Are Joining the Church

One further question remains: Who are the people who are joining the churches in these stories? Are they faithful Christians from other denominations or other UCC congregations who have recently moved? Are they among the unfaithful who have drifted away and have been attracted to a new understanding of church? Or are they converts to the Christian faith? While all new members may be cause for celebration, evangelism is primarily concerned with the last two groups. A healthy future for the church is not to be found in some congregations growing at the expense of others—the moving of members from one congregation to another, which the new congregation pridefully claims as a success—but in the conversion of non-Christians to the gospel. Perhaps only churches doing the latter have the right to celebrate growth.

Juan Carlos Ortiz, an Argentinean Pentecostal pastor, in his book *Call to Discipleship* writes: "God began speaking to me about the condition of my church. He said that we were not growing. My reply was, 'Lord, we *are* growing. We have gone from one hundred to six hundred in two years.' And God said, 'You are not growing; you are getting fat!' "

What do we mean by growth? Is it numbers or faithfulness of life or both? Some have suggested that in this post-Constantinian era the faithful church will need to withdraw from the culture so as to build a solid foundation for later growth. Perhaps this is an age when mainline Protestant churches have become so secularized that growth will only make them fat, and, worse, they will be building on sand.

Such is a radical critique of mainline Protestantism. It is a position no serious Christian can dismiss out of hand, even as we celebrate the "Good News in Growing Churches." And there is good news in these stories worth celebrating. Nevertheless, the purpose of this postscript is not to applaud faithful life but to raise hard questions about the price of worldly success.

Perhaps the church will grow most faithfully in racial and ethnic minority congregations and in congregations led by women clergy who have not been as secularized as have the more typical congregations led by white male clergy. Secularism—the heresy of the present era—is focused on the masculine, rational, human, material, active dimensions of Christianity; it denies and neglects the sacred, which is focused on the feminine, intuitive, divine, nonmaterial, contemplative dimensions of Christianity. Or will churches be so concerned to grow that they permit the secularization of the church to win out, making the church into a popular, prosperous religious institution serving individual, privatized religious needs and personal social needs of people in a de-sacralized society? If that occurs, where is the Good News?

There are many more serious questions that need to be asked amid the enthusiasm for growing churches, but perhaps I have raised a few that will be useful in the common quest to have churches grow in the Good News!

JOHN H. WESTERHOFF III, professor of
theology and Christian nurture,
Duke University Divinity School